The Amazing Story of Arundel-on-the-Bay

1600s to Today

Developed and Written By

The Arundel-on-the-Bay History Project

Aris T. Allen Jr.

Philip Allen

Marc L. Apter, Chair

Wilma Coble

Edie Dolberg

Pamela Duncan

Richard Marc Grigsby

Robert Meissner, Editor

John Moses

Richard Napoli

Karen J. Neale

Bill Semenuk

Arend J. Thomas, III

The 1890 Plat of Arundel-on-the-Bay

(See Figure 12, Chapter 2 for details)

Linden Ave
Redwood Ave
Sycamore Ave
Walnut Ave
Cedar Ave
Maple Ave
Lake Ave

Printed in the United States of America.

ISBN-13: 978-0692195512 (Pamela T. Duncan)
ISBN-10: 0692195513

Printed by CreateSpace, An Amazon.com Company
First printing, October 2018

For more information contact:
Property Owners of Arundel-on-the-Bay
The History Project
P.O.Box 4665
Annapolis, MD 21403

Arundelonthebay.org

MarcA1030@gmail.com

Graphic Design by Karen Tobin
Modern Visual Solutions
(Special thanks to Shirley Hopkins)
Annapolis, MD

Cover Photograph

Margaret Taylor Randall

(With unidentified young man)

Margaret Taylor Randall was a photographer, the daughter of Dr. Burton Randall of Annapolis. An image of her at work along the shoreline of Arundel-on-the-Bay can be found in Chapter 3, at page 64.

She was born at the Carlisle Barracks in Pennsylvania on January 14, 1861 where her father was serving as a surgeon in the Army during the Civil War. Her mother, Mary Virginia Taylor, was a niece of Zachary Taylor, president of the United States from 1849-50. In 1865 the family lived in New Utrecht, Kings N.Y. while her father served there; later, he became medical director of the hospital established on the Naval Academy grounds.

Herself a descendant from a well-known Annapolis family, Margaret Randall married Joseph Muse Worthington MD (1846-1914) in 1895. The marriage produced five children born between 1895 and 1904: Virginia, John, Margaret, Joseph, and Anna. A member of St. Anne's Church in Annapolis for more than 85 years, she died in Annapolis on February 17, 1959 at the age of 98 and is buried in the church cemetery.

Seven of her photographs are included in the George Forbes Collection of the Maryland State Archives. Forbes (1873-1941) accumulated 2,000 photographs, most taken by professional photographers between 1890 and 1910, which he used for lectures and history-related events in Annapolis.

Historians Review

The Amazing History of Arundel-on-the-Bay 1600s to Today

Burton K. Kummerow, Former President and CEO and Historian-in-Residence, Maryland Historical Society

Community spirit is getting less attention these days in our politically divided nation. There is, however, a drumbeat of local success stories pulsing through the republic. One of those stories has come out of Arundel-on-the-Bay, a pleasant little Chesapeake Bay beach community dotted on an appendix of land that stretches south from Annapolis. During the last 130 years, Washington and Baltimore families have been enjoying summers on the Bay while pioneering women's suffrage and facing civil rights issues as they endured hurricanes and the inevitable advance of the water that surrounded them. ***"The Amazing Story of Arundel-on-the-Bay"*** *is a new illustrated chronicle of generations of families that have loved and endured a special, precarious piece of Chesapeake real estate. The entire community has put this tale together and its spirit in the telling is an inspiration for all of us.*

Jane W. McWilliams, Author of *Bay Ridge on the Chesapeake* and *Annapolis-City on the Severn*

This is the story of a community written with respect and pride by members of that community. Frank, personal, and engaging, ***The Amazing Story of Arundel-on-the Bay, 1600's to Today*** *celebrates one of the oldest summer communities on the western shore of the Chesapeake Bay.*

Although residents over the decades have enjoyed the same benefits as other Bayside communities: swimming, boating, fishing, crabbing, cool summer breezes, and that vacation feeling even in winter, Arundel-on-the Bay is unique among them for its racial history. Settled before the turn of the 20th century as a majority-white summer community for Washington, D.C. families, with only a few African-American property owners, the development became almost exclusively black at mid century, populated by professional people of color, most of them with winter homes in the District. Eventually the advantages of waterfront living, coupled with increased construction, brought white families back to the peninsula, and today Arundel-on-the-Bay sails into the 21st century as a fully integrated neighborhood of mostly year-round residents, sharing community events and working together to achieve community objectives.

It is an "Amazing Story" indeed!

Ellen O. Moyer, former Mayor of Annapolis and author of many articles on local history

Arundel-on-the-Bay founded in the 1890's as a summer home paradise on the Chesapeake Bay is still very much alive. Its residents have done masterful research to describe this once tiny municipality and the vision of the Washington, D.C. elite founders. America's changing culture after WWII also changed Arundel-on-the-Bay to the community it is today. This book, ***"The Amazing Story of Arundel-on-the-Bay"*** *is a must read for anyone interested in culture and social history and the dynamic challenges and relationships that shape a community*

Dedications

Richard Marc Grigsby

(July 10, 1947–February 8, 2016)

Marc was an enthusiastic participant in the deliberations of the History Project Group. He made available to us his startling beautiful images of Arundel-on-the-Bay, the Chesapeake Bay, and wildlife–so many too wonderful it was difficult to choose which to include in the book. Clearly a book of Grigsby images alone would be a treasure to those who love the Bay region!

Marc, his wife Dale, and their son Michael renovated his maternal grandmother's property at Arundel-on-the-Bay beginning in 1981. As Dale indicated in the program for the celebration of his life, they built a house around a house to preserve the existing structure, particularly the fir flooring of the original house. She notes: "The house that exists today, that includes Grandma Anna's fir flooring in the center, was completed in the spring of 1983….the original wood stoves serve as the source of heat for the house even today."

Marc graduated from Roosevelt High School in the District, enlisted in the Air Force, and afterward received a Bachelor of Science degree in Police Science from New Mexico State University. His professional career, for which he was given many awards, included service on the White House Security detail and in the Prince George's County Police Department and the Transportation Security Agency. His fascinating pursuits after his retirement included being a doting grandfather and extensive travel and photography. Our memories of Marc are clear in our minds–as a down-to-earth pragmatic person, a caring neighbor and loving friend, and as the first person out after a storm to assist the community in recovery. Several of his photographs are placed throughout the book of views from our community.

Pamela Duncan

Rick Napoli

(March 7, 1955–December 7, 2013)

Richard P. Napoli moved to Arundel-on-the-Bay in late 2004 and lived there until his death in December 2013. Rick liked living in Arundel-on-the-Bay and truly enjoyed the last two years when he was retired. Rick made friends in the community, first through daily walks, then through volunteering as the treasurer and with the Arundel-on-the-Bay history project.

Rick was a native New Yorker, born in the Bronx. He lived in New York through college, earning at BA in social sciences from the State University of New York at Purchase. Rick moved to the Washington, D.C. area, earning an MA in museum administration from George Washington University. At mid-career Rick attended the Attingham School. Rick spent most of his career in Washington, D.C. managing a federal agency organization that supports White House operations.

Rick was attracted to the Bay as an ocean kayaker and to the area as a cyclist on its winding country roads. He had a wide range of interests, from the outdoors to history, art and antiques. In his later years Rick was drawn back into scholarly research. This was a passion from his teenage years when Rick was an amateur archaeologist, that during his career he channeled into work-related projects. When Rick retired it led to his work on the Arundel-on-the-Bay history project which focused on archival research.

Josefa O'Malley

Louise Kent Linkins Bezdek Seely

(February 13, 1913–February 15, 2018)

We lost Louise on February 15, 2018 at the age of 105 and 2 days. A friend and critic of our work since I met her in Florida in 2012, Louise reviewed two complete drafts of our book. She made meticulous marginal notes and wrote dozens of letters and notes explaining portions of our history that only she could have comprehended. She allowed me to scan all of the photos in her picture albums, many of which are in the book. Her family's span, from 1895 to 1972, represents the longest and most complete memory of anyone in our community. The community itself only began in 1890 and her Great Uncle, former congressman Lewis E. Payson, was one of the early residents and a commissioner of the town. On several occasions we had her recollections and her son Hugo's friend, Tommy Carroll Worthington, on the same event; namely the 1933 hurricane. It was precious to hear each of them calling the other out on one point or another. Hugo's memories of riding on the horse-drawn trash wagon were so vivid that I think of him (and the flies) every time I see those photos. The most valuable contribution in my mind was Hugo's and Louise's recollection of life between the black and white areas of the community. Legends are challenged and folklore debunked. Her insight and her father's close friendship with the John Wesley (Wes) Harris family helped us to stitch together several loose ends in our history. She is survived by her sons, Hugo F. Bezdek III and James C. Bezdek, 6 grandchildren and many great and great-great grandchildren. She moved to Atlantic Beach, Florida in 1992 and was active there in volunteer activities including the library and the Beaches Baptist Hospital where she knitted hats and mittens for newborns continuously until her death.

Bill Semenuk

Thomas Carroll Worthington Jr

(September 8, 1929–November 22, 2017)

Tom was an enthusiastic contributor to the History Project Group. He spent his summers at his grandfather's home on "the point" from 1929 until the 1960s. He gave several interviews, wrote numerous e-mails, answered many questions from the group, and made available to us his family albums and movies from the 1920s through the 1960s.

From his photos we have been able to contact over a dozen residents who lived here from 1929 until the 1970s and to record recollections from the 1933 hurricane, the 1916 fire, the post civil rights act changes and much more. He gave us never-before seen images of Arundel-on-the-Bay, Thomas's Island, Chesapeake Bay log canoes, and more.

Tom's grandfather owned the William H. Thomas Clothing and Tailor shop on Main Street in downtown Annapolis, which later became the home of the Stevens Hardware store. Tom followed his father into the family real estate business, Worthington & Associates. They were instrumental in passing along the historic post-1947 Arundel-on-the-Bay real estate sales to the Carroll Hynson firm.

Tom graduated from the Severn School and attended Johns Hopkins University. He served his country in various overseas assignments for the U.S. Government. An avid hunter and fly fisherman he, together with his wife Linda, traveled to Canada, Africa, Scotland, and widely in this country.

In addition to our Arundel-on-the-Bay book, he has made numerous contributions to *Over the Bridge,* the pictorial history of Eastport. Tom cherished his membership in the historic Ancient South River Club, where we presented our fledgling book results in 2016.

Bill Semenuk

Preface

In February 2011 a group of Arundel-on-the-Bay residents gathered at the home of Marc Apter, then a member of the Board of Directors of the Property Owners Association, to join the effort convened by him to write the history of the community. Collegially, over coffee, juice, fruit, lox and bagels, and sweet rolls, a series of discussions led to an outline of a book and its chapter headings. Research and writing responsibilities evolved as did the questions which needed answers. Since, many wonderful people have provided their memories and photographs. We are especially thankful for the contributions of Louise Linkins Seely and Thomas Carroll Worthington Jr.

Throughout our history residents of Arundel-on-the-Bay have enjoyed the Chesapeake Bay as a natural resource of great beauty and found that the bonds of family life and friendship were strengthened while spending time on its shores. At the same time, each generation has recognized the need to contend with the problems life by the shore brings—damage from hurricanes and other storms, land erosion, and the maintenance of infrastructure and community services.

We have been continually surprised during our work, particularly to discover the shift in the physical form of our community and its built environment, and in the nature of its population. We are delighted to share this product of our endeavors, a compendium of life at one place on the shore of the Chesapeake Bay over a period of four centuries.

The History Project Group: Aris T. Allen Jr., Philip Allen, Marc L. Apter, Wilma Coble, Edie Dolberg, Pamela T. Duncan, Richard Marc Grigsby,* Bob Meissner, John Moses, Rick Napoli,* Karen J. Neale, Bill Semenuk, and Arend Thomas III.

*Deceased

Osprey Nest and Kayaker on the Bayfront. *Photograph by Marc Grigsby*

Foreword

Kurt L. Schmoke
President
University of Baltimore

Enlightening and inspiring. That is the history of the community known as Arundel-on-the-Bay. It was my beautiful wife who introduced me to this lovely place. Throughout her formative years growing up in Baltimore, Patricia had the great pleasure of spending part of each summer at a waterfront house owned by her grandparents in the neighboring community known as Oyster Harbor. She dreamed of one day owning a home in this area, and she was particularly drawn to Arundel-on-the-Bay by meeting a number of people who lived or visited there. By pure chance, a physician who practiced in Baltimore and owned a home in Arundel-on-the-Bay passed away, and his executor was keen on selling the property to another Baltimore-based physician. Enter Dr. Patricia Schmoke. She took one look at the property, which abuts Fishing Creek, and it was love at first sight. I looked at the same property and saw a decaying cottage suffering from years of deferred maintenance. Unlike my wife, my eyes were not drawn to the water, and the birds of the Chesapeake that were little more than a stone's throw away.

We purchased our little slice of Arundel-on-the-Bay paradise with the thought of it being a nice weekend getaway place. However, over a short period of time, the definition of weekend changed, and the days of residence in Arundel-on-the-Bay got longer and longer, until we made the decision to become permanent residents of the community. We were drawn to the contemporary pleasures of a place set between a great bay and a modest creek. What we did not know until reading this history, were the stories of the wonderfully diverse individuals who have enriched the quality of life of this place.

These pages reveal that Arundel-on-the-Bay has travelled a long and winding road from summer resort to a year round vibrant community. As one who once commuted daily from Arundel-on-the-Bay to Washington, D.C., I read with interest—and with envy—the fact that the community was served for decades by train service that went to Washington's Union Station in about an hour and a half. I was also surprised to learn that there was an amusement park in the nearby Bay Ridge neighborhood that in its day was considered one of the top recreation attractions on the East Coast.

The political history of Arundel-on-the-Bay is also of great interest. Early in the 20th century, Arundel-on-the-Bay had two political marks of distinction. First, it was at one time the smallest incorporated township in the United States. Only one person lived here year-round, making it truly a one-man town. Second, prior to the passage of the 19th Amendment to the U.S. Constitution, Arundel-on-the-Bay was the only jurisdiction in the State of Maryland that extended the right to vote to women. At the time, the extension of women's suffrage was considered so unusual that it was the subject of out-of-state press coverage at the annual elections of the town commissioners.

Today, Arundel-on-the-Bay is a racially mixed community of recent arrivals such as myself, and long-time residents who have been here for decades. This book confronts the very complicated story of the community as it concerns race relations. Complicated is the correct term to be used, for one will find that although the community was founded by investors who in 1890 largely created a whites-only summer resort, African Americans purchased property as early as 1893. In an interesting example of what is described as the Arundel-on-the-Bay "conundrum of race," at the same time that AOTB commissioners were enacting racially-restrictive covenants on the sale of property, white residents of the community were using the services of an African American doctor (who lived on the north side of the community) for emergency medical care. There would come a time when the resort community would shift from an all-white to an almost all-black community, but the recent history is one of not only embracing racial diversity but also celebrating it.

No foreword would be complete without a mention of the history of Arundel-on-the-Bay's encounter with the forces of nature. The location of the community along the Chesapeake Bay is a source of joy and pleasure to the residents. However, throughout the history of Arundel-on-the-Bay there have been challenges with the forces of nature that have brought about profound changes to the community. Stories are recounted of families dealing with hurricanes, typhoid fever, and a great fire that swept through the resort in the early part of the last century, calling into question whether the community would survive. The resilient people, with their love of this environment, revived Arundel-on-the-Bay, allowing it to grow from a resort of 33 cottages to a community of nearly 800 people. It is my hope that you will not only enjoy this history, but also draw from it both insight and inspiration.

Fishing Creek Churning, Hurricane Isabel, 2003. ***Photograph by Marc Grigsby***

Table of Contents

Photograph by Marc Grigsby

Chapter One

The Early Experience

Philip Allen

Our peninsula has attracted migrant hunters, gatherers, and warriors toward the Chesapeake for eons, but as a place of steady residence, it had to grow up rather rapidly—over the past 125 years. Although Arundel-on-the-Bay played no conspicuous role in history, even in the regional or local narratives, this beautiful outpost witnessed centuries of lively commercial and military traffic on the Bay. It's true that Captain John Smith's first maps and journals (1608 and 1612) indicate no sign of settlement along the coast between the Susquehanna and Patuxent Rivers; and that current inventories of "Indian" towns and tribes show no such installations there.[1] Indeed, Arundel-on-the-Bay sat at the farthest end of the region's "Middle Neck"—the mid-region between Broadneck to the north and South River Hundred. It remained an interested bystander for more than two centuries while Annapolis was emerging sporadically into a prosperous capital city.

Before the Maryland Colony

Modern scientific teams have been uncovering abundant evidence of pre-colonial residence and transience at various sites around the Severn and South Rivers—if not precisely at our place, not yet. We know, moreover, that Native Americans prospered along the Patuxent until they succumbed to contact with the weapons and diseases carried by English colonists in and around St. Mary's City. Algonquin language groups like the Piscataway circulated for nearly a millennium among Chesapeake camps and villages in forest clearings along nearby rivers, as they hunted, fished, and grew corn and other food crops. This activity began to decline in the latter sixteenth century when marauding Susquehannock (Iroquois-speaking) bands expelled the more docile Piscataway southward from our region; to make matters worse, the Powhatan also raided from the south, leaving our coasts a kind of "no man's land."[2]

Hence, until archaeologists peel off some of Arundel-on-the-Bay's surface to disclose evidence of Native American habitation (arrowheads, shards, shells, bead work, maybe even burial sites), we can only conjecture how and when humans frequented our bailiwick before they began leaving written records.

In the absence of such evidence, we suppose those Native Americans to have been transient hunters and fisher-folk, for the peninsula offered them an abundance of forest and water life, as well as good shelter for small boats. They sojourned on this extremity, between the peninsulas now named Bay Ridge to the north and Thomas Point to the south, beneath stands of red and white oak, sassafras, cedar, tulip poplar, hickory, sweet gum, and native chestnut trees, and among lower layers of dogwood, holly, red maple, and

Figure 1: Arundel on the Bay's typical bird – osprey parent about to feed chicks in their home-made nest. ***Photo by Marc Grigsby.***

flowering bush. Through this terrestrial endowment circulated deer, bear, fox, wild boar, squirrels, and rabbits, and above them a host of migratory birds and residential gulls, birds of prey, woodpeckers, hummingbirds, and mockingbirds. The waters abounded in aquatic fowl and fish (including sturgeon), terrapin, crabs, and oysters, some of them reportedly huge.

Thus, while welcoming people in search of food, the peninsula reminded them, as it does ourselves, that they were here thanks to the indulgence of The Bay.

The Chesapeake

That bay is the largest estuary on the American continent, nearly 200 miles in length and 30 miles wide at the Potomac's mouth, although it narrows to only four miles between Annapolis and Kent Island. Its 4,000 miles of shoreline rim great rivers, tidal creeks, shallow coves, wetlands, and myriad islands – although not so many now, as erosion has cost the Bay some of its land endowment. The watershed extends northward into New York State via the Susquehanna, and westward into Appalachia, thanks to the Potomac. What is now Arundel-on-the-Bay occupied at most 130 acres – over 300 acres when combined with Oyster Harbor, still less than a half-mile square – on the Middle Neck at 38 degrees 55 minutes north latitude and 76 degrees 27 minutes 30 seconds west longitude.

Although subject to robust storms, often at inconvenient moments, the Chesapeake's climate, currents, and tides are normally gentle. Its shallow shoulders on either side of the deep channel, while perilous to unsuspecting boaters, encourage prodigious flora and fauna when sunlight is allowed in. That deep central channel is actually the ancient bed of the Susquehanna River as it foraged down toward the Atlantic, fed by melting glaciers in the late Pleistocene ("ice age") ending about 12,000 years ago. The rivers to our north carry fresh water (and much debris) into this segment of the Bay, while Virginia's capes toward the mouth are force-fed by incoming heavy salt water.

Early European Settlers

Enjoyment of the Chesapeake's bounty devolved rapidly to the British colonists – mostly non-conformist Protestants–who began moving into Southern Maryland after King Charles I's grant of a proprietary charter to Cecilius (Cecil) Calvert, second Lord Baltimore, in 1632. The territory had already been explored by William Claiborne, who set up a trading mission for fur trappers on Kent Island in the 1620s and who persisted in challenging Lord Baltimore for political control of the province. No doubt these trappers and traders knew our peninsula, but they did not put down roots here. Many of the earliest settlers came in search of religious breathing room promised by the Roman Catholic Calverts and subsequently under Maryland's Toleration Act of 1649. They came at first from Anglican Virginia and were eventually joined by immigrants arriving directly from England at St. Mary's. The newcomers either booked passage on their own or were "transported"–arriving in debt (indenture) to those who paid their passage. As their servitude expired, white and (for a brief period) African immigrants took parcels of land, some of it also claimed by Native Americans.

Relations with the native population had begun cordially, but they deteriorated as land acquisitions eroded what the original inhabitants regarded as their own. In 1650, following the alleged murder of an Englishman, the Maryland General Assembly at St. Mary's prohibited "any Indians" from entering the new Anne Arundel County without prior authorization. In 1652, after desultory hostilities, the Susquehanna nation was defeated by the Maryland Anglos; in exchange for peace, the Susquehannock ceded rights to land on both eastern and western shores of the Bay and were eventually absorbed by the Iroquois Senecas. From an estimated population of 6,500 in the early seventeenth century (the majority of them Algonquin speaking), Maryland's native population dwindled to only about 140 by 1756.

From the outset, immigrants brought their families with them, as well as livestock, tobacco seedlings, seed corn, and "servants" (white and black), most of them bonded for a specific number of years before slavery set into the Maryland economy. Some colonists trickled from St. Mary's into the more fertile lands that in 1650 became Anne Arundel County; the new county was named for Cecilius Calvert's recently deceased wife, whose father had sought a New World sanctuary for Roman Catholics as early as 1605. These predominantly Puritan (non-conformist Anglican) settlers, joined by Quakers, Roman Catholics, and others, were attracted by the 50-acre tracts offered along the Severn and South Rivers through Land Office grants from the proprietor Lord Baltimore. The most prudent settlers had their claims surveyed and subsequently patented by the Land Office.[3] By 1652, at least 87 families (some 400 people) had settled in our county, growing Oronoco tobacco in what has been called "reasonably good poor man's country"–good that is, for those who survived the inhospitable climate and other threats to health.[4]

In the 1660s, however, as European immigration declined and illness took its toll on many already here, African captives and native-born African Americans became increasingly crucial on the labor-intensive tobacco plantations. The demand intensified during boom years for tobacco, as in 1697-1707. For both economic and racial reasons, that work force fell under a caste system that condemned them to lifelong servitude, precluded freedom of movement, and denied them access to the courts until 1864. The condition of children followed that of the mothers, thus bonding even the progeny of European fathers to fields and households. By 1860, the population of Annapolis (4,529) was nearly 30 percent African American; while almost two-thirds of those town dwellers were "free blacks," few African Americans lived freely in rural spaces like our peninsula.

Figure 2. Augustine Hermann map of "Virginia, Maryland" 1670. Arundel-on-the-Bay peninsula peeks out between the Severn and South Rivers, see highlighted area. ***Collection of the Maryland State Archives.***

The Calvert monopoly was promptly challenged by champions of the Puritan Parliament that succeeded England's monarchy after the assassination of Charles I in 1649. In 1655, the two factions fought the Battle of the Severn off what is now Horn Point in contemporary Eastport; they concluded peace two years later. In 1689, following another period of turmoil, King William III and Queen Mary II assumed Crown authority over the Roman Catholic Calverts' erstwhile domain. The colony was restored to the fifth Baron Baltimore in 1714 after his conversion to the Anglican faith. By 1708, when our county's first town was chartered, it was named Annapolis after Mary's sister, who had already succeeded her to the throne as Queen Anne. Under the provisional name of Ann Arundel Town, however, Annapolis had already supplanted St. Mary's as capital of the Maryland province in 1695.[5]

Disappointing the Calverts who advocated development of urban life along the Bay, most of the early planters lived on their estates, not in towns. They traded in and out of sheltered private landings reached by lighters from ships at anchor, rather than via central port sites. The budding exception was Providence across the Severn from what is now Annapolis, which offered port facilities (including access to slave traders), ship's supplies, and refitting industries. Even after the transfer of those facilities across the Severn to present-day Annapolis, the shallow harbor and scarcity of timber in the hinterland – in addition to "fear of the [timber-eating] worm" (*teredo navalis*) – restrained urban port development. Decline of the Severn's port was hastened by collapses in price of over-abundant tobacco on London markets in the late 17th and again in the early 18th centuries. In any case, the Annapolis capital gradually yielded oceanic prominence to Baltimore and the Patapsco with their wider, more populous hinterland, deeper port, and cooler water temperature. Boasting little protective escarpment ("fall line") close to shore, young Anne Arundel County produced few other towns, and certainly none on our own small peninsula. Nevertheless, at nearby London Towne (now Edgewater) across the South River, Col. William Burgess, in partnership with his brother-in-law Richard Beard, conducted much trade in commodities and slaves with England and the Caribbean until his death in 1686.

While denied the temptations of urban and mercantile life, the Middle Neck forest did invite Anglo colonists into its seventeenth century precincts–like the Native Americans who had been frequenting them for centuries. Nevertheless, the descriptions that follow for that century remain largely conjecture, for want of solid documentary and archaeological evidence. Here, just four miles to the southeast of Annapolis, there are intimations of a track running through our densely forested peninsula to intersect with the road to "Tolleys Point" (now Bay Ridge); farther north, that pathway connects with routes to Annapolis and to the South River across from London Towne.[6] No such track appears in Augustine Hermann's map, drawn in 1670 for the Lord Proprietor, but Hermann did place one tiny symbol sitting lonely and unarticulated on Arundel-on-the-Bay's peninsula, resembling several images that designate "plantations" along the Severn and South Rivers.[7]

If Hermann's wee symbol is accurate rather than arbitrary, it's likely that by 1670 our dense forest was giving way gradually to cultivation of tobacco, corn, and vegetables, some cattle, hogs, and poultry (horses became common only in the late 18th century). As the land grant process evolved, Tidewater plantations tended to average about 300 acres, putting them at a distance of roughly one-half mile from one-another. What are now Arundel-on-the-Bay and Oyster Harbor were bordered on the north by Richard Beard's "Dock" (currently Fishing Creek Farms) and Walter Smith's "Rest" on Cherrystone (Cherrytree) Creek; that creek empties into the South River near what are now Duvall Creek and Kitty Duvall Drive, just beyond the junction of Thomas Point and Arundel-on-the-Bay roads. North of those properties stood Samuel Withers' "Outlet," at the crossroads with the Bay Ridge-Annapolis highway.

This land and its shores were worked no doubt by tenants of absentee landowners with their families, slaves, and indentured servants. Life in the Middle Neck was hard-scrabble, but the clay and loam soils proved courteous enough, and the inhabitants could manage if they survived the ravages of childbirth and disease (especially smallpox and scarlet fever). Gradual decline of the tobacco market, especially from the mid-18th century, enforced a diversification of economic activity against the threat of poverty in Annapolis's rural environs. Land was converted to corn, wheat, flax, and pasture, instead of being entirely dedicated to tobacco's insatiable appetite for soil and labor. Livestock was raised for meat and sometimes for manure to fertilize croplands; there seems to have been very little dairy in the regional diet. Only in the subsequent century did a seafood industry burgeon to absorb labor and energy from the Bay littoral.

While tobacco remained the local cash crop, it demanded intense labor in cleared forest plots, and it was vulnerable to boom-bust market cycles in England, continental Europe, and the West Indies. Until Revolutionary times, those who got rich here tended to be land speculators and entrepreneurs (including shippers and slave traders). Farming could reward only those women and men who were willing to sacrifice consumer pleasures for the toil exacted by the tobacco cycle, and who cleared sufficient space for crop rotation and pasture. Most farm families merely clung to the land where the demand for labor virtually precluded cultivation of crafts and the finer arts. Farmers bought furniture, clothing, and even tools from importers, often paying in tobacco rather than currency. Unusually cold weather at the end of the 17th century exacerbated the hardships caused by recessionary periods in 1686-1696 and 1708-1714. When conditions improved, plantations could expand production of root vegetables, fruit (especially apples), pork, mutton, and game, fish and oysters, as well as beverages like cider, beer, and (some) milk in seasons when freshened cows had surpluses; high summer temperatures appear to have discouraged butter and cheese making.

It is doubtful that any of the planter-owners built permanent dwellings for themselves on our territory – let alone the grand manor houses typical of prosperous tidewater plantations elsewhere. They or their tenants often lived as though in camps, retreating for the winter to more comfortable lodgings on some home estate. In places with seasonal activity like our own they erected small, rude, fragile, unpainted frame dwellings (not log cabins) with dirt floors. Proprietors, tenants, and servant or slave families usually occupied the same dwelling until time and finances permitted the addition of out-buildings. None of these structures has survived to our times. For the landed colonial elite, our modest peninsula had neither the attractions of Annapolis nor the secure landings and anchorages of more sheltered sites. As Wilstach comments, "the planters rarely built along the exposed bay side [preferring] home sites in the rivers and creeks, in the lie of a point if possible."[8] As for the creek side, the original opening (gut) into South River was too narrow and too shallow to permit mercantile shipping. In 1852, a new break was cut through the beach, giving small craft access from creek into Bay, but aggravating erosion; as a result the entire east-west island that once linked the tips of Arundel-on-the-Bay and today's Thomas Point has disappeared.

Figure 3. Remnant of Thomas Island (now vanished), see highlighted area; photographed in 1924 by island owner Garnett Clark, with Thomas Point Lighthouse in upper left corner, Thomas Point peninsula in center. ***Image from Thomas C. Worthington Collection provided by Sandy Clark to Bill Semenuk.***

The Landowner Lineage

So, who were those 17th and 18th century proprietors who failed to appreciate the advantages so evident to modern residents of Arundel-on-the-Bay? Although many court records are either missing–in consequence of a fire in 1705–or unclear, we can trace (or guess at) some of the transfers of property in our neighborhood from the 17th through the 19th centuries. As it happens, we must begin with a mystery. Drawing from the first book of surveys prepared for the Lord Proprietor by Master Robert Burle, the "John Hammond mapp" constructed by 20th-century historian James Moss attributes ownership of some 280 acres on our peninsula to one William Pennington.[9] Surveyed in 1650 as "Pennington's Ponds," this holding, if Moss is accurate, seems to have been ephemeral, for the title appears nowhere else in the surviving records. Still, the "ponds" (or at least one of them) might have designated our Fishing Creek, often termed "Fishing Cove." The cove was then virtually enclosed on the south by the not-yet-eroded island bridge from what is now Thomas Point in the west to "Philip Thomas Poynt" just southeast of Arundel-on-the-Bay's own point today. Hence, it *might* have been thought of as a "pond," and we can conjecture that Pennington failed to patent his claim. We also don't know for certain who acquired it from him and when.

The Pennington clan did earn more categorical attention elsewhere in the land records. We learn that the original William Pennington "received" some land in 1661 from Nathaniel and Mary Utie after "transporting" himself to the province. Pennington's sons, William and Thomas, left orphaned by their father's death in 1670, were raised as wards of the province by Colonel Burgess, the distinguished resident of London Towne, and by Captain Richard Hill, a major figure in Annapolitan and Bay Ridge history, whose descendant, Joseph Hill, purchased at least part of our peninsula in 1712. Those orphaned sons were themselves prosperous enough to have acquired real estate in St. Anne's (Annapolis) and St. Margaret's (Broadneck) parishes, although none of it is identifiable with "Pennington's Ponds" or today's Arundel-on-the-Bay. Moreover, the original William Pennington, although unable perhaps to patent his local "ponds," conveyed some land (but which? and when?) to one Ralph Williams; yet we do not know what Williams might have done with that mysterious parcel.

In the absence of precise records, it is possible that Pennington's un-patented ponds were sold before 1670, the probable year of William Pennington's death, to one Robert Davidge, who had immigrated into the county several years earlier. We know that Davidge tried to patent what he called "Davidge's Meadows" several times beginning in 1655. He succeeded only in 1705, with a name change to "Davidge's Purchase," designating what is now Oyster Harbor down to Fishing Creek and continuing into a northern fragment of the Thomas Point peninsula. In 1739, Davidge's planter heirs re-patented their Thomas Point farm and acquired various others. However, it seems probable that the then contiguous acreage now identified as Arundel-on-the-Bay and Thomas Point was granted by Lord Baltimore to Philip Thomas who patented it in 1665. Himself progenitor of a notable line, Thomas had arrived at St. Mary's from Bristol in 1651 with his wife Sarah and three children. He was granted some 500 acres on "the west of the Chesapeake," including 121 acres of what had been known as Fuller's Point but later took Thomas' name; that was of course when the "point" enclosed Fishing Creek to the south through the now vanished island joining the tip of Arundel-on-the-Bay. The original designation was to Captain William Fuller, who was to organize an insurrection against Lord Baltimore's governor William Stone, ending in the Battle of the Severn in 1656. In May 1658, Thomas joined with Fuller in the Anne Arundel delegation to the negotiations with Stone that led to an amicable compromise. Thomas thereupon abandoned politics and, like many others in the neighborhood, joined the Society of Friends. Unlike other regions of the colonies, Quakers seem to have dwelt amicably alongside Anglicans and others in tolerant 17th century western Chesapeake.

Beginning in 1664, Thomas and his descendants expanded their original holdings, and eventually produced three governors of Maryland as well as several members of

Congress. They parted with Fuller's Thomas Point and The Barrens in 1705, the year that Davidge first succeeded in patenting his neighboring "purchase"—and the year that fire destroyed many earlier records. It was then that the Thomas family sold their 121 acres to one John Prindiwill, another planter, for 55 pounds Sterling (the equivalent of $9,800 today), who resold them promptly for 60 pounds to a shipwright named Robert Johnson. We don't know what Johnson did with his acquisition.

Chain of Hills and Chases

The chain of title resumes, and with improved clarity. In 1712, 1,410 acres of Anne Arundel County were purchased by Joseph Hill from his Philadelphia merchant brother Richard. This Joseph Hill died in 1724. This vast property included 135 acres designated "The Barrens," a tract that seems virtually coextensive with today's Arundel-on-the-Bay. The designation Barrens (aka Bearrens, even Barrons) may imply an absence of agricultural and maritime production in our forested neighborhood, but most of the area is regularly referred to as farmland, and Hill was willing to pay for it. A descendant, Captain Richard Hill, had been a prominent Annapolis town official, merchant, and proprietor of portions of present day Hillsmere, Bay Ridge, Annapolis Roads, and Eastport. In 1750, eleven years before he died, his descendant, Joseph Hill, deeded the Barrens to his granddaughter, Henrietta Margaret Hill Ogle, wife of Benjamin Ogle, subsequently governor of Maryland. Known as "Henry Margaret," the governor's wife, herself a descendant of the Thomas clan, owned more than 2,000 acres of Anne Arundel, but the Ogle family seemed perpetually in need of money—and that's where Jeremiah Chase comes in.

Jeremiah Townley Chase (1748-1828) was a second cousin to Samuel Chase, one of four Maryland signers of the Declaration of Independence. A distinguished citizen in his own right, Jeremiah Chase served as chief judge of the Maryland Court of Appeals after a term in Congress in 1783-84, and as mayor of Annapolis, where he welcomed George Washington in 1783 and the Marquis de Lafayette in 1785.

Judge Chase was also an avid collector of Maryland real estate and a shrewd land speculator. During and after the Revolution, he bought up property left by British subjects and Tory loyalists, as well as parcels whose owners had neglected to survey and patent within the required two-year period. Chase commanded admirable credit, enabling him to delay payment for his own acquisitions until after the formal surveys were completed, so that he eventually accumulated interests in several thousand acres of Maryland. In 1789, after some internal Davidge family transfers, he acquired "The Purchase" from Ezekial Davidge, making him the owner of Oyster Harbor and much of Thomas Point. Three years later, he also acquired The Barrens from Benjamin Ogle, making him full owner of our immediate neighborhood—Arundel-on-the-Bay, Oyster Harbor, and Thomas Point. Chase paid 653 pounds for the Barrens' 135 acres, the equivalent of $85,600 in current U.S. dollars. This tenfold increase in value from the mere 60 pounds ($10,000) paid in 1705 suggests that, assuming Chase knew his property values, the "barren" tract that became Arundel-on-the-Bay had been much improved by 1792.

In 1823, toward the close of his elaborate last will and testament—after meticulously designating property bequests to four other fortunate children and grandchildren —Jeremiah Townley Chase dictated the following, almost as an afterthought:

> I give and devise unto my dear daughter Hester Ann and the heirs of her body lawfully begotten all the rest of my lands lying on Oyster and Fishing Creeks South River and

Figure 4: Map of Anne Arundel County, 1860 by Simon J. Martenet, showing Hester Chase ownership of the peninsula lower right, with the Thomas Point Island and former Light House at bottom. ***Collection of the Maryland State Archives.***

the bay including Thomas' point and adjoining the lands devised unto my daughter Lockerman.[10]

The last reference was to Frances Chase Lockerman (also spelled Loockermann), Hester Ann's older sister, who earlier in the document inherited the current Thomas Point peninsula and the island that still bridged the two peninsulas. In 1824, Chase chopped seven acres off that property (part of the connecting island) for sale to the Federal Government as a site for the first light-house in our vicinity; the government also obtained a right of way through 71 acres leading to the lighthouse site.

Upon her father's death in 1828, "dear daughter Hester Ann" at 37 years of age thus became the sole owner of the future Arundel-on-the-Bay and Oyster Harbor. The detail from *A Map of Anne Arundel County*, by Simon J. Martenet (Fig. 4), shows "Miss H. Chase" as the proprietor of our peninsula, at least to the junction of what is now Magnolia Avenue with the Bay.[11]

Remaining unmarried (and otherwise unproductive of "lawfully begotten" heirs) until her own death in 1875, Hester Ann Chase also inherited a share of her father's Annapolis residence–the historic Hammond Harwood House–on the corner of Maryland Avenue and King George Street, which he had bought in 1811, as well as household furniture and other possessions in Annapolis. She also acquired five bonded servants, rights to rental income in Baltimore, and bank stock. Some of that inheritance had to be sold – along with legacies contributed by Chase's other children – to pay the debts of her father's estate after 1828. Nevertheless, residing at 22 Maryland Avenue, the Chase-Lloyd House, which she purchased in 1847, Hester Ann Chase retained sufficient wealth to be called "the town's wealthiest woman."[12] She was an original investor in the Annapolis Gas and Light and the Annapolis Water Companies. Under Jeremiah Chase's will, the slaves bequeathed to Hester Ann and her siblings were to have been emancipated at specified intervals after his death, some of them unconditionally, others on condition of "behaving themselves well and faithfully in the mean time." We do not know which, if any, lived or worked in Arundel-on-the-Bay.

Although Hester Ann Chase was clearly the owner of the Arundel-on-the-Bay peninsula, we can discover no evidence that she (or any of the Chase dynasty) ever resided or even sojourned there. She bequeathed the Barrens and her share of Davidge's Purchase by her will of 1873 to her niece, Matilda Chase, who thereupon left them to her sister, Hester Ann Ridout, née Chase. Exceedingly wealthy in her own right, Ms. Ridout devised the holdings in 1886 onto her cousin, Richard M. Chase, who in turn transferred them in September 1890–as tracts known as "The Fishing Creek" (the erstwhile Barrens) and "Thomas Point Farm" (Davidge's Purchase) – to the Chesapeake and Columbia Investment Company "in consideration of the sum of one dollar."[13] While we are unsure of any collateral interests that might have accrued to Richard or other Chases from the sale, it is probable that $8,500 changed hands in the transaction–again only a fraction of what Jeremiah Chase paid for The Barrens alone. So, after this chain of terrestrial "begats," our beloved Middle Neck seemed cheaply disposed of for development.

Alarums and Excursions

While soon worth far more than the purchase price, our bailiwick probably remained rather barren and (at Oyster Harbor) quite swampy at the time of its sale. Moreover, it participated in historical change mainly by ricochet. Four miles to the north as crows flew, Annapolis experienced indirect effects from the French and Indian War (1754 to 1763) as well as colonist protests over British exactions like the Stamp Act (1774), but these impositions fell upon trades people and other middle-class folk, not the peasantry of the Middle Neck. Urban residents abandoned their city in 1775-1776, anticipating invasion by the Redcoats, but they fled to the north and west of Annapolis, not into our forests. Annapolis

Figure 5: Thomas Point Light House, current site. ***Photo by Marc Grigsby***

and its hinterland glanced at the American Revolution from their perch on the Chesapeake, but did not feel the shock of war directly, even though the British did blockade the Bay until 1781. In August 1777, Admiral Richard Howe's fleet of 260 ships sailed past on their way to disembark British troops for the invasion of Philadelphia, and they sailed back again, saving Annapolitans—but offending their sensibilities—by disdainfully bypassing the state capital. None of that migration touched the Arundel-on-the-Bay backwater—unless its farms had to contribute provisions to support the billeting of friendly soldiers in the town.

"There would be no lighthouse to warn of that treacherous patch for another twelve years"

So, our predecessors in rural Anne Arundel were spared the hostilities that afflicted other places prominent in the annals of American military history. They escaped the habitual vicissitudes that accompany warfare conscription, destruction of property, ruinous billeting of troops, and the crime and corruption of a contractor economy. But they also remained on the margins of cultural and technical changes that were converting Annapolis into a significant if modest metropolis. As the Articles of Confederation gave way to the Constitution of the United States, that small nearby capital city acted as a political and cultural bridge between colonial and revolutionary America, into the founding of our republic. By contrast, the Arundel-on-the-Bay peninsula had to await the decisions of the Chesapeake and Columbia Investment Company after 1890 to begin to enjoy the social and economic progress pledged by the new America.

Naval activity became a bit more exciting during the 1812 war. In February 1813 the British again blockaded the Bay but did not challenge the two forts built on the Severn to defend Annapolis. They did send a fleet in April of that year to harass other parts of the littoral, anchoring off Tolly's Point; but they turned back on 12 May without troubling the Annapolis area – although residents fled the town once again, and not for the last time. In that return voyage, however, a British sloop-of-war ran aground on the shoal over a mile offshore from Thomas Point just outside the mouth of the South River (there would be no lighthouse to warn of that treacherous patch for another twelve years). For a time, the Annapolis garrison considered improvising an earthwork battery on the Point to destroy the enemy vessel, but the plan proved unfeasible. It might even have been dangerous, for the sloop had signaled for help to larger warships that could have wiped out the battery and even attacked Annapolis if the city's defenders had been preoccupied elsewhere. A British frigate eventually arrived to haul the sloop off the shoal.[14]

Later in that war, the British attacked Kent Island but not the western shore of the bay, and a frigate with four schooners captured a packet boat from Cambridge in the waters off Thomas Point. The British fleet passed again several times, including on the way to assault Baltimore, and some even ran aground off Kent Island, but without stopping to disturb Annapolis or its environs. The attack on Washington proceeded via Bladensburg, not Annapolis as was feared, and our forebears remained unscathed while the nation's capital burned. For its part, the future Arundel-on-the-Bay remained absorbed in its mainly agricultural preoccupations from one war to the next–and beyond that.

Tightly garrisoned and carefully neutralized by Federal forces in the Civil War, Anne Arundel County remained sympathetic to secession, hostile to President Lincoln, and overwhelmingly opposed to the emancipation of slaves. Eighty percent voted in November 1864 against the state convention decision for emancipation; a majority of Annapolis electors voted no. Lincoln's 1864 reelection received only 12 percent support in the county. He was even obstructed by ice off Thomas Point in February 1865 while proceeding to his futile negotiations with Confederate delegates aboard the *River Queen* at Hampton Roads, Virginia. In 1870, Maryland refused to ratify the 15th Amendment to the Constitution, which guaranteed the right to vote to men regardless of race, color, or previous condition of servitude.

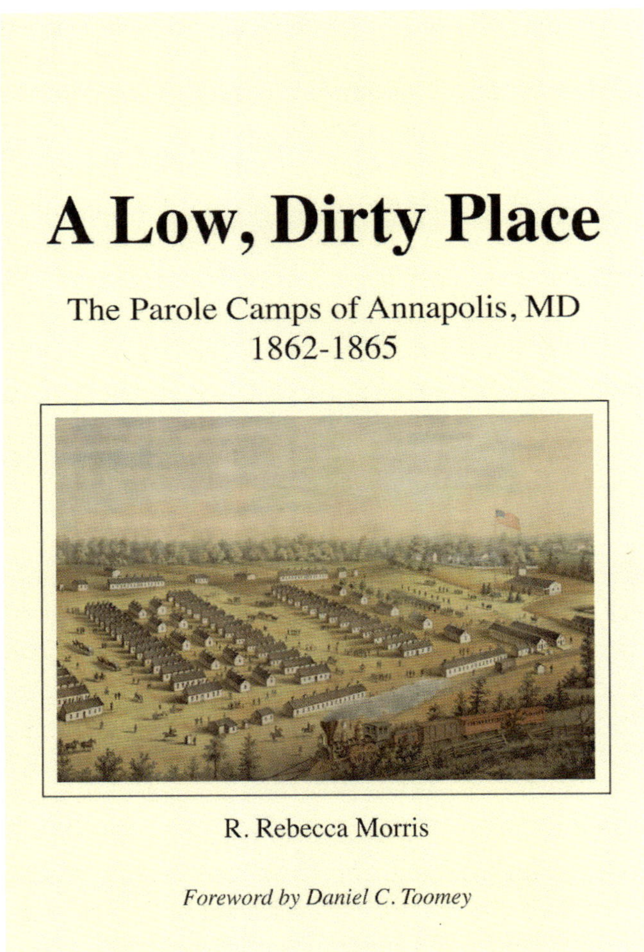

Figure 6: R. Rebecca Morris, *A Low, Dirty Place,* 2012, book cover, showing the camp at Parole near Annapolis.

The U.S. Naval School (now Naval Academy) had opened in Annapolis in 1845, but the town lost that distinction temporarily to Newport, R.I., out of concern for the academy's security during the Civil War. The city even had to house an unruly camp for repatriated Union prisoners from 1862 to 1865. This "low, dirty" installation, known as Parole, is well treated in a recent monograph by Arundel-on-the-Bay resident Rebecca Morris.[15]

Combined with the uncongenial Union presence in the city, the perils of Parole induced many urban residents to take flight to country places, none of them located hereabouts, so far as we know. Despite the pro-secession sentiments of the county population, local merchants and farmers profited from more than four years of occupation by Union troops who needed shelter and nourishment. City residents returned gradually to Annapolis as the Federal occupation kept the peace, although some of them fled once again in July 1864 on a false alarm of Confederate invasion from the west.

Roots of Modernity

Until the exchange between Richard Chase and the Chesapeake & Columbia Company at the end of the 19th century, prosperity had been slow to come to our neighborhood. No longer wilderness, yet remote from the whirl of civilization, our morsel of the Arundel patrimony remained a neglected ward of an inattentive Bay. 19th century steamboat traffic called at longer piers in deeper water, including the widely popular Bay Ridge resort from 1880.[16] Arundel-on-the-Bay seemed dependent on smaller scale traffic harvesting the Bay, and on overland connections with the rest of Maryland. This thumb of land in the western Chesapeake was linked with Annapolis either by boat or by circuitous land routes–what are now roughly Forest Drive, Spa Road, and West Street–until 1870 when the Spa Creek Bridge allowed more direct passage via an enlivened Eastport.

Peace-loving commerce on the bay has been facilitated for nearly two centuries by a lighthouse first erected in 1825 on seven acres of Federal land (acquired from Jeremiah Chase) at the southeast (Arundel-on-the-Bay) corner of the peninsula. The original lighthouse was a round stone caisson structure, 30 feet high, 18 feet wide across at the base, and nine feet wide at the top. The site proved of minimal help to shipping; it sat too far from the shoal that runs from today's Thomas Point toward the bay's distant channel, and the ground eroded constantly under it. So the lighthouse was rebuilt to the west in 1840 on a bluff behind the shoal at what is now the county's Thomas Point Park; the new facility was equipped with strong Fresnel lenses in 1855, emitting a red light every twenty seconds. Still ineffective and vulnerable to erosion, the land-based caisson collapsed on February 28, 1894. It had been replaced in November 1875 by a cheaper, more efficient structure, planted in the water atop the perilous shoal, one and one-half miles from the Arundel-on-the-Bay point. This is the current hexagonal "screw-pile" lighthouse–modeled on British prototypes. Its 10-inch wrought-iron piles plunge more than 22 feet down into the middle bay floor, buttressed by masses of rip-rap and iron ice-breakers. Despite its sturdy design, the edifice was seriously damaged by ice storms in 1877 and 1933, forcing evacuation and extensive repairs to the facility and equipment.

Thomas Point was one of 68 Chesapeake lighthouses at the turn of the 20th century (34 remain today), eleven of screw-pile design. Ten of those have been dismantled or moved, but the Thomas Point screw-pile stands today in sight of our Narragansett Avenue point. In 1975, responding to protests by state officials and recreational boaters, the Coast Guard abandoned plans to remove it, preserving the structure for nomination to the National Register of Historic Places; it is one of ten lighthouses to enjoy status as a National Historic Landmark.

Between its pilings and beacon tower, the sea-rooted Thomas Point Light provided a two-story living-work space, including a cabin with two bedrooms. It became the last of the screw-piles to retain its human crew; the light and foghorn were not automated until 1986. Now jointly owned by the City of Annapolis and the U.S. Lighthouse Society, it is maintained and restored–and opened to the public in summer season–by the city, county, and volunteers from Annapolis' Maritime Museum and the Chesapeake chapter of the U.S. Lighthouse Society. The Coast Guard maintains its navigational aids so that Thomas Point's flashing lights still function to direct bay traffic.[17]

Labor-intensive plantations absorbed a gradual rise in county population (unlike Annapolis city, which expanded only in fits and starts); Anne Arundel probably had about 30,000 inhabitants by 1840. Probably nearly half of the increase consisted of slaves, despite the influence of Quakers who drew converts steadily over the decades as they agitated for abolition. If indeed the "peculiar institution" extended into our peninsula, as is likely, we do not know how well, or ill, slaves fared in Arundel-on-the-Bay–or whether Quakers had any abolitionist influence here. There is evidence nonetheless of a continuing debate; somewhere nearby in 1799, John Chew, a prosperous descendant of Philip Thomas, was obliged to free 100 of his family's bonds-people in order to join the Society of Friends.

But our vicinity also included the Duval family, descended from Mareen Duval, a French Huguenot who arrived among the first indentures in mid-17th century and who died prosperously in Anne Arundel County in 1684. Part of the family estates lay along Duvall Creek just west of contemporary Oyster Harbor, and there's little doubt that they were worked by slaves. Yet, in a line some ten generations from Mareen Duval, through Ann Durham, his mother, is Barack Obama, 44th President of the United States – and the first of African descent.

View of the Bay at Our Southernmost Point. ***Photograph by Marc Grigsby***

Endnotes

1. Semmes, Raphael. *Captains and Mariners of Early Maryland.* Baltimore, MD: Johns Hopkins University Press, 1937.

2. See Cunningham, Isabel Shipley. *The Pasadena Peninsula: a Closer Look at the Land Between Two Rivers*. Pasadena, MD: Pasadena Business Association, 2001.

3. Patents were official instruments recording parcels of land certified by an official surveyor and given identifying names. From 1634 to 1776 (except for a period of Crown control from 1689 to 1714), the Lords Baltimore, Proprietors of Maryland, technically "owned" all land in the colony as a perpetual fiefdom, whether the tracts had been patented or not. Grantees owed semi-annual "quit rents" to the Calverts but were free to sell or bequeath their holdings.

4. Carr, Lois Green; Morgan, Philip D.; and Russo, Jean Burrell. *Colonial Chesapeake Society*. Williamsburg, VA: Institute of Early American History and Culture, 1988.

5. McWilliams, Jane Wilson. *Annapolis: City on the Severn*. Baltimore: Johns Hopkins University Press, 2011, pp. 16-18. This is a rich, masterfully executed account of our urban neighbor.

6. The track appears in a reconstructed and possibly fictitious map by James E. Moss, in *Providence: Ye Lost Town at Severn in Mary Land.* Baltimore, MD: Maryland Historical Society, 1976, Map No. 1.

7. *Map of Virginia and Maryland*, by Augustine Herrmann, 1670. Washington, D.C.: Library of Congress, Geography and Map Division. See Papenfuse, Edward C., and Coale III, Joseph M. *The Maryland State Archives Atlas of Historical Maps of Maryland.* Baltimore, MD: Johns Hopkins University Press, 2003.

8. Wilstach, Paul. *Tidewater Maryland*. Indianapolis, IN: Bobbs-Merrill, 1945, p. 277.

9. Moss, *Providence,* Appendix [1], p.491. See Papenfuse, Edward C., and Coale III, Joseph M., *The Maryland State Archives Atlas of Historical Maps of Maryland*. Baltimore: Johns Hopkins University Press, 2003

10. Anne Arundel County Court, Register of Wills, 1817-1828, *Jeremiah T. Chase*, May 20, 1828, pp. 362-376 [punctuation and capitalization as in original].

11. *Map of Anne Arundel County, 1860* by Simon J. Martenet. Collection of the Maryland State Archives. Reproduced with permission.

12. McWilliams, *Annapolis,* p. 193 and p. 431, n. 264.

13. Deed from Richard M. Chase to Chesapeake and Columbia Investment Co., recorded 17 September 1890. Anne Arundel County Land Records, SH 37, 507, located through mdlandrec.net, AA Co page.

14. See George, Christopher T. *Terror on the Chesapeake: the War of 1812 on the Bay.* Shippensburg, PA: White Mane Books, 2000, p. 61; *Maryland Gazette and Political Intelligencer,* 13 May 1813; *Easton Republican Star,* 12 July 1814.

15. Morris, R. Rebecca. *A Low, Dirty Place: the Parole Camps of Annapolis, MD, 1862-1865.* Linthicum, MD: Ann Arrundell County Historical Society, 2012.

16. See McWilliams, Jane Wilson, and Patterson, Carol Cushard, *Bay Ridge on the Chesapeake: an Illustrated History*. Annapolis, MD: Brighton Editions, 1986.

17. For more on the Thomas Point and other lighthouses see De Gast, Robert, *The Lighthouses of the Chesapeake*. Baltimore, MD: Johns Hopkins University Press, 1973; Vojtec, Pat, *Lighting the Bay: Tales of Chesapeake Lighthouses*. Centreville, MD: Tidewater Publishers, 1996; Holland, F. Ross, *Maryland Lighthouses of the Chesapeake Bay*. Crownsville, MD: Maryland Historical Trust Press, 1997; Wendy Winters, "A Little Castle on the Bay," *The Capital-Gazette*, Annapolis, August 3, 2013, pp. B.1-B.4.

The author gratefully acknowledges valuable assistance in preparing this chapter from the following:

Staff of the Maryland State Archives, especially **Emily Oland Squires** and **Allison Seyler**

Jane Wilson McWilliams, scholar of Annapolis and Bay Ridge

Archaeologists **James King** and **Al Luckenbach**

Anne Arundel County Assistant Librarian (retired) **Cynthia Hackett**

Photographer **Marc Grigsby**

Graphic artist **Jameson Allen**

Osprey Over the Bay. *Photograph by Marc Grigsby*

Chapter Two

The Chesapeake & Columbia Investment Company: The 1890s

Pamela Duncan

Introduction

Seven enterprising Washingtonians founded Arundel-on-the-Bay in 1890. Handwritten minutes of their early deliberations as the Chesapeake & Columbia Investment Company, not previously known to have survived, were found at the Kiplinger Library of the Historical Society of Washington, D.C. These and other documents donated to the library in 1988 by John Van Sant from the estate of his father Frank, an attorney and town commissioner, have made this history possible.

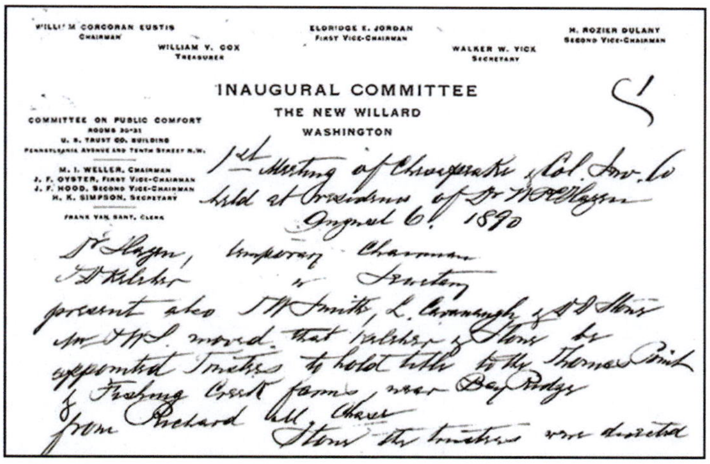

WILLIAM CORCORAN EUSTIS, CHAIRMAN
WILLIAM V. COX, TREASURER
ELDRIDGE E. JORDAN, FIRST VICE-CHAIRMAN
WALKER W. VICK, SECRETARY
H. ROZIER DULANY, SECOND VICE-CHAIRMAN

INAUGURAL COMMITTEE
THE NEW WILLARD
WASHINGTON

COMMITTEE ON PUBLIC COMFORT
ROOMS 30-31
U. S. TRUST CO. BUILDING
PENNSYLVANIA AVENUE AND TENTH STREET N.W.

M. I. WELLER, CHAIRMAN
J. F. OYSTER, FIRST VICE-CHAIRMAN
J. F. HOOD, SECOND VICE-CHAIRMAN
H. K. SIMPSON, SECRETARY

FRANK VAN SANT, CLERK

1st Meeting of Chesapeake & Col. Inv. Co
held at residence of Dr W C Hazen
August 6. 1890
Dr Hazen, temporary Chairman
T D Keleher " Secretary
present also T W Smith, L. Cavanaugh & D D Stone
Mr T W S. moved that Keleher & Stone be
appointed Trustees to hold title to the Thomas Point
& Fishing Creek farms, near Bay Ridge
from Richard Hill, Chase
Stone the trustees were directed

Figure 1: This handwritten summary of the early meetings of the Chesapeake & Columbia Investment Company, developers of Arundel-on-the-Bay, was prepared in 1914. ***The Historical Society of Washington, D.C.***

What follows is a detailed account of the formation of a summer community in its dynamic geographical and social context–most notably the business and professional evolution of late 19th and early 20th century Washington, D.C. from which Arundel-on-the-Bay draws its human substance.

The founders–the key figures in this story–were lumber merchant Thomas W. Smith, banker Nicholas H. Shea, surgeon William C. Hazen, grocer Lawrence C. Cavanaugh, government clerk Timothy D. Keleher, attorney William J. Rannells, and real estate manager David D. Stone. Our platted streets are the physical representation of their efforts. The occasional well-water pump or horseshoe found in a yard, an old house or two, and some wooden porch or lawn furniture are the rare relics of this bygone, and very different, era.

We need to use our imaginations to envision the Arundel-on-the-Bay they created. A frontage road made of oyster shells–known as Chesapeake Avenue–ran along the length of the community's eastern shore. A narrow wooden boardwalk, four feet in width and illuminated with gas lamps, stretched from Cedar Avenue on the north, alongside and east of Chesapeake Avenue to the end of the peninsula, then called Point Pleasant. The community itself was a forested area, served by shell and dirt roads accommodating horse-drawn wagons. It would grow to contain some 30 wooden cottages, stables, and assorted outbuildings; community piers and a dancing pavilion; and fishing and hunting club houses, guest houses, and tent camps.

Figure 2: The Thomas Point Shoal Light Station in 1885, *U. S. Light-House Board, historic photograph by Major Jared A. Smith.*[1]

This endowment came to life in summer. Ladies, in the full-length white summer dresses of the time, carried parasols to shield their complexions from the sun as they strolled with their families and guests. Dances, yachting, fishing and duck hunting, card parties, and watermelon and crab feasts made up an active social calendar. Saturday evening parties on the long community pier into the Bay at Chestnut Avenue featured programs of song, readings, and rhetoric. Young people's events, such as the Wednesday dances or "hops," were chaperoned.

Picnics were held on Thomas's Point Island which the community owned. The resort's yacht, *The Arundel*, ferried parties to Annapolis and on other excursions. The Naval Academy training vessel, the *U.S.S. Constellation*, often anchored offshore. Gas lights and outdoor privies being the rule, a bailiff employed by the investment company lit and extinguished the lights on schedule and enforced standards covering the set-up of outdoor privies, assisted by another employee—a town scavenger—who disposed of the contents.

The Context of the Times

Figure 3: A sailboat on the Chesapeake Bay, shown on a postcard sent from Queenstown to Baltimore, Md. in 1908. *Collection of the author.*

Seaside bathing came into vogue for the masses after 1840 with the development of railroad access to the coasts. Cape May, N. J., known as America's oldest seaside resort, was incorporated in 1848 and exclusive places such as Newport, R. I., where the wealthy began to build summer cottages in the mid-19th century, became vacation destinations. At the same time, entrepreneurs scouted for and developed recreational sites along the Chesapeake Bay.

The active economic climate of post-Civil War Washington, D.C., drew people seeking to profit in the building boom or in the provision of services a city needed.[2] Veterans of the war flocked to the capital to take clerkships in government. The founders and first purchasers of lots at Arundel-on-the-Bay were among them, becoming prosperous builders, bankers, lawyers, merchants, and businessmen in the railroad and emerging electrical supply industry. By 1890 the resources, financiers, and a spirit of entrepreneurship were in place for the development of our community.

Figure 4: An old-fashioned wooden glider at Arundel-on-the-Bay. *Photo by Pamela Duncan.*

Especially important to the success of a summer resort on the shores of the Chesapeake Bay was the availability of a passenger railroad network which allowed more people to seek waterside residential ownership. Such a rail line was available from Annapolis to the nearby Bay Ridge Resort, which was then linked to Arundel-on-the-Bay by its founders via a summer-car line along the waterfront known as the "Blackberry Train." This rail

Figure 5: The Bay Ridge Resort which opened in 1880 was known as "The Queen Resort of the Chesapeake." A summer-car rail line ran from the park to Arundel-on-the-Bay beginning in 1892. ***Howard H. Hopkins, photographer, ca 1906, Robert G. Merrick Archives of Maryland Historical Photographs, Maryland State Archives.***

Figure 6: The long steamboat pier off Tolley Point at the Bay Ridge Resort in 1895 can be seen as highlighted in the background from the shoreline of Arundel-on-the-Bay. ***The Annapolis I Remember Collection, Maryland State Archives.***

line played an essential role in the development of the community and is discussed in detail in Chapter Three.

Access to our shoreline by automobile would be possible only after the turn of the century; Henry Ford's Model T was introduced to the public in 1908. Even so, a trip by automobile from Washington, D.C., to Arundel-on-the-Bay took nine hours in the early years, as contrasted to one hour and a half by train.

"Women voted in the annual elections at Arundel- on- the-Bay beginning in 1891, the only place in the State of Maryland where this civic participation was possible until the ratification of the 19th Amendment to the U.S. Constitution in 1920..."

The times were lively. In 1890 professional baseball began, the Weather Bureau was founded, Native Americans were massacred at Wounded Knee, punch cards were devised, Yosemite was protected as a national park, and the center for immigration at Ellis Island opened. Our founders would experience the assassination of a president, William McKinley, in 1901; the Wright brothers' first flight of 1903; and the sinking of the great ocean liner, the *Titanic*, in 1912. They would pay federal income tax for the first time in 1913 and their sons would go off to fight in World War I after the United States entered it in 1917.

While the first woman was hired as a White House staffer in 1890, women did not have the right to vote at the time. At Arundel-on-the-Bay, however, women voted in the annual community elections from their beginning in 1891, the only place in the State of Maryland where this civic participation was possible until the ratification of the 19th Amendment to the U.S. Constitution in 1920.

In 1890, the Daughters of the American Revolution was founded; the National Association for the Advancement of Colored People began in 1909. Life at Arundel-on-the-Bay reflected the racial stratification of the times, as the community was largely white until after 1949, yet there *always* were African American property owners at Arundel-on-the-Bay. One of the early purchasers was Laura Douglass, the second wife of Frederick Douglass's son Charles, who bought a lot in 1893. Several other African American families located nearby on Cedar and Chesapeake Avenues.[3] Before the settlement was begun, African Americans were among the tent campers on the bluffs and under the trees of Cedar Grove on what was to become Arundel-on-the-Bay.[4]

Figure 7: Banker Nicholas Henry Shea (1843-1917), treasurer of the Chesapeake & Columbia Investment Co., was responsible for naming the north-south streets after prominent sea-side resorts and the east-west streets after the trees that grew at Arundel-on-the-Bay. ***Historical Society of Washington, D.C.***

A Claim that Banker Nicholas Shea was the "Father of Arundel-on-the-Bay"

According to an unpublished family history, three directors of the Federal American Bank in Washington, D. C.—Nicholas H. Shea, Charles B. Lyddane, and the bank president John Poole—sailed to Bay Ridge in 1880 to purchase land for Arundel-on-the-Bay. The author, Edwin J. Madill, was the husband of Margaret Agnes Shea, a granddaughter of founder Nicholas Henry Shea. Writing in 1988, Madill designated Shea as the "father of Arundel-on-the-Bay."[5]

As told by Madill, Shea built the family's Idle Wild cottage on a bluff overlooking the Bay soon after the sailing trip. Madill also reported the existence of a railroad from the port at the Bay Ridge resort to the north, which was used to transport residents and the lumber and furnishings for the cottages being built, and of a pavilion, dubbed "The Arundel Country Club," constructed just north of the Shea family cottage.

Figure 8: An early photograph of Idle Wild, one of the first seven cottages constructed for the officers of the Investment Co. in 1891. Cottages were given names before numbered street addresses were used. The cottage of Nicholas Shea, at 1365 Chestnut Avenue, stands today. ***Historical Society of Washington, D.C.***

Figure 9: John Poole, a prominent banker in the District of Columbia, was said to assist in scouting to purchase land for building Arundel-on-the-Bay. ***Harris T. Ewing Collection, Prints & Photographs Division, Library of Congress.***

While Shea, Lyddane, and Poole may well have been involved in scouting for an eventual purchase of land for Arundel-on-the-Bay, it is unlikely, because of the differences in their ages, that the expedition took place as early as 1880, although the three were associated in banking. Shea was vice president of the Commerce National Bank in the District of Columbia from its beginning in 1904, John Poole joined the bank as a cashier in 1909 and became a director in 1911, and Charles B. Lyddane later was hired as an assistant cashier. Poole founded the Federal National Bank in 1913, of which Shea and Lyddane would become directors.

The Purchase of Land from Richard M. Chase of Annapolis

Despite Madill's assertions, there is no public record of a purchase of land by Nicholas Shea in 1880. In fact, his deed for two lots purchased from the Chesapeake & Columbia Investment Co. is dated May 10, 1891, although, just to confuse matters, the Maryland Department of Taxation and Assessments gives the year of construction of the Shea cottage as 1880. While the idea of Arundel-on-the-Bay may have existed in the minds of dreamers some years before, we can only designate with any official certainty the founding to have been September 16, 1890–the date of the deed of purchase by the Chesapeake & Columbia Investment Co. of more than 350 acres of land from Richard M. Chase of Annapolis.

Chase, born in 1827, was a grandson of Revolutionary War figure Jeremiah Townley Chase (1748-1828), an Annapolis lawyer and judge who had begun to amass land on the Annapolis Neck in 1798 with a 690-acre purchase from Benjamin Ogle. Over the next 30 years, Jeremiah Chase's holdings were enlarged to nearly 1,100 acres.[6] The intra-family transfers of the land owned by Jeremiah T. Chase which ultimately comprised Arundel-on-the-Bay are discussed in Chapter One. Richard M. Chase's father, Richard M. Chase Sr. (1784-1853), was the eldest child of Jeremiah Chase and his wife, Hester Baldwin Chase.

Figure 10: Jeremiah Townley Chase, colonial patriot, Chief Justice of the Maryland State Court of Appeals, member of the Maryland legislature, and Mayor of Annapolis amassed the land on which Arundel-on-the-Bay was developed. ***New York Public Library Digital Image.***

Richard Moale Chase began his career as a merchant in the 6th Ward of Baltimore, as recorded in the 1850 federal census, where he lived with three of his siblings; Hester Ann Chase, born in 1825, William born in 1829, and Sarah born in 1835. Their mother, Mary Marriott Chase, died in 1836. By 1854, he was in Annapolis as a clerk to the U.S. Superintendant of the Naval Academy and appears in U.S. Naval and Marine registers as secretary to the Naval Academy until 1899. Chase also was a member of the Maryland General Assembly and on the Board of Visitors and Governors of St. John's College.[7] He never married, boarding in Annapolis along with his sisters Hester A. Chase, who lived with him as reported in the 1860 census, and consistently with Sarah H. Chase, known as Sallie, and later her daughter Mary, known as Mollie, according to the censuses of 1860, 1870, and 1880.

Planning Arundel-on-the-Bay

The first meeting to plan Arundel-on-the-Bay was held on August 6, 1890, at 511 East Capital Street SE in the District of Columbia, the home of Dr. William C. Hazen.[8] In addition to Hazen who served as temporary chairman, those present were Timothy Keleher, acting as temporary secretary; Thomas Smith, Lawrence Cavanaugh, David Stone, and Nicholas Shea. Keleher and Stone were designated trustees to hold title to the two tracts of land which were to be purchased–the Thomas Point and Fishing Creek Farms and Thomas's Point Island–and to collect $8,500 needed from members of the company for the transaction. These funds were used to pay the title insurance premiums in March of 1891.

Figure 11: Richard M. Chase, U.S. Naval Academy Secretary, in his office, c. 1895-1905. In 1890, Mr. Chase sold the land for Arundel-on-the-Bay to the Chesapeake & Columbia Investment Co. ***George Forbes Collection, Maryland State Archives.***

Meeting a few weeks later, Stone recommended incorporation of the investment company under Virginia law and subdivision of the property.[9] John Duvall, a civil engineer of Annapolis, a descendant of one of the early families of Anne Arundel County and whose father also had been a surveyor in Annapolis, was hired to plat the community in lots of 50 by 150 feet.[10]

At a third meeting on September 4, 1890, the company name was adopted. It was agreed to capitalize the venture at $100,000 raised from the sale of 2,000 shares at $50 each. An election of officers resulted in Smith being chosen president; Hazen, vice president; Shea, treasurer; Stone, general manager; Cavanaugh, inspector of grounds; and Assistant Attorney General William J. Rannells, counsel. Each company member who built a house worth $1,000 before June 1, 1891 was to receive his lot free. As oystering, fishing, and shooting for ducks or rabbits were popular pursuits of the time, the company allocated $2,000 to build a club house and agreed to advertise for a contractor to undertake the project. The application of Lawrence Costigan to be foreman for building Arundel-on-the-Bay was reviewed and he was ultimately hired.

The plat subdivided the 279 acres of Tract No. 1, consisting of the Thomas Point and Fishing Creek farms, into approximately 350 lots. Thirteen acres of the land, west of Cohasset Avenue and north of Cedar Avenue comprising what would have been 37 blocks if subdivided, were not included in the initial plat and were designated as "The Farm." A farmhouse, barn, and corn crib were on this site which was leased for rental income. Tract No. 2, the 71 acres of Thomas Point Island, also was not included in the plat.

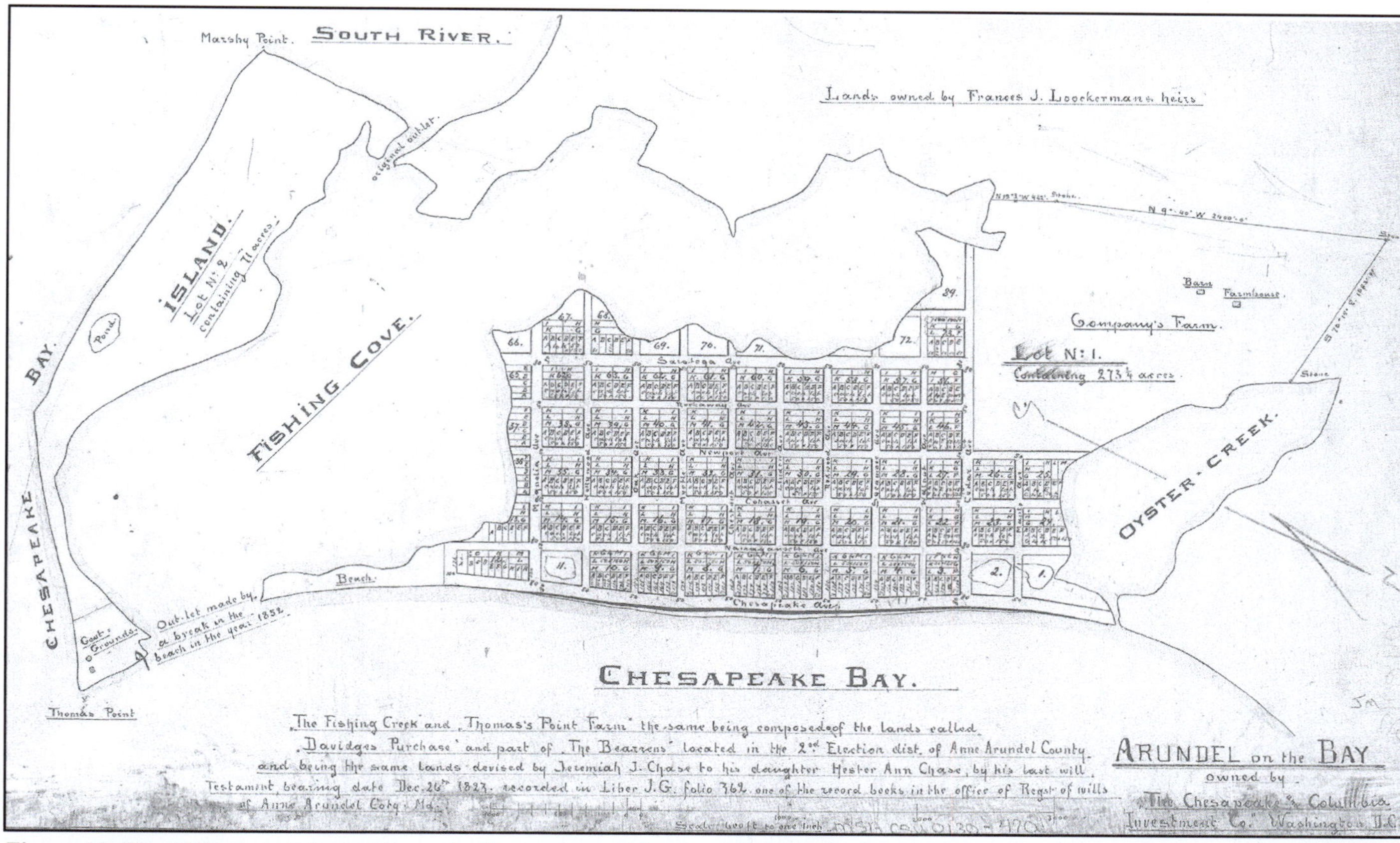

Figure 12: The 1890 plat of Arundel-on-the-Bay prepared for the Chesapeake & Columbia Investment Co. by civil engineer John Duvall of Annapolis. The blocks were numbered 1-89 beginning with No. 1 at the lower right and the lots within each block labeled A-K, as necessary. An original outlet from Fishing Cove to the South River is shown at the top left; on the bottom left is the outlet made by a break in the beach in 1852. Note that sections of the original subdivided area and the company farm now make up the community of Oyster Harbor. ***SH 37, p. 508a, Land Records, Anne Arundel County Circuit Court. See expanded plat on inside cover.***

Figure 13: A wealthy businessman from Washington, D.C., Arundel-on-the-Bay founder Thomas Wilson Smith (1846-1919) served as president of Arundel-on-the-Bay from 1890 until his death in 1919. ***Washington Post: A History of the City of Washington, Its Men & Institutions, 1903, p. 1001.***

A Closer Look at the Seven Founders

President **Thomas Wilson Smith** was born in Gordonville, Pa., on January 1, 1846. He attended public schools and the Columbia Institute of Columbia, Pa., and at the age of 16 studied pharmacy and became licensed in that field. He served in the militia of Lancaster County, Pa., during the time of raids in the area led by Confederate Gen. Jubal Early. In 1863, Smith moved with his father to Montgomery County, Md., and worked with him on the farm he leased near the Cabin John Bridge.

In 1868 they moved to the District of Columbia, where Smith became a general clerk for George W. Linville & Co., located at Second Street and Indiana Avenue NW. Smith served as a lumber inspector for the District of Columbia for two years, a position to which he was elected at a joint convention of the Board of Aldermen and the Common Council during the administration of Sayles J. Bowen (1868-70), the first Republican mayor of the District and outspoken supporter of emancipation. Smith became a partner in the Linville business, which was later sold and in which he retained a financial interest. In 1872 he married Caroline Gatchell of Chester County, Pa., and they settled at 616 East Capitol Street.

In 1874 Smith founded his own firm, the Thomas W. Smith Lumber Co. Specializing in finished doors, moldings, and cabinet work, the firm's products were in great demand in Washington's booming construction economy. With a lumber yard at the corner of First Street and Indiana Avenue NW, the highly successful business grew to encompass a

Figure 14: The headquarters building of the Thomas Smith Lumber Company on the northeast corner of First & C streets NW, now the site of the International Brotherhood of Teamsters in Washington D.C., ca. 1900-1909. ***Historical Society of Washington, D.C. Photograph by Joseph E. Bishop.***

large shed and mill employing more than 100 people and filling nearly the entire block, now the site of Union Station. Stock and building materials were stored there, while drying kilns were located on the Anacostia River near the Anacostia channel with capacity to keep 100,000 linear feet of lumber dry in 27 rooms. After fire destroyed the original mill, a new one was built on Fourth Street SE; after fire destroyed the second location the mill was rebuilt at First and N Streets SE. Location of his facilities near the Anacostia River gave Smith ease of transportation for his products.

In 1895, Smith also entered the ice business on the Georgetown waterfront, and rebuilt an old mill at Potomac and Grace Streets for the purpose.[11] Smith's businesses were immediately profitable and well-run, enabling him to give attention to civic and charitable work.

Smith's civic activities were extensive. He was president of the National Capital Bank, a director of the Washington Loan & Trust Co., and vice-president of the East Washington Savings Bank. He was the elected president for two years of the Washington Board of Trade and organized and served for 20 years as president of the East Washington Citizens Association. He was president of the Eastern Dispensary and Casualty Hospital at Third and East Capitol streets which he helped develop. Smith was a trustee of American University and a manager of a citywide group known as Associated Charities. He also was a member of the National Civil Service Reform League, the Columbia Historical Society, the B.B. French Masonic Lodge, the Methodist Episcopal Church, the Republican Party, and he was a significant donor to the Y.M.C.A. Smith reportedly turned down the efforts of Presidents Cleveland and Harrison to appoint him a District of Columbia commissioner.

In addition to the at least 16 lots Smith would eventually purchase at Arundel-on-the-Bay, he owned an apartment house at 676 Fourth Street NE, row houses in the 200 block of Indiana Avenue NW, later family homes at 1867 and 2334 Columbia Road NW, property in northeast Washington's Deanwood neighborhood, and a farmhouse at 3426 Newton Street in Mount Rainier, Md.[12] Recognized as one of Washington's wealthiest and most influential businessmen and civic leaders, at his death in 1919 Smith's estate was worth over a million dollars. In 1930 it was written:

> Thomas W. Smith played a part in the up-building of the nation's capital that entitles him to generous recognition as one of Washington's best citizens, a man who was generous, progressive and broad-minded, and one who enjoyed the confidence and esteem of citizens of all classes as well as his own business associates and personal friends.[13]

Figure 15: A founder of Arundel-on-the-Bay, Dr. William C. Hazen celebrating his 91st birthday. ***Washington Evening Star, April 1941.***

Vice President **William Patterson Clark Hazen** was born in 1852 in Lower Mount Bethel Township, Pa. He lived in New Jersey and Pennsylvania before coming to the District of Columbia to attend medical school at Georgetown University, from which he graduated in 1877. Hazen married Catherine Wood in 1878, and he practiced medicine as a surgeon from offices in his home at 511 East Capitol Street SE. The couple had four daughters; Emma, Florence, Bessie, and Catherine.

Hazen was a member of the Washington Academy of Sciences and authored articles which were published in *The Medical and Surgical Reporter* and *The Journal of the American Medical Association* in 1900 and *The Transactions of the Sixth International Congress on Tuberculosis* in 1908. He was involved with Smith in establishing the Medical & Surgical Society of the District of Columbia in 1888 and served as its president in 1897. Both were directors of the Eastern Dispensary & Casualty Hospital at 700-708 Massachusetts Avenue NE, stockholders in the Washington Railway & Electric Co., directors of the National Capital Bank of Washington, and active in the Washington Board of Trade. Hazen also was among a group of promoters of the East Washington Belt Line Railway Co., an electric road to run along M Street, Virginia Avenue, U Street, and Tennessee Avenue. He owned a seven story apartment building at Eighth and F streets NE near Gallaudet College and property purchased from Smith in Deanwood in northeast Washington. Hazen was a member of the Almas Temple of the Shriners. The last surviving of the original founders, he died in 1944.[14]

Figure 16: Margaret O'Toole Shea (1854-1905), wife of Arundel-on-the-Bay founder Nicholas Henry Shea, was born in Ireland. ***Historical Society of Washington, D.C.***

Treasurer **Nicholas Henry Shea**, whose parents were native to Ireland, was born in West Va. in 1843. After living in a variety of places in Maryland, the family moved to Washington, D.C., in 1850. In 1875 he married Margaret O'Toole, who was born in Ireland. The couple had seven children and lived at 1451 Fairmont Street NW in the District.

Shea opened N. H. Shea, Wholesale Groceries and Liquor Rectifier at the corner of Seventh Street and Pennsylvania Avenue NW, the current site of the Federal Bureau of Investigation headquarters. His listing in the *Washington D.C. City Directory of 1896* as a "wholesale grocer" describes Shea as a "jobber in staple and fancy groceries, grocers' sundries, wines and liquor." (A rectifier is one who blends, packages, and sells alcoholic products.)

In addition to being vice president and a director of the Commerce National Bank, organized in Washington, D.C., in 1904, Shea was a director of the Washington Loan & Trust Co., as was Thomas Smith. He was a board member of the District Title Insurance Co. and a benefactor of the St. Josephs Male Orphans Asylum, as was future Arundel-on-the-Bay resident Michael I. Weller. The headquarters of his Commerce National Bank at 1405 G Street NW, designed by prominent architect Waddy Wood, was completed in 1917, the year of Shea's death.[15]

Secretary **Timothy Ducey Keleher** was born in Connecticut in 1852. He married his wife Nellie in 1878 and moved to the District of Columbia around 1880. A disbursing clerk in the Office of the Auditor of the Treasurer in the Post Office Department, Keleher became a division chief in 1896. As a notary public, Keleher's signature was on early deeds of sale and he was reimbursed a finder's fee on at least one occasion.

Keleher was out of the area for some years afterward. From 1898 to 1901 he was a paymaster at the rank of captain in the U.S. Army in the then-Department of California and the Philippine Islands and the family lived in Manila from 1903 to 1905. In May 1905 he was posted to Burlington, Vt., to head the paymaster's department outpost there and in 1911 was honorably discharged from the Army at the rank of major. On two occasions, he was treated at Walter Reed Central Hospital – as it was known – in June 1910 and again in September 1916. Timothy Keleher died on December 3, 1916, and is buried at Arlington Cemetery.[16]

Inspector of Grounds **Lawrence C. Cavanaugh** was born in Ireland in 1847 and immigrated to the United States in 1860. He married his wife Annie in Washington, D.C., in 1875. Annie's parents were born in France, but Annie was born in Washington. They lived at 608 East Capitol Street SE, on the same block as Thomas W. Smith and one block from Dr. Hazen. Widowed, Cavanaugh married Emma Josephine Leonberger Courtenay in 1902, mother of a five-year-old son, Edward Courtenay Jr. Their son, Lawrence J. Cavanaugh Jr., was born in 1904.[17]

In an April 1878 newspaper article, Cavanaugh was identified as a grocer who had been appointed by the District commissioners to furnish supplies from the $5,000 charity fund in his police district. His name appears in Washington newspapers between 1866 and the latter decades of the 19th century for real estate transactions, as well as on two occasions when he was assaulted and robbed. Cavanaugh served as a member of the Inaugural Committee for President Grover Cleveland in 1893.

Cavanaugh was secretary of the Chesapeake & Columbia Investment Co. from 1895 until 1900. A trustee of the Knights of Columbus St. Peters Branch No. 129, Cavanaugh was a member of the Irish National League, as were other early Arundel-on-the-Bay property owners Nicholas Shea and James Somerville.

The current entrance from the Chesapeake Bay to Oyster Creek, between the Oyster Harbor and Venice Beach communities to the north of Arundel-on-the-Bay, was once known as the Cavanaugh Canal. Cavanaugh served as the inspector of grounds for Arundel-on-the-Bay, supervising the maintenance of the canal and other infrastructure, so it is likely the waterway was named after him. Mr. Cavanaugh died at home in Washington, D.C., on October 2, 1910.[18]

Figure 17: Co-founder of Arundel-on-the-Bay and counsel of the Chesapeake & Columbia Investment Co., William J. Rannells shown when he served at the rank of captain with an Ohio unit in the Union Army in the Civil War. ***Brad R. Pruden Collection, Ancestry.com.***

Manager **David D. Stone**, an attorney involved in real estate with offices at various locations in Washington, D.C., handled advertising and property sales for Arundel-on-the-Bay. In 1892 his residence was 2021 Massachusetts Avenue NW. In 1896 his firm, David D. Stone and Sons, included his sons Charles P. and Robert Stone and was described as being engaged in real estate and insurance sales. Stone died in 1904.

Counsel **William J. Rannells** was born in Mason, Ky., in 1839 and moved as a child to Ohio. He served in the Civil War as captain of Company 1, 75th Ohio, and practiced law there before coming to the District to become an assistant attorney general at the Department of Justice. *Boyd's City Directory of the City of Washington for 1892* lists Rannells as president of the Washington Improvement & Investment Co. of 617 F Street NW. He died in 1895 at the age of 56 and is buried in the District of Columbia at Rock Creek Cemetery.[19]

Developing the Community Began in 1890

After filing the charter of the Chesapeake & Columbia Investment Co., the founders ordered a corporate seal and appointed a committee on by-laws. By late October, 1,400 shares of the corporation – 200 each by the seven paying $2 apiece – were subscribed.

Banker Nicholas Shea can be credited with the idea of naming the north-south streets after prominent resort communities and the east-west streets after the types of trees present at the site. His motion at a meeting of Jan. 9, 1891, resulted in the selection of Chesapeake, Narragansett, Cohasset, Newport, Rockaway (today's Rockway), and Saratoga Avenues as names for the north-south streets and Cedar, Walnut, Sycamore, Redwood, Linden, Chestnut, Myrtle, Oak, Hollywood, and Magnolia Avenues for the east-west streets.

Arundel-on-the-Bay as the formal name of the community was voted on the motion of Timothy Keleher on Jan. 20, 1891, after which the plat map was sent to be lithographed. $75 was allocated to buy up oyster rights and funds were pledged for the purchase of an

Figure 18: Advertisements like this one from July 1, 1892, appeared weekly in the *Washington Post*.

80-foot wide right-of-way to the north of Arundel-on-the-Bay. For the price of $150, the right-of-way was purchased from the estate of the heirs of Chastity Brashears on July 20, 1891. Surveyor John Duvall again was engaged to lay out the road on this right-of-way along the shoreline to connect the new Chesapeake Avenue at Arundel-on-the-Bay with the resort at Bay Ridge.

According to Edwin Madill, Arundel-on-the-Bay was named for Thomas Arundel who was made Bishop of Ely and later became Archbishop of York and Archbishop of Canterbury. From this position, he crowned King Henry IV. As Madill explained, Arundel was known for "defending the rights of the Church against attempts of Parliament to limit those rights."[20]

Readers will find numerous references to Chesapeake Avenue in this history. Once the Chesapeake Bay frontage street of the burgeoning community and the connecting street to Bay Ridge, it ultimately succumbed to storms. Now the only reference to Chesapeake Avenue is the stretch of shoreline known as Chesapeake Walk between Walnut and Linden Avenues. A remnant of the old street also extends north on private property along the shore from Walnut Avenue.

A number of actions were taken by the founders meeting in March 1891: they ordered an artesian well dug which was to supply every cottage with potable water, determined the form of deed to be used for the lots, decided to plant 500 shade trees and 60 peach trees and specified other garden fruits and vegetables, and selected George N. Walker of Hyattsville, Md., to build seven cottages along the coast for the officers. The solicitation for the well, which appeared in the *Baltimore Sun* of March 31, 1891, read:

> Artesian Well Contractors to drive a well of sufficient depth to produce 10,000 gallons daily, furnish Wind Engine, 6,000 gallon tank, Frame to set tank on, thirty feet above earth, at 'Arundel on the Bay' one mile south of Bay Ridge.

The contract of $330 was awarded to John E. Robinson of 1301 Market Street in Philadelphia on April 15, 1891.

General Manager David Stone, who had the task of promoting the community and handling sales, painted a most enticing portrait of what Arundel-on-the-Bay had to offer in the Washington area *Sunday Herald and Weekly National Intelligencer* of April 19, 1891:

> This is to be a cottage city, and from the desirability of its location promises to be as beautiful and thriving a resort as may be found on the Chesapeake...
>
> Situated on a high bluff, with the waves of the bay dashing against its base, with a beautiful undulating plain back from the bay in the rear. The other two sides are almost surrounded by the waters of Fishing Cove and Oyster Bay. Arundel-on-the-Bay forms a peninsula and commands from its elevation varied and beautiful views of the bay and surrounding country. Heavily wooded down to the very verge of the bluff with tall oaks, chestnuts, hickories, hollies, maples, pines and cedars, it presents that rare combination, shade and beach, seldom to be found at any sea-side resort.
>
> Three-quarters of a mile to the north of Arundel-on-the-Bay is Bay Ridge, the 'Coney Island of the South,' with its myriad attractions, and reached by a short drive

> in the company's wagonettes over a beautiful shell road, fanned by the breezes of the bay; or, for those who prefer it, by a short sail in the company's jaunty little steam yacht 'Arundel...
>
> Some very fine woods centre [sic] here and afford delightful drives past verdant farms and through deep, shady woods. Then to the south of Arundel is Fishing Cove, celebrated for its oysters and terrapins, as well as ducks in the game season.
>
> The Cove affords a welcome harbor for fishermen of the Chesapeake when overtaken by storms and, being land-locked, it is at all times a perfectly safe place for rowing and sailing...A long beach of firm white sand on the bay front gradually sloping outward, affords absolutely safe salt-water bathing. Across Fishing Cove is Thomas's Point Island, containing seventy acres of primeval forest, owned by our company, affording one of the finest picnic grounds imaginable for the use of the cottagers. On its western extremity is the picturesque old Thomas's Point lighthouse, now abandoned by the Government. South River, here five or six miles wide, on the south side of the Island, is a famous fishing ground, and has long been noted as a ducking shore.
>
> The company expects to erect a modern inn, costly and elegant in all its appointments, with handsome and spacious grounds; a clubhouse, with pavilion, bowling alleys, boathouses, with landing wharves for the cottager's use, and altogether, it will be the model resort of the Chesapeake.

Arundel-on-the-Bay was the first planned residential community built on the Annapolis Neck, the area between the Severn and South rivers and Route 50 and the Chesapeake Bay. Among our immediate neighbors, Bay Ridge, the amusement park begun in 1880, was subdivided for residential development first as Brighton Beach by the Bay Ridge Improvement Co. in 1894 and later by the Bay Ridge Realty Co. in 1922.[21] Only four lots in the Brighton Beach development were sold. Highland Beach, the community of prominent African Americans to the north of Arundel-on-the-Bay, was founded in 1893. Venice Beach, next to Highland Beach, was begun in 1922, and Oyster Harbor, the community directly adjacent to Arundel-on-the-Bay on the north, was developed in 1947 from land originally owned by the Chesapeake & Columbia Investment Co.[22]

The peninsula was never going to be a getaway just for members of the investment company. It was time to sell Arundel-on-the-Bay. Stone's sales campaign was well-honed when he declared that Arundel-on-the-Bay "combines all the advantages of Bay Ridge without the annoyance of the large crowds."[23] Sales began in earnest in May 1891. Lots priced from $150 to $400 were advertised as available "on easy terms." Carpenters were sought to work on frame cottages for the company officers.

Cottages for the Officers of the Investment Company and Other Construction in 1891

Between 1891 and 1893, the seven officers acquired lots in Arundel-on-the-Bay, with Smith purchasing six lots and Cavanaugh four. Construction of their cottages began in the spring of 1891 along Chesapeake Avenue, described by Stone "as the shell road which runs along the pretty beach and makes a beautiful drive to Bay Ridge."[24] Lumber for the houses arrived by ship, while window sashes, doors, and blinds were transported by rail.

The cottages of the investment company officers faced the bay. Smith's and Stone's cottages stood on either side of Sycamore Avenue, Rannells' and Keleher's cottages bracketed Redwood Avenue, Hazen's and a second cottage built for Smith were across from each other at Linden Avenue, and Shea's Idle Wild was on the south side of Chestnut Avenue.[25] Waterfront lots were sold to the early buyers for $400, although some deeds noted considerations of $30 or less, perhaps given away for promotional purposes. Lots off the waterfront were less costly.

Figure 19: Idle Wild in March 2014, one of the oldest properties in Arundel-on-the-Bay. A bench for observing the Bay was installed by Landscape Chair Roy N. Karten. ***Photo by R. M. Grigsby.***

On May 20, 1891 a party of 62 persons, including the officers of the company and their guests, 25 of whom were ladies, set out from Annapolis to inspect the new resort. As reported in the *Washington Post:*

> At Annapolis a steam yacht in waiting conveyed the excursionists to their destination. The sail of six miles down the bay was heartily enjoyed, particularly by the lady contingent. An elegant *al fresco* lunch, spread on the bluff overlooking the broad Chesapeake…
>
> Seven handsome cottages, six of them nearly completed, are well under way, and will be ready for occupancy June 15. These will be used as the Summer homes of the officers of the association. The South River Gun and Fishing Club are erecting a commodious clubhouse that will soon be completed.[26]

Late in May 1891 saw the beginning of a pier at Walnut Avenue, for which the company paid $700, as well as the construction of a 12-foot-wide plank roadway to the north and bridges over the Cavanaugh Canal at Oyster Creek to connect the frontage road, Chesapeake Avenue, to the resort at Bay Ridge.

Manager Stone announced in the May 31 edition of the *Sunday Herald and Weekly National Intelligencer* that 100 of the 500 available lots had been sold:

> Arundel-on-the-Bay is also proving a great success, and lots there are being rapidly disposed off…Many cottages have already been erected, costing from $800 to $3,000, and many more are now being or shortly will be put up.…As a resort for those who wish to be near the city, and at the same time enjoy the salt air, it cannot be surpassed…[27]

Anne Arundel County land records for 1891 show 16 transactions involving the investment company, including 11 deeds of purchase for lots and the purchase of oyster bed rights. (Other sales were made and the deeds never recorded.) John B. Doyle, Timothy Keleher and his brother Peter J. Keleher, and Terance J. Gorman, the latter two both clerks in the 6th Auditor's Office of the Post Office Department–executed deeds of riparian consent for five acres of land for oyster rights, "for the purpose of Protecting, Preserving, Depositing, Bedding and Sowing Oysters" under state law.[28] Timothy Keleher executed three such deeds. Five acres of ground for oyster sowing also were obtained by contractor George N. Walker.[29] The oyster sites were located on the flats of Fishing Creek.

In June, Smith reported that testing of the water from the artesian well found it to be too salty for use. The officers accepted a bid of $3,000 for community development work recommended by supervising civil engineer Percival G. Williams of Annapolis. This included filling areas not subdivided on the plat–blocks two (Chesapeake Ave. north of Cedar Ave.) and 11 (Chesapeake Ave. between Hollywood and Magnolia avenues)–with dirt moved from grading streets, filling low ground in block 10 (Chesapeake Ave. between Oak and Hollywood avenues), and bringing blocks 14 and 15 (bounded by Narragansett, Cohasset, Magnolia, and Hollywood avenues) to grade. $135 was set aside to pay for the building of a scow. Smith's lumber company provided materials for the various projects as shown in the bill of lading at Figure 21.

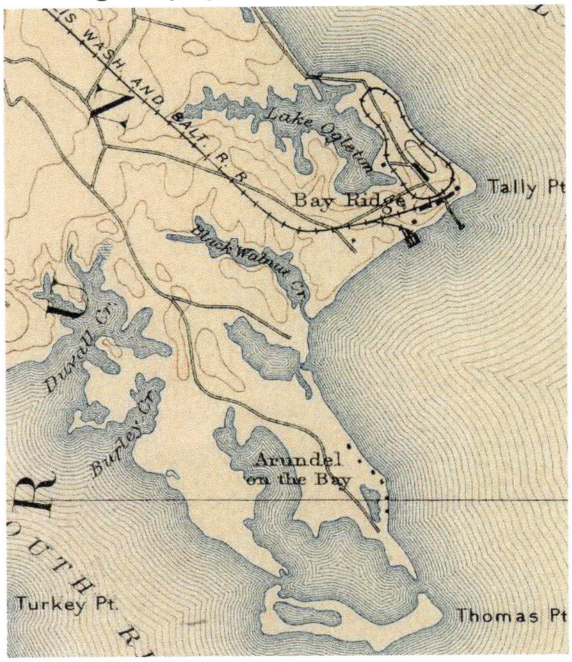

Figure 20: The first cottages at Arundel-on-the-Bay, denoted by the black dots along the coast, are shown on the 1892 map of the *U.S. Geological Survey*.

Lumber, nails, tar paper, second-hand lumber, terra cotta pipe, street lamps, screws, oak lumber, and a variety of other materials were ordered. Handwritten notes on the ledger indicate that the materials were for construction of a boardwalk, a pier, an outboard walk, for well tops, and for pile drivers. The words "Walnut Creek" indicate construction activity there. This invoice totaled $160.24.

Efforts to sell lots at Arundel-on-the-Bay were coordinated with promotion of the Bay Ridge resort. In mid-June 1891, B&O Railroad officials escorted a group of newspapermen, including F. H. Noyes of the *Washington Evening Star*, from Washington to the opening of the resort, after which they "motored" by yacht to Arundel-on-the-Bay. There it was announced that "a modern inn, a club-house and pavilion, bowling alleys, and a 600-foot pier are among the desires of the owners..."[30]

By mid-summer 1891 several improvements included a stage line between Arundel-on-the-Bay and Bay Ridge and a four-foot-wide boardwalk running along the Bay side of Chesapeake Avenue from the Walnut Avenue pier to the south side of Chestnut Avenue. Two additional wells, requested of Robinson, the Philadelphia well contractor, were completed by early August. At a meeting on August 27, the officers agreed that the Sisters of the Holy Cross could have a 25 percent discount on any lots they might purchase.

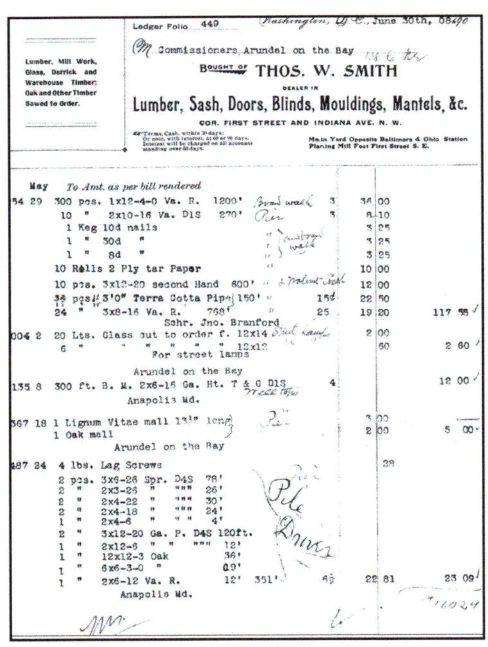
Ledger Folio 449 Washington, D.C., June 30th, 1890

M Commissioners Arundel on the Bay

Bought of THOS. W. SMITH

Dealer in

Lumber, Sash, Doors, Blinds, Mouldings, Mantels, &c.

COR. FIRST STREET AND INDIANA AVE. N. W.

Lumber, Mill Work, Glass, Derrick and Warehouse Timber; Oak and Other Timber Sawed to Order.

Terms, Cash, within 30 days; Or note, with interest, at 60 or 90 days. Interest will be charged on all accounts standing over 60 days.

Main Yard Opposite Baltimore & Ohio Station
Planing Mill Foot First Street S. E.

May To Amt. as per bill rendered
54 29 300 pcs. 1x12-4-0 Va. R. 1200' Board walk 3 36 00
10 " 2x10-16 Va. D1S 270' Pier 3 8 10
1 Keg 10d nails 3 25
1 " 30d " 3 25
1 " 8d " 3 25
10 Rolls 2 Ply tar Paper 10 00
10 pcs. 3x12-20 second Hand 600' Walnut Creek 12 00
36 pcs. 12" 3'0" Terra Cotta Pipe 150' 15¢ 22 50
24 " 3x8-16 Va. R. 768' 25 19 20 117 55
Schr. Jno. Branford
004 2 20 Lts. Glass cut to order f. 12x14 Street Lamps 2 00
6 " " " " " " 12x12 60 2 60
For street lamps
Arundel on the Bay
135 8 300 ft. B. M. 2x6-16 Ga. Ht. T & G D1S Well tops 4 12 00
Anapolis Md.
367 18 1 Lignum Vitae mall 13½" long Pier 3 00
1 Oak mall 2 00 5 00
Arundel on the Bay
487 24 4 lbs. Lag Screws 28
2 pcs. 3x6-26 Spr. D4S 78'
2 " 2x3-26 " " 26'
2 " 2x4-22 " " 30'
2 " 2x4-18 " " 24'
1 " 2x4-6 " " 4'
2 " 3x12-20 Ga. P. D4S 120ft.
1 " 2x12-6 " " " 12'
1 " 12x12-3 Oak 36'
1 " 6x6-3-0 " 09'
1 " 2x6-12 Va. R. 12' 351' Pile Drivers 6½ 22 81 23 09
Anapolis Md.
160 24

Figure 21: The bill of lading for lumber for the construction of the Arundel-on-the-Bay boardwalk and pier, ledger Folio 449, Thos. W. Smith "Dealer in Lumber, Sash, Doors, Blinds, Mouldings, Mantels, & etc." *Historical Society of Washington, D.C.*

Members of the 6th Battalion encamped at Bay Ridge for a week in August and visited Arundel-on-the-Bay. Among the activities in September 1891: engagement of Capt. Baldwin of Annapolis as a watchman at a salary of $45 per month; he and his wife and son were allowed a house and two acres to cultivate; delivery of the 35-foot yacht *Arundel*, at a cost of $520; and planting of 2,000 bushels of oysters costing 25 cents each. On September 24, attendees of the first annual meeting of the investment company in Alexandria, Va., learned that a capitalization of $70,000 had been raised through purchases of stock in the corporation.

In late October 1891, work was begun to fill in block 15, to bridge the ditches crossing streets, to cut trees to make Newport Avenue, and to add a driveway to Magnolia Avenue from a wharf on the bay. Lawrence Costigan, who had been the foreman for construction efforts since the fall of

1890 and whose services had been suspended in mid-October 1891, was rehired to grade the land with a plow to help build streets and dig ditches two feet deep and 20 inches wide along them.

Marketing continued late into the year. Officers advertised in the *Washington Evening Star* of November 25, 1891, for friends "who might have been overlooked in the issuance of invitations to attend a Thanksgiving Day oyster roast and turkey shoot on Thomas Point at Fishing Creek...you are cordially invited to join the party." Tickets were sold at the

Figure 22: Early residents of Arundel-on-the-Bay could get to and through the community by train, bicycle, horse, and horse-and-buggy as shown in this 1890 photograph of a horse-drawn wagon, with Margaret Taylor Randall (1861-1959), an accomplished photographer of Annapolis, in the first seat. *The Annapolis I Remember Collection, Maryland State Archives.*

B&O depot in the District. The special train transported 375 attendees on November 26, departing from Washington, D.C. at 9:15 a.m. and returning from Bay Ridge at 4:30 p.m.

The Pioneering Buyers of 1891

Sixty-three real estate transactions of the Chesapeake & Columbia Investment Co., beginning in1891 through1908 when the reports ended, are recorded in the Grantor Index to Land Records for Anne Arundel County. In addition to the purchases of company officers Smith, Stone, and Keleher, nine lots were listed as sold in 1891. Among the first to buy was James L. Parsons Jr. (1847-1917), owner of a contracting firm that built portions of Lansburghs and the Woolworth department stores in Washington, D.C. His lot, which he received for $5, was on the northern side of Linden Avenue, just inland of company officer Hazen's property on Chesapeake Avenue. German-born Rudolph Bleifus (1834-1905), keeper of a saloon at 12 Fourth St. NE in Washington, D.C., and wife Katherina bought the second lot south of Walnut Avenue on Chesapeake Avenue for $400.

Samuel Gelston, a business partner of contractor George N. Walker, builder of the first seven cottages, who also operated out of the lumber offices of Smith, bought a frontage lot for $450 with his wife Elizabeth. Born in New York in 1828, Gelston listed his occupation at the Navy Yard in 1880 as a machinist and later as a foreman and clerk. The couple and their 11 children lived at 630 East Capitol Street SE, on the same block as founders Thomas Smith and Lawrence Cavanaugh. Gelston's property was on Chesapeake Avenue on the second lot south of Sycamore Avenue, next door to Stone's cottage on the street corner.

Samuel A. Drury, partner in Arms & Drury, a real estate brokerage with a significant loan business in Washington, D.C., also purchased in 1891, choosing a lot on Chesapeake Avenue just south of Magnolia Avenue on Point Pleasant for which he paid $450. Minnie M. Weisen bought two frontage lots on Chesapeake Avenue between Redwood and Linden avenues at a cost of $800 and James N. Gray bought two lots on the corner of Cohasset and Redwood avenues for $450.

Promotional Efforts and Lot Purchasers of 1892

Beginning in the spring, Thomas Smith advertised a Decoration Day excursion to Arundel-on-the-Bay from the B&O railroad station in Washington, D.C., urging prospective purchasers to spend the day and inspect the lots. Servicemen from the District and Maryland, members of a military encampment at Bay Ridge during a week in August, also were invited to have a look.

Figure 23: The McIntyre family, a presence on Narragansett Avenue in Arundel-on-the-Bay at their Rose Cottage for many years, photographed c. 1910 next to their grocery on K Street NW in Washington, D.C. Standing, from the left is Agnes Agatha Clementine (Peg) McIntyre (1896-1994), John Thomas McIntyre (1867-1920), Martha Clementine Thorn McIntyre (1845-1918), and Peter J. McIntyre (1839-1919). Standing on the far right is Mary Alma McIntyre (1898-1984). ***With permission of Jack Gray of Suffolk, Va., Ancestry.com.***

Five additional deeds for lots purchased from the Chesapeake & Columbia Investment Co. were recorded in 1892.[31] This included one at $250 by Peter John McIntyre, born in Ireland in 1839, and his wife Martha Clementine Thorn, a native of Georgetown and born in 1845. Their Rose Cottage stood on Narragansett Avenue at the southwest corner of Walnut Avenue. McIntyre and his wife were proprietors of a grocery store at 2534 K Street NW in the District over which the family with eleven children lived. Later, McIntyre listed his occupation as master builder. He also opened a restaurant at 955 26th Street NW.[32]

Mary S. Heinecke and her husband Charles T. Heinecke, a clerk in the Pension Office, bought two lots on Chesapeake Avenue between Sycamore and Redwood avenues for $800. Their Cedar Cottage, completed by July 1891, was described by a newspaper columnist as "one of the most charming spots on the bay." The Heineke sons, who vacationed at the family's cottage throughout their lives were George B. Heinecke, a physician who lived in the Brightwood section of the District, and Howard Heinecke, who practiced law in Plainfield, N.J.[34] The Heineckes' daughter Francina, or "May" as she was called,

Figure 24: Cottages on Chesapeake Avenue at the waterfront of Arundel-on-the-Bay in 1892 with a summer house and the Chesapeake Bay to the right. The woman walking with a young boy is Margaret Taylor Randall of Annapolis. *Photo courtesy of Arundel-on-the-Bay resident Wilma Coble. MdHR G 182-777, Special Collections, Maryland State Archives.*

died in a freak lightning accident at Arundel-on-the-Bay in the summer of 1893. The horrible story of the accident was told in both the *Washington Post* [35] and the *Baltimore Sun*:

> She had been standing on the porch of her father's cottage, at Arundel on the Bay, watching the progress of a storm which came up suddenly. A large chestnut tree in front of the cottage was shattered, and splinters of the tree struck the young girl, who was only a few feet away. The electric current which shattered the tree caused the instant death of Miss Heinecke.[36]

Records show that John W. Reynolds purchased two lots on Narragansett Avenue at the intersection of Magnolia Avenue for $500. T.W. Tomey was given two lots on the hillside overlooking Fishing Creek at the corner of Hollywood and Rockaway Avenues for $30. Property sales for the year wrapped up in December with the purchase of a deed in trust by the National Capital Brewing Co. at $600 for three lots on Magnolia Avenue – the southernmost street of the peninsula – on the eastern side of Newport Avenue.[37]

Brewing Family Dynasties at Arundel-on-the-Bay

The brewing company purchase was the first of two local brewers who summered at Arundel-on-the-Bay. He was Albert Carry (1852-1925), born in Hohenzollern, Germany, who made his home at 135 12th Street NE.

Figure 25: Albert Carry and his wife, Anna. ***George Didden Spring Distinguished Lecture Series, May 24, 2000, Historical Society of Washington, D.C.***

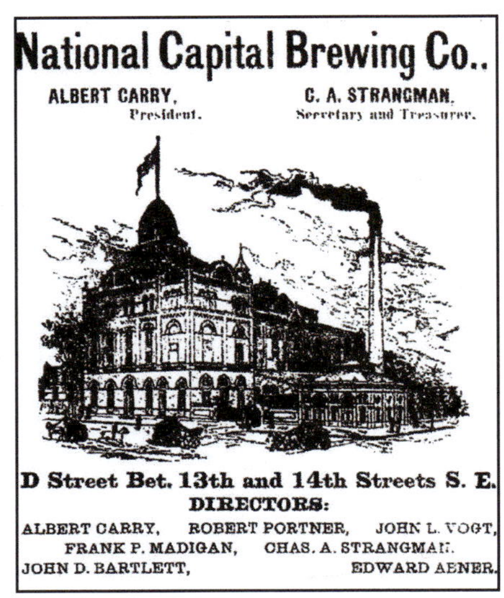

Figure 27: A National Capital Brewing Company advertisement. ***Sunday Herald, February 22, 1891.***

Figure 26: This vintage beer tray shows the Maerzen Beer Red Label containing a lithograph of the Christian Heurich Brewing Co. as it looked c. 1900-1909. Built in 1895, the brewery was located in the Foggy Bottom neighborhood of Washington, D.C. on the site now occupied by the John F. Kennedy for the Performing Arts. It replaced the original company brewery near Dupont Circle which had been damaged by fire. ***Historical Society of Washington, D.C.***

The other brewer was Christian Heurich Jr. (1902-1979), who would take over Heurich Brewery after his father's death in 1945. His purchases of six lots on the Bay front between Myrtle and Oak avenues were completed in early

Figure 28: Diamond Beer Label, National Capitol Brewing Company. ***George Didden Lecture, Historical Society of Washington, D.C.***

Figure 29: Christian Heurich Jr., a member of a Washington D.C., brewing family, owned a vacation home at 1363 Myrtle Avenue in Arundel-on-the-Bay beginning in 1939. Heurich is shown above, far right in a white shirt, with the Heurich Brewery baseball team. ***Historical Society of Washington, D. C.***

1939. His mailbox was a beer keg fastened to a tree. The Heurich family as Arundel-on-the-Bay residents also is discussed in Chapter Five.

Albert Carry moved to Washington, D.C., from Cincinnati, Ohio, where he had been brew master for the John Houch Co. His National Capital Brewing Co., founded in 1887 and occupying an entire block at 13th and D streets SE, marketed its beer under such brand names as Bock, Imperial Export, Crystal, Diamond, and Ruby. Carry earned the appellation as the man "who brought ice cream and beer to Capitol Hill," when, after Prohibition was enacted, he reformulated his business and sold Carry Ice Cream.

Carry also was a founder and vice president of the National Capital Bank of Washington, a Director of the American Security Bank, and a founder and director of the Annapolis Savings & Trust Co. The family home, or "mansion," as it was known, was located near the brewery at 12th and B Streets SE, and they owned another summer home, Red Gables, in Suitland, Md. According to the Historic American Buildings Survey Report DC-794, covering a four-family building at 501-503 11th Street NW which had been developed by Carry and later contained the landmarked Whitlows Restaurant, Carry "became one of Washington's most distinguished citizens."

Prominent Builders from the District Purchase Lots in 1893

As he had done in1892, Thomas Smith again organized a Decoration Day excursion from the B&O station in Washington, D.C. "A lunch will be served free, and a splendid opportunity given to view this beautiful little cottage city," the advertisement read. On June 24, the following advertisement was placed in the *Evening Star*:

> Do you intend to purchase a summer home? If so don't buy until you see Arundel-on-the-Bay, the healthiest and most beautiful cottage city accessible to Washington and Baltimore. Located one mile south of Bay Ridge in a magnificent hard-wood forest on a high bluff overlooking Chesapeake bay. Hourly trains on the Arundel-on-the-Bay

railroad from Bay Ridge...Boating, bathing, crabbing, fishing. Twenty beautiful cottages already erected and occupied by Washingtonians.

Business men in either Washington or Baltimore can spend the day at business in either city and take dinner with their families at the seaside and have plenty of time to enjoy the luxury of a salt water bath before dining. Returning the next morning arrive in the city by 8:30...

When at Bay Ridge run over to see us. Any of the officers or employees of the company will take pleasure in showing you around. We will not show you on paper a long list of contemplated improvements. Our improvements, costing over $40,000, are completed and speak for themselves. A free pass, good for three months transportation from either Washington or Baltimore, furnished those who build. For further information apply to the officers of the company.

By the end of 1893, a total of 13 sales for the year were recorded. Purchasers as tenants in common included John Gould and Ames Furbee Medford, Chief of the Division of Auditors for the War Department, who lived with his wife Laura and family at 138 C Street NE in the District. Their one lot and a portion of another, obtained for $400, were located on Chesapeake Avenue south of Magnolia Avenue on the southernmost block in the community on the spit of land called the Point, or Point Pleasant. Many of the entertainments detailed in newspaper social columns took place at the Medford cottage, which was known as The Gables.[40] Medford's yacht was called *The PDQ.*

Figure 30: The architect's drawing of the Barr Building located on the east side of the 900 block of 17th Street NW and built for Arundel-on-the-Bay resident Lester Arrington Barr. Constructed in 1927, the building was listed on the National Register of Historic Places in 2013. ***Historical Society of Washington, D.C.***

William W. Calvo was another buyer in 1893, taking an inner lot for $300 on the north side of Redwood Avenue between Chesapeake and Narragansett avenues. Born in South Carolina in 1859—the son of an Englishman who had been born in Nassau, The Bahamas—Calvo moved to the District of Columbia in 1880. In 1891, his occupation was listed in a city directory as salesman. In 1895 his business address was 821 Market Space NW, in 1896 it was 784 Fifth Street NW, and, according to the 1910 census, he was then a merchant and a boarder at an estate in Fauquier County, Va. We also know that he was a member of the Grand Lodge of Free and Accepted Masons.

Franklin T. Sanner and Lester A. Barr, as tenants in common, were given two scenic Magnolia Avenue frontage lots overlooking the Bay on the eastern side of Rockaway Avenue for $30. They were business partners as Barr & Sanner in the 1890s operating out of offices at 1363 Columbia Road in the District. Both remained at Arundel-on-the-Bay for a significant period. In 1894, Sanner bought a lot on Chesapeake Avenue between Redwood and Linden avenues and built a house. Barr sold his interest in the Arundel-on-the-Bay property in 1921.

Through John L. Barr & Sons, the family later commissioned the Barr Building in downtown Washington, D.C., designed by architect B. Stanley Simmons with whom Barr often worked on building projects. Barr developed, built, owned, and for many years lived at the stately Wyoming Apartments built in 1905 at 2022 Columbia Road NW in the District. Later architect Simmons designed 2120 Leroy Place NW as a home for Barr.

Barr was born in Hagerstown, Md., in 1854. His household at the time of his purchase at Arundel-on-the-Bay comprised his wife Ida Stewart of North Carolina and five children, including their son Lester S. Barr, who was born at Arundel-on-the-Bay on the Fourth of July, 1893, and later worked in the real estate and insurance business.[41] A June 7, 1921, news article reported Barr's wife among the attendees at an Arts Club luncheon for Grace Coolidge, wife of then-Vice President Calvin Coolidge.[42]

Barr, who began his career as a plasterer, rose to an active role in building and civic life in the District. Others who were to own property at Arundel-on-the-Bay were members of boards of directors on which Barr served. He was a director of the American National Bank, as were 'Arundelites' T. Berry Linton, James F. Shea, and Thomas Somerville. Barr was active in the Board of Trade, as were Sanner and community founder Thomas Smith. He belonged to the Washington Commandery No. 1 of the Knights Templar and was elected to membership in the Columbia Historical Society in 1910. In 1914, Barr was a member of a Committee of 100, which opposed any change to District tax law, as were 'Arundelites' Edwin C. Graham, Frank Sanner, Nicholas Shea, and J. I. and Michael I. Weller. Barr died in 1937, leaving an estate worth more than $970,000.[43]

Figure 31: Arundel-on-the-Bay property owner Franklin Sanner's daughter, Miss Laura Sanner, was featured in a society column in 1905. *The Washington Times, Aug. 16, 1905.*

Barr's business partner, Franklin Thearle Sanner (1851-1916), was a bricklayer by trade. He became a contractor responsible for much residential housing in Washington, D.C., including an apartment building of 1905 that stretched along the south side of Massachusetts Avenue between 14th and 15th streets NW; the building's estimated value at the time was $200,000.[44] In 1907 Sanner became vice president and a director of the National City Bank at 1405 G Street NW and was a director of the Merchants and Mechanics Bank. He maintained offices at 18th Street and Columbia Road NW in Mount Pleasant, and resided in L'Aiglon Mansion overlooking Rock Creek Park at 1808 Adams Mill Road NW. Designed by architect Simmons, the house was built in 1906. In addition to Arundel-on-the-Bay, the family vacationed in Atlantic City and the Adirondacks. Mr. Sanner died at home at the age of 63; his estate was estimated to be worth $275,000, most of it in real estate.[45]

The third prominent builder of housing in the District purchasing at Arundel-on-the-Bay in 1893 was Charles Gessford (1831-1894), and his wife Elizabeth Evans Gessford. He reportedly built more houses than anyone else in Washington, D.C. in the years between 1875 and 1895.

Residing at 661 South Carolina Avenue SE, Gessford began his career as a carpenter's apprentice, became a carpenter builder and later a speculator in real estate. According to the Capital Hill History Project, Gessford was representative of the hard-scrabble wave of German, southern European, and Irish immigrants who found their way to Washington after the Civil War and were able, for the most part, to prosper in the building boom of the time. The Gessford cottage at Arundel-on-the-Bay was on the southern side of Redwood Avenue just inland of Chesapeake Avenue on a lot costing $400.[46]

Figure 32: An early Somerville company factory building with Civil War armaments shown in the Washington D.C. yard. The company still has facilities in Annapolis. ***Thomas Somerville Co.***

Figure 33: Thomas Somerville Sr., a Scottish immigrant born in 1831, founded the family business. The Somerville family bought property in Arundel-on-the-Bay in 1893. ***Thomas Somerville Co.***

Two well-known businessmen also purchased lots in 1893. Henry Murray bought one lot for $400 on Chesapeake Avenue midway between Oak and Hollywood Avenues and Thomas Somerville chose two lots for $800 on Chesapeake Avenue just south of Myrtle Avenue.[47]

Somerville Sr., born in Scotland in 1831, came to the United States around 1860. In 1861 he founded Thomas Somerville & Sons, originally called the National Brass Works, with offices in the District of Columbia at 727 13th Street NW and a foundry at 1320 13th Street NW. The sons who would later join the business were James W., born in 1851, and Thomas Jr., born in 1857. According to company history, the early success of the business was in castings and fittings for cannons and howitzers during the Civil War. Expanded in 1896 to include plumbing supplies, Somerville today operates in 21 locations with 10 stores–including one on Route 2 in Annapolis–and a central distribution facility.[48]

James W. Somerville, son of the company founder and listed in the census of 1900 as a dealer of plumbing, served as one of the first seven commissioners and treasurer of the Town of Arundel-on-the-Bay from 1898 until he left the area for California in 1902. Returning to Washington around 1910, a bookkeeper by profession he served in that role at the family firm. Beautifully located on the Bay front, the Thomas Somerville Chesapeake Avenue lots were bought by sisters Ada E., Eleanor S., Florence E., Edith Maude, and Mary Margaret Harris in 1916. Their brother, John H. (Jack) Harris, constructed a cottage he called Oak View for them on the site of today's 1363 Myrtle Avenue.

Also purchasing in 1893 was Jennie W. Matthews, whose lot costing $400 was on Chesapeake Avenue in the area called the Point, south of Magnolia Avenue. Wife of artist George B. Matthews, their cottage was called The Studio.[49] Matthews worked for the Architect of the Capitol between 1928 and 1935, retouching and repainting the frescoes of Constantino Brumidi in the U.S. Senate's famed Brumidi Corridors.

Kate Canfield and her husband Henry W. Canfield, an official at the War Department, bought on Chesapeake Avenue between Myrtle and Oak avenues south of the Somerville lots, and George W. Driver purchased two lots on Chesapeake Avenue just north of Oak Avenue. Company president Smith's purchase of an additional lot on Chesapeake Avenue at the northern corner of Sycamore Avenue, and vice president Hazen's of two lots at the northern side of Chestnut Avenue on Chesapeake Avenue, also were recorded in1893.

Postal Service at Arundel-on-the-Bay

Lawrence Cavanaugh owned two cottages diagonally across from one another at the corner of Narragansett and Redwood avenues. In August 1893, he became a postmaster and established a post office in the cottage on the southeast corner. As the *Washington Post* noted, this new post office was a boon to the community: "It is much more convenient now for the residents to obtain their mail than last year, when they were obliged to go to Bay Ridge."[50] James Keleher, son of founder Timothy Keleher,

Figure 34: Photograph of a portrait of Patrick Henry by artist George B. Matthews, whose cottage on the Point at Arundel-on-the-Bay was called The Studio. Descendants of Patrick Henry's sisters were early property owners and summer residents of Arundel-on-the-Bay. Matthews helped repair the famous Brumidi Corridors of the U.S. Senate. *Library of Congress*.

served with Cavanaugh as assistant postmaster. Beginning in 1896, twice daily collections and deliveries were made at mail boxes at major corners, and newspapers were delivered on the day they were issued. Jeanette Medford assisted in 1901 and T. Berry Linton was appointed postmaster in July 1905.[51] The cottage serving as post office later became the home of caretaker George Tyler, his wife Annie who became postmistress in 1906, and their children. In 1913, a lending library operated at the post office. Residents of Highland Beach received mail at the Arundel-on-the-Bay post office until their own was established in 1917.

Social Doings and other Events of 1893

A grand party was reported in the *Washington Post* in August 1893:

> The dance given last night by the residents of Arundel to their friends and neighbors turned out to be a success in every way. Only those holding invitations were granted admission to the Bay Ridge dancing pavilion, which was filled nearly to its utmost capacity. A portion of the Fifth Regiment Band of Baltimore furnished music. The dancing ceased about 11 o'clock...The party then took the train to Arundel, at which place it arrived after an eight minutes run.[52]

Ambitious plans for 1894 were disclosed in *Post* a few days later:

> At the opening of next season, Arundel will have a spacious and magnificent hotel capable of accommodating about 500 people. In connection with the hotel a large dancing pavilion will be erected. The Arundel Railroad will have its terminus at the corner of Chestnut and Narragansett avenues, immediately in rear of the proposed hotel. The net receipts from the road this year are over double those of last year, and it is expected next season will be more profitable still.[53]

The *Washington Post* of August 29 noted that the training ship *U.S.S. Constellation* was anchored off Thomas Point at Arundel-on-the-Bay after returning from its annual cruise to the Canary Islands and that "during the two days of anchorage the naval cadets have made frequent foraging trips to the inland in search of fruit and melons."[54] On September 5, 1893, it was reported that "a private hop was given at Bay Ridge last night to the young ladies at Arundel on the Bay and Brighton Villa (an area near Bay Ridge) by the young gentlemen of Annapolis."[55] Society columns wrote that the cottages of Mr. Barr, Mrs. Barker, Mr. Matthews, and the Farnsworth family were built[56] and that a storm tore up the railroad tracks along the beach and flooded the Van Zandt cottage.[57] In December 1893 corporate assets of $120,906 were reported at the annual meeting of the Chesapeake & Columbia Investment Co. Smith, Hazen, Cavanaugh, Shea, and Rannells were reelected as officers.

The Douglass Family: African American Property Ownership in 1893

Although there is no explicit written record that the founders of Arundel-on-the-Bay intended it to be white-only, racial segregation was the practice in real estate sales of the time. Yet several lots were sold to African Americans during the initial marketing, and there was an African American presence at the northern end of Arundel-on-the-Bay from the very beginning. Current Arundel-on-the-Bay resident and history project participant, John Moses, relates that the extended family of his African American maternal grandfather, Cornelius Ridgely, tent-camped "in the country" on a bluff called Cedar Grove at today's Arundel-on-the-Bay. Ridgely was a descendant of William Bishop of Annapolis, a slave born in 1802 who received his freedom in 1822.

In a sale recorded in October 1893, Laura Antoinette Haley Douglass, an African American woman, paid $400 for a lot on Chesapeake Avenue near the intersection with Cedar Avenue. Laura was a daughter-in-law of the famed abolitionist Frederick Douglass through her marriage to his youngest son, Charles Remond Douglass.[59] A few months earlier, as recorded in May 1893, Alice Jane Haley Colbert, Laura's sister, had bought a lot on Cedar Avenue between the Bay and Narragansett Avenue, around the corner from the Douglass purchase. Mrs. Colbert was a dressmaker and her husband Robert was employed at the Bureau of Printing and Engraving. The family lived at 1629 O St. NW.[60] How these sales came to be and what, if any, relationship there was between the Douglass family and the founders of Arundel-on-the-Bay remains a mystery.

Figure 35: Alice Jane Haley Colbert, sister of Laura Douglass, purchased a lot on Cedar Avenue at Arundel-on-the-Bay in May 1893. *Frederick Douglass Family Album. Courtesy of Joellen ElBashir, Curator, Manuscript Division, Moorland-Spingarn Research Center, Howard University.*

It is certain that the Douglass family would have been known to the founders of Arundel on-the-Bay because of the prominence of the patriarch, Frederick Douglass, who lived in Washington, D.C. from about 1872 until his death in 1895. Biographer and genealogist Joseph L. Douglas Jr. writes that "following the Civil War, if not earlier, the Frederick Douglass Family did indeed merit characterization as the 'first family' in black America."[61]

Because the Douglass home on Capitol Hill at Third & A streets NE was within the boundaries of the East Washington Citizens Association, begun by Arundel-on-the-Bay President Thomas W. Smith to advance the interests of that portion of the District, perhaps the family was known to Arundel-on-the-Bay founders. The founders, some of whom were of Irish descent, might have particularly respected Frederick Douglass for his advocacy of Irish home rule. Douglass traveled to Ireland in 1845, as part of a two-year stay in the British Isles, and there he met and became inspired by Irish nationalist Daniel O'Connell, and in the 1880's was outspoken in his support for Irish nationalism.[62]

Certainly the Charles Douglass purchase from the Brashears family of land adjoining the Arundel-on-the-Bay tract would have brought the family to the attention of Thomas Smith and his colleagues. Although Charles and Laura Douglass enjoyed previous visits to the Bay Ridge resort—and despite the fact that the resort advertised to African Americans in the *Washington Bee*—the couple experienced an incident of racial indignity there during an 1892 visit; this led to their purchase of land for Highland Beach.[63]

The purchase was arranged in the fall of 1892. On April 10, 1893, two-thirds interest in 40 acres of the Brashears' tract was put in the name of Joseph Henry Douglass, Charles' son from his first marriage, and Charles then filed the plat for Highland Beach. He and his family spent that summer clearing the land and building their Highland Beach cottage. A deed of partition conveyed the remainder of the tract to Douglass on September 6, 1893.[64] Thus construction at Highland Beach began slightly more than two years after the work at Arundel-on-the-Bay.

Why would Charles and Laura Douglass buy a lot in Arundel-on-the-Bay at the same time they were developing Highland Beach? Perhaps the purchase was made so that they would own property directly on the Chesapeake shoreline. Their own cottage at Highland

Figure 36: Charles R. Douglass (1844-1920), the youngest son of American abolitionist Frederick Douglass, in 1904. His second wife, Laura Antoinette Haley (1854-1928), purchased a lot at Arundel-on-the-Bay in 1893. One historian cited the creation of Highland Beach as Charles Douglass's foremost achievement. *The Colored American, September 1904.*

Beach and the cottage later begun for Frederick Douglass next door were 500 feet inland of the bay.[65] More likely the purchase was made to accommodate the family during the summer of 1893 which–according to a letter from their son Haley to his grandfather– they spent at the beach. Certainly the already-cleared Arundel-on-the-Bay sites were easily accessible by rail from Bay Ridge on the summer cars.

The historical record is not clear as to where the Douglass family actually lived during the summer of 1893. Perhaps cottages had been built for them at Arundel-on-the-Bay, or they tent-camped at the Cedar Avenue grove on the newly purchased lots, or lived in an already existing structure remaining from the Brashears' farm. Why, also, did the Colberts buy a lot at Arundel-on-the-Bay rather than at the new Highland Beach? Perhaps they, too, were already familiar with the Cedar Avenue area and the nearby beach and had tent-camped there in previous years. Maybe there was a cottage or tent on their lot which they shared with the Charles Douglass family in the summer of 1893.

Contemporaneous newspaper stories about the peninsula offer no clarity as to these questions, or as to any social relationships between residents of Highland Beach and those of Arundel-on-the-Bay. In fact, the whole area was referred to as Arundel-on-the-Bay. For example, the *Washington Bee* and other sources might report on social events, the guest list of which might be entirely African American, but describe them as having taken place at Arundel-on-the-Bay. Poet Paul Laurence Dunbar, who bought a lot at Highland Beach in 1902, characterized Arundel-on-the-Bay as "the Negroes' Bar Harbor."[66] This confusion in nomenclature was because Highland Beach had no post office until 1917 and its residents got their mail from the post office at Arundel-on-the-Bay. After Highland Beach was incorporated in 1922, it was referred to by its own name.

Figure 37: Haley George Douglass (1881-1954), the son of Charles and Laura Douglass, lived with his parents at Arundel-on-the-Bay in the summer of 1893. A graduate of Harvard University in 1905, Haley Douglass taught at Dunbar High School in the District, and was mayor of Highland Beach from 1928-1953. *Frederick Douglas Historical Site, National Park Service.*

Tax assessments for 1894 at Arundel-on-the-Bay list two Douglass frame buildings (cottages) valued at $600 each. These must have been two cottages built on the lots owned by the Haley sisters at Arundel-on-the-Bay, not those at Highland Beach, even given the confusing terminology. The Charles Douglass cottage at Highland Beach was completed in the summer of 1894; however, the home for Frederick Douglass, also begun in the summer of 1893, was not complete at the time of his death on Feb. 20, 1895, and so would not have been a part of a 1894 tax assessment.

Laura Douglass sold her lot at Arundel-on-the-Bay in January 1916 for $400 to Dr. Austin M. Curtis, one of the nation's most outstanding African American surgeons. As early as 1900, newspapers reported that Dr. Curtis and his family were vacationing at Arundel-on-the-Bay.[67] He and his wife were guests at a party at the Charles R. and Laura Douglass home in Highland Beach in July 1901.[68] Attended by 50 people, the party was described as having four tables set up for whist, negligee dancers in the parlors, and the porches illuminated by Japanese lanterns. Dr. Curtis also appears on the list of eligible property owners at Arundel-on-the-Bay for purposes of voting in 1911. More about the Curtis family at Arundel-on-the-Bay can be found in Chapter Five.

Figure 38: Charles Lenox Remond, considered the first black abolitionist speaker whose name is given Charles Remond Douglass. ***Massachusetts Historical Society.***[72]

Charles Douglass, born in Lynn, Mass., likely was given his middle name in honor of Massachusetts abolitionist and orator Charles Lenox Remond (1810-1873), reportedly the first black public speaker on abolition.[69]

The *Washington Bee* of Feb. 23, 1907, reported that Arundel-on-the-Bay vacationers Doctors A. M. Curtis and William G. Lofton were attendees at the annual dinner of the Pen & Pencil Society, a group formed to commemorate the birth of Frederick Douglass.

Deals for Some Purchasers in 1894

At the beginning of 1894 only one waterfront lot at Arundel-on-the-Bay remained unsold according to an advertisement placed by B. T. Welch, now handling sales.[70] Many of the deeds of purchase recorded in 1894 were for the low price of $30 per lot. This may have been a down payment, or a gift of President Smith. The announcement of the annual Decoration Day sales event in the May 22 edition of the *Evening Star* read:

> Arundel on the Bay. For sale in this charming subdivision. Prices, $175 to $500. Payments to suit purchasers... salt water resort accessible to Washington. 23 Cottages already built... ...Woodland and Salt Breezes. See and be convinced. Excursion on May 30, 1894. Take regular 8:30 a.m. train from B. and O. Station. Returning, reach Washington, 5:20 p.m. Particulars from B. T. WELCH, Jr. 600 F St. NW.

The excursion was to give prospective purchasers "a chance for a quiet day" to look over the property. The rail fare was to be refunded to anyone purchasing a lot.[71] Smith's furnished six-room Geneva Cottage was advertised as available for a four- month rental at a cost of $150 and property owners also offered tents for rental to prospective tent campers.

Nine lots were recorded as sold in 1894. Buyers included businessman Leidy Shimer Depue, owner of a flour and seed company with offices in the District at 820 Fourth Street SW. His grain elevators and mill were located at Harpers Ferry, W. Va. By 1923 he was in candy manufacturing. His two lots at Arundel-on-the-Bay for which he paid $60 were on Chesapeake and Narragansett Avenues between Walnut and Sycamore Avenues.[73]

Figure 39: Henry T. Offterdinger, founder of a cigar factory in Washington, D.C., bought bay front property at Arundel-on-the-Bay in 1894. ***Washington with its Points of Interest Illustrated, NY: Mercantile Illustrating Co., 1894, p.230.***

E. Clarence Colford, who incorporated the Santa Clara Refrigerating Co. to make and sell ice in Cuba, also received a lot for $30 in 1894.[74] Born in Cuba in 1865, he came to Washington, D.C., and worked initially as a clerk and a bookkeeper. Colford's Cuba Libre cottage was located on Chesapeake Avenue between Chestnut and Myrtle avenues. He and his wife Ida lived at 1867 V Street NW in the District, where he was a member of the Carroll Council of the Knights of Columbus.

Henry T. Offterdinger, owner of the Offterdinger Cigar Factory at 506 Ninth Street NW and the maker of "Deer Head" cigars, received a lot in 1894 for $30 on Chesapeake Avenue at Myrtle Avenue.[75] When he became vice president of the Lincoln National Bank at Seventh & D streets NW, his son Frederick took over the cigar operation. His son Theodore sold stocks and bonds. Active in the National Civil Service Improvement Association of the Businessmen of the United States, which in 1911 was advocating for increased pay for civil service workers, Offterdinger also served on committees of the chamber of commerce and retail merchants with fellow Arundel-on-the-Bay property owner Edwin C. Graham.

Thomas Berry Linton, a marine engineer who was born in the District in 1865 and lived with his wife Mabel at 1000 26th Street NW, purchased a lot in 1894 for $325. Their cottage, built in 1895 on Sycamore Avenue at Narragansett Avenue, which had not been used for many years, has been restored and expanded.

According to reports in the society pages, Arundel-on-the-Bay's summer residents in 1894 included David S. and Anna Barker Tallerday, who celebrated their wedding on Sycamore Avenue, and James C. Courts in his newly completed cottage. Also on hand were the Barrs, the Semmes, the Heinecke and Towers families, Capt. and Mrs. Van Zandt, and Alice J. Colbert and family.

Tallerday served in the Civil War as a member of the 38th Ohio Volunteer Infantry. He entered business as an owner of eight stables in southwest Washington; by 1894 his occupation was listed in city directories as a broker.

James C. Courts was born in Fairfield, Texas, in 1855. He began work on Capitol Hill as a messenger, rising to Principal Clerk of the U.S. House of Representatives Committee on Appropriations. Mentioned several times in connection with Arundel-on-the-Bay in the *Evening Star* column, "Heard and Seen Here and There," a poem detailing his wish to spend Christmas at Arundel-on-the-Bay was published on Dec. 25, 1909:

Sir James gazed deep into the coals, in pleasant reverie
"A Courts I am," he quote aloud, "a Courts of Tennessee."
But weaned I am from mine ancient home, I've been so long away,
And I'll spend my Christmas 1909 at Arundel-on-the-Bay.
Tis there I hie with quickened steps whenever work is through,
And of I take for company a husky friend or two.
I remember one who went to loaf; his blessed name was Ray.
But he sawed four cords of hickory wood at Arundel-on-the-Bay.
A good friend dug my cistern and another bore my well,
Another painted shutters and it took him quite a spell:
But I was glad to have him and I like my friends to stay,
For labor's scarce and mighty dear at Arundel-on-the-Bay.

But now a worry sears my mind, for what am I to do?
I've scanned a list of all my friends; I fear I've run them through.
And when, with warmth and urgency, 'Please come again' I say,
They shake their heads and spurn the dust of Arundel-on-the-Bay.
I know a fat newspaper man, I think I'll ask him down.
I'll tell him he should rest awhile, he hustles so in town.
He hefts about two-fifty now. I wonder what he'd weigh.
After he had visited Arundel-on-the Bay."
The coals fell down, the flames flared up; Sir James shook off his cares.
"Thanks to my husky friends," said he, "I do not need repairs.
So to my villa warm and snug I'll go some time today.
And spend a happy Christmas at Arundel-on-the-Bay.[76]

In an April 1910 column it was written facetiously:

Courts....clerk of the House Committee on Appropriations, secretary of the U.S. Bonding Commission, chairman of the board of public works of Arundel on the Bay, Vice President of the Arundel and Annapolis Transportation Company, treasurer of the Arundel Cistern Supply Company has begun to invite friends down to his Arundel home. His friends say that labor is scarce at Arundel on the Bay and that Mr. Court's house needs painting.[77]

Upon his return from a trip to Panama "alligator hunting," it was reported that "Sir" Courts was "met by the entire present population of Arundel on the Bay whose name is Smith."[78] In 1913, Courts was described as: "the redoubtable Courts, whose memory contains more anecdotes of political strategy than most men, and whose broad vision makes national campaign snarls appear like tiny knots on the threads of a spool of silk."[79]

Figure 40: The Thomas Berry Linton House, constructed in 1895 at 1359 Sycamore Avenue and now being renovated, has not been used for many years. Of modest design, the house featured a porch running on two sides with decorative fish-scale shingle siding in the gable ends. ***Photograph by Bill Semenuk, May 2016.***

Charles W. Semmes and his brother E. E. Semmes founded the Semmes Motor Line in 1912. Renamed the Semmes Motor Car Co., it sold Hudson automobiles, Dodge trucks, and later the Wilcox truck from a showroom located at 2827 M Street NW in the District.

Mark Edwards Tower was born in 1864 in the District. He joined the Navy at the age of 15 and sailed on the USS. *Constitution*, famously known as "Old Ironsides," where he was deafened by cannon fire and received a disability discharge in 1882. He learned the printing trade from his father and worked for 15 years at the *Washington Post* and for 25 more years as a linotype operator at the Government Printing Office. Mr. Tower was a nephew of John Thomas Tower, the first Public Printer of the United States and Mayor of the District of Columbia from 1854 to 1856. He was a member of the Columbia Typographical Union and the Samuel Gompers Chapter of the Masons.[80] Bayview, the Towers' cottage, was one of the seven original cottages built in 1891 on Chesapeake Avenue, on the site of today's 1360 Chestnut Avenue. Tower offered the property for sale in 1910: "For sale, well-furnished 6 rm cottage-large corner lot; stable and chicken house, in best location, facing bay."[81]

A party held by the Smiths was reported in the *Washington Evening Star* of August 11, 1894: "Wednesday evening there was given a dance at Arundel-on-the-Bay by Mr. and Mrs. Thos. W. Smith. The younger portion of the visitors indulging in dancing till a late hour, when all sat down to a substantial repast."

The Original Thomas Point Shoal Light Station Collapses in 1894

On Feb. 28, 1894, the stone tower of the Thomas Point Shoal Light Station originally constructed in 1825 by John Donahoo–who built eleven others around the Bay in the same time period–fell down. The tower, at first 100 feet from the shoreline, had been relocated in 1838 and rebuilt using original materials to a height of 33 feet by Winslow

Figure 41: The Semmes Motor Company, 2827 M Street NW, Washington, D.C. and a T.A. Cannon Co. truck of its manufacture, 1926. ***Library of Congress.***

Lewis before it was abandoned for the present structure located in the Bay in 1873, see Chapter One.

The land on which the original light stood—at one time the eastern extension of Thomas Point—can be seen at the bottom edge of this chapter's Figure 12 and in Figure 4 of Chapter One. Erosion separated this strip from the rest of Thomas Point, and the remaining fragment continued to erode, shrinking seven acres to about two. This two-acre tract was sold by the U.S. government in 1914 for $426 to Garnett Y. Clark of Ellicott City, Md. As the land eroded still more, descendants of Clark moved their home on the island to Magnolia Avenue in Arundel-on-the-Bay.[82]

A Dancing Pavilion, Entertainments, and More Cottages in 1895

Smith advertised Arundel-on-the-Bay throughout the summer of 1895 as an "ideal resort." Cottages costing $750 could be constructed for buyers within one month, he pledged. The lots of 25 feet by 150 feet were priced between $50 and $150. It was said in the advertisement, "About 25 cottages now finished are owned by Washington people, and the society of the place is good."[83] On June 12 an advertisement in the *Washington Evening Star* described Arundel-on-the-Bay:

> The ideal summer resort, combining as it does, the hard-wood shady forests of the mountains with the cool, invigorating salt-water breezes of the ocean. 25 cottages of prominent Washingtonians...

In 1895, a dancing pavilion was erected between Tower's Bayview Cottage and Shea's Idle Wild on Chesapeake Avenue at Chestnut Avenue. The woman's auxiliary, founded the previous year, advocated construction of the pavilion primarily as a site for social gatherings, but the community found other uses, such as a place to vote in the annual elections and a gathering place for Sunday religious services. Smith's wife Catherine organized a "Saturday Night Club" to plan entertainments and she served as the club's president. Jeanette Medford served as secretary and Emma Towers as treasurer. In the following years, the pavilion would continue to inspire society columnists at the *Washington Post* with such notes as this one from July 1896: "...the Saturday evening club gave an enjoyable lawn fete and dance in the pavilion."[84]

In other *Washington Post* society columns it was reported:

> On Wednesday evening the pavilion was given over to the juvenile society. The grounds and pavilion were bright with their usual attractive decorations and the little ones, numbering half a hundred, made merry. Games and dancing were enjoyed to the utmost by the children, and seats were arranged for the comfort of the older ones.[85]

> Saturday evening the pavilion was the scene of its usual hop. The decorations and illuminations were as attractive as usual, but, owing to the intense heat, the floor was only half filled at any time. Seats were arranged through the grounds and made a pleasant resting place. The feature of this evening was the raffling of a fine water color picture, donated by the painter, Mrs. A. Medford, who is an artist of no poor ability. A large number were present.[86]

Among the entertainments enjoyed by Arundel-on-the-Bay residents in the summer of 1895 was a day trip to Baltimore on the steamer Columbia, which departed from Bay Ridge.[87] A party given at The Gables, the cottage of the Medfords, was described as:

> A real old-fashioned taffy boil...after the taffy had reach (ed) the state of perfection, a bright golden hue, games were enjoyed. The evening was finished with a dance. Musical selections were rendered...and a well-known elocutionist...gave a recitation...[88]

What happened in the community was of interest to those in the *Washington Post's* area of circulation. Clearly, people wanted to read about what was happening to their friends and neighbors off for the summer. Other newspaper reports of the charms of life at Arundel-on-the-Bay included:

- Entertained friends at a bathing party. The water was all that could be desired, and after the party returned to terra firma, refreshments were served on the lawn.
- The pier extends 400' out in the bay and is a favorite resort after sundown.[89]
- An old-fashioned all-day picnic was held at Thomas' Island. Baskets were taken along and lunch was spread upon the green lawn under the shade of the grand old trees.
- The yacht 'Dorothy' carried a sailing party to Annapolis, where they went on a sight-seeing expedition.
- The little steam launch 'Arundel,' the property of Mr. Thomas W. Smith, carried a pleasure party to Kent Island. This is a most delightful trip of five miles across the bay.[90]
- Bicycling is as great a fad here as in the city, in defiance of the sandy roads.[91]
- On Tuesday evening the sojourners in this resort were entertained in a delightful manner...A large number had collected upon the end of the pier to enjoy the cool breeze and the beautiful moonlight. Miss Murphy recited several difficult selections and although hardly more than a child, showed remarkable talent . . .
- Boating, fishing and crabbing parties are the popular fad.[92]
- A common sight on the boardwalk is the indefatigable fisherman armed with rod and rockfish.[93]
- Mr. (F.I.) Sanner caught five immense black bass the other morning before breakfast, fishing from the end of the little pier in front of his place.[94]

Card games were popular: "On Monday evening 'Bay View Cottage,' the home of Mr. and Mrs. Mark E. Towers was the scene of a gay assembly, the occasion being a euchre party."[95] Euchre was a card game for 2-4 players using a modified deck of nine through the ace in which five cards are dealt to each player and three tricks must be taken to win a hand. Some cheating, such as "stealing the deal," is an accepted part of the game.

According to newspaper reports, cottages opened in 1895 included those of Chester H. Beatty, former U.S. Rep. Lewis E. Payson, and Captain and Mrs. William B. Brown and their daughter Mrs. Weston (Lucinda) Flint. Born in 1873, Chester Hopkins Beatty received his dental degree from George Washington University in 1894 and practiced dentistry in the District. He married Adda B. Carr. His brother, Dr. Louis K. Beatty, was one of the founders of Casualty Hospital, where Thomas Smith and William C. Hazen served as directors. Beatty joined the 32nd Infantry in May 1918 as a first lieutenant and served in France between June 1918 and February 1919. The 1930 Census records him as resident in a rooming house in Dayton, Ohio, and a widower.

Figure 42: Arundel-on-the-Bay resident former congressman Lewis Payson in 1898. He represented the same district in Illinois as had Abraham Lincoln. ***Courtesy of Louise Linkins Seely, great-niece of Payson.***

A Former Congressman, Elected from the District Abraham Lincoln Represented, Buys at Arundel-on-the-Bay

Former U.S. Rep. Lewis Payson, who purchased the Samuel Drury property on Chesapeake Avenue south of Magnolia Avenue, was a District of Columbia lawyer. He was a member of the U.S. House of Representatives from 1880 to 1890 (the 47th through the 51st Congresses) and elected from the district represented by Abraham Lincoln, the 9th District of Illinois. An expert in land law, Payson appeared before the courts and in Congress on behalf of influential clients, including John D. Rockefeller, the Harriman

Figure 43: Chelsea Cottage c. 1900, the Arundel-on-the-Bay home of former U.S. Rep. Lewis Payson. Facing the Chesapeake Bay on Chesapeake Avenue, south of the Magnolia Avenue right-of-way, the cottage was built in 1895. The image is taken from the bay looking southwest; the kitchen and other service buildings are to the rear shown on the right. The home was sold to newspaper man and humorist Philander Johnson in 1909, bought by William Linkins in 1914, and purchased by Clyde and Wilma Coble in 1971 from descendants of the Linkins family. The house burned in a fire of mysterious origin in 1980. ***Maryland State Archives.***

interests, and the Newport News Shipping & Drydock Co. His family describes him as a lobbyist who mainly represented the interests of western railroads.

Payson built Chelsea Cottage on Chesapeake Avenue in 1895. Born in 1851 in Providence, R.I., he lived at 1229 Massachusetts Avenue NW in the District. At his death in 1909, his estate was valued at $900,000.[96]

Five deeds of purchase were recorded with Anne Arundel County in 1895. They were those of Capt. Brown ($400), Dr. George C. Burton ($400), and Julia E. Farnsworth ($30), along with the purchases of additional single lots by previous owners David D. Stone ($30) and Peter McIntyre ($275). The Farnsworth property was on the northern side of Sycamore Avenue, inland of Chesapeake Avenue. George Burton was a physician practicing at 907 H Street NE and later at 810 H Street NE. His cottage was built in 1895 on Chesapeake Avenue between Myrtle and Oak Avenues next to the Somerville lots.

The Brown/Flint cottage was located on Magnolia Avenue between Chesapeake and Narragansett Avenues next door to former Rep. Payson. The lot was purchased in 1894. Col. Weston Flint, who married the Brown's daughter, was a lawyer, journalist, and educator who served in the Civil War and was U.S. Consul to China from 1871 to 1874. Born in 1835 in western New York, where his father had a farm, Flint began his career as editor and publisher of a St. Louis newspaper. He later became secretary/treasurer of the Washington public library and subsequently served as librarian of the Patent Office, where he completed a 700-page catalog of its holdings. Flint was Secretary of the Board of Managers of the Anthropological Society of the District of Columbia and a member of the Sons of the American Revolution. The Flint residence in Washington, D.C., was 917 12th Street NW. Flint died in 1906 and is buried at the Rock Creek Cemetery. Their son, Weston, was born in 1884.

A Descendant of Martha Washington among Purchasers in 1896 and 1897

Eight deeds were recorded in 1896 and one in 1897. Among those purchasing was Willie Anna Watson Peters, born in 1860 in Virginia and the wife of Jesse David Bright Peters (1845-1945), a descendent of Martha Washington. In 1890, when Jesse Peters applied for membership in the Sons of the American Revolution, he cited as his relevant ancestor Thomas Peters of Pennsylvania, the husband of Martha Washington's granddaughter Martha Parke Custis.[97] In 1880, Jesse Peters was an intern at Mount Vernon; he later became a government clerk.

Willie Anna operated a grocery at 1009 E St. NW in the District. The family, which included four children; Jessie, Willie, Hetty, and Harold, resided at 918 N St. NW. The Peters' cottage, built in 1896, was on Sycamore Avenue near the corner of Narragansett Avenue, the lot costing $300. According to the 1920 federal census, the Jesse Peters family was living in Tampa, Fla.

Charles A. Wissing, who was gifted a lot for $10 in 1896, was born in Denmark in 1842 and immigrated to the United States in 1861. His wife Ellen, a native of Maryland and born in 1845, worked as a cook. Charles was a fireman serving at a variety of locations around the city, including St. Elizabeth's Hospital. The Wissing cottage, built in 1896, was on Chesapeake Avenue at the corner south of Oak Avenue.[98]

George W. Driver and his wife Mary came from New York to the District in the 1880s. He was a popular restaurant owner, saloonkeeper, and a seller of wines, liquors, and cigars from a business at 605 Pennsylvania Avenue NW. In 1896 the Drivers purchased a corner lot on Chesapeake Avenue on the north side of Oak Avenue for $400.

Figure 44: Weston Flint, U.S. Consul to China from 1871-74, enjoyed a family cottage on Magnolia Avenue at Arundel-on-the-Bay. ***View Media-Ancestry. com, 1894 family reunion.***

Driver provided his customers an annual satiric publication entitled *Facts of Interest to Voters.* When he sold his restaurant in 1905, the headline read "The Premier Establishment of the National Capital." The story recounted:

> The admirable location of this famous establishment, being close to the Pennsylvania depot, hotels, and to the car lines, makes it a fashionable meeting place of gentlemen. It is a fact that visitors from everywhere will drop into 'Driver's old stand' and recall pleasant things which occurred long ago.[99]

Lots also were sold to Joseph H. Milans, Wm.W. Mortimer ($30), Lena Morgenweck, and Sarah Jane Oram ($30). Milans was a lawyer, director of the Dimes Savings Bank, and later Grand Commander of the Knights Templar of the District of Columbia. Morgenweck lived in the District at 12 Fourth St. NE. Oram of Baltimore purchased the southernmost lot on Point Pleasant.

Mortimer, whose listed address in 1910 was 1755 Columbia Rd. NW and in 1920 was 2627 Adams Mill Rd. NW, was a division chief at the Patent Office, having begun there as a draftsman. Mrs. Mortimer, the former Katherine B. Bowen, was a 1908 graduate of the Providence Hospital School of Nursing. Their cottage was on the north side of Myrtle Avenue at the corner of Narragansett Avenue on the site of today's 1360 Myrtle Avenue.

Tent Camps at Arundel-on-the-Bay

In July 1896 newspapers began mentioning a number of tent camps that were springing up at Arundel-on-the-Bay. Camping was a new pastime for many Americans, perhaps inspired by early catalogs from Abercrombie & Fitch, founded in 1892 and calling itself the "greatest Sporting Goods Store in the World." Campsites were given bucolic names like Camp Sub Silva and Camp White Oaks. According to newspaper reports, tent visitors created Camp Ohio in Cedar Grove– a site at the northern end of the community, Camp Pleasant on The Point, and the Copper Party Camp on Narragansett Avenue. As one news story said:

> ... numbers of ladies and gentlemen have erected their tents upon their annual camping ground on the picturesque bluff overlooking the Bay. The camp is composed principally of Mount Pleasant (D.C.) people, from which it derives its name of Camp Pleasant.

The *Washington Post* commented on the Copper Party Camp:

> ...one of the most unique camps in this locality is occupied by a party of young lawyers from Washington. The camp is situated on Narragansett Avenue, and is fantastically decorated with cedars and other plants; in the sand surrounding the tent oyster shells are arranged to form the words, "Copper Party" such being the independent political [sic] these gentlemen represent.[100]

Another group from Mount Pleasant, calling themselves the "None Such," "have erected tents upon the beautiful bluff overlooking the bay, and their canvas homes make quite a little settlement," it was reported.[101] "President N. E. Young of the National Baseball League, and family, who have been in camp at Arundel, broke camp August 30," the *Post* reported on September 1. The organist and choirmaster of Epiphany Parish camped on Redwood Avenue in July.[102]

Figure 45: A picturesque tent on the lawn of Chelsea Cottage at Arundel-on-the-Bay in 1916. ***Photograph courtesy of Louise Linkins Seely, who is shown learning to garden at the age of two.***

Descendants of Colonial Patriot Patrick Henry at Arundel-on-the-Bay

In September 1893 the *New York Times* reported the death of Mary R. Garland Cabell at a cottage at Arundel-on-the-Bay. Mrs. Cabell was a niece of Patrick Henry, the daughter of his sister Mary Jane. In 1897 her granddaughter, Jennie Van Zandt O'Neill, obtained a lot in the community for $30. Newspaper reports indicated that Jennie's parents, Capt. Nicholas Biddle Henry Van Zandt and Jane Henry Meredith Cabell, were occupying a cottage in the community before that purchase, which might have been where Mary Cabell died. These stories included a reference to the Van Zandt's cottage, The Anchorage, being flooded in 1893 and a society column in 1894 stating that the couple was "in residence."

Figure 46: Arundel-on-the-Bay property owner Jennie Van Zandt O'Neill, shown here in her passport photograph of 1915, was a descendant of Mary Jane Henry, a sister of famed colonial orator and pamphleteer Patrick Henry. ***Ancestry.com.***

Capt. Van Zandt, born in Virginia in 1822, had a colorful Navy career that included travels to the Far East and his capture as a Confederate naval officer. A brief synopsis of the naval career of Van Zandt is offered as a sidebar to this chapter. A long-time resident of Georgetown, he died in 1900 and is buried at Georgetown's Oak Hill Cemetery.

Van Zandt's wife, Jane Henry Meredith, born in Virginia in 1830, was named for Patrick Henry. After moving to Washington, D.C., Jane Meredith was introduced to her future husband by her elderly cousin Dolley Madison, wife of the fourth president.

Mrs. Van Zandt purportedly knew personally every First Lady of her time and was a close friend of Mrs. Alexander Hamilton, the widow of the first Secretary of the Treasury. Much beloved, Jane Van Zandt died at Arundel-on-the-Bay on Feb. 2, 1915.[103]

Figure 47: Capt. Nicholas Van Zandt, Arundel-on-the-Bay resident, fought in the Mexican war and later for the Confederacy in the Civil War. He was a great-grandson of Lucy Henry, a sister of Patrick Henry. ***Photograph of portrait, National Historical Society, Journal of American History, Vol. 6, 1912, p. 708.***

Figure 48: Jane Henry Meredith Cabell Van Zandt, a great-granddaughter of Mary Jane Henry, a sister of colonial patriot Patrick Henry, Mrs. Van Zandt died at Arundel-on-the-Bay in 1915 at the age of 85. ***Photograph of a portrait, National Historical Society, Journal of American History, Vol. 6, 1912, p.705.***

Details of Van Zandt's Naval Career by James W. Cheevers, Senior Curator, U.S. Naval Academy Museum, Annapolis, Maryland:

Van Zandt entered the U.S. Navy as a Midshipman on October 19, 1841, and served until December 1861, when he resigned and became a Lieutenant in the Confederates States Navy in which he served throughout the Civil War.

In the fall of 1841 he was assigned to the USS *Columbia*, a frigate, which over the next three years took him off the coast of Brazil and to other ports in South America and then to ports in the Mediterranean during his education and training at sea in the "school of hard knocks." He kept journals which were examined daily by the captain of the frigate.

After returning home in early 1845, he was soon reassigned to a ship-of-the-line, USS *Columbus*, which was fitted out for an extensive tour in the East Indies. Departing on June 4, 1845, for Canton, China, the ship's Commodore delivered a ratified copy of the first American commercial treaty with China. Protecting American interests along the coast of China until April 1846, *Columbus* sailed to Japan and attempted an official visit on July 19, without success. It was seven years later when Commodore Matthew C. Perry finally negotiated a successful treaty with Japan. Because of the Mexican War, the *Columbus* was recalled to the western hemisphere, first arriving at Valparaiso, Chile, where orders were found to proceed to Monterey, California. The ship patrolled the central California coast until July 26, 1846, when it departed San Francisco for Norfolk, arriving on March 3, 1848.

Upon his return, Van Zandt was sent to the new Naval School at Annapolis where he was given examinations. He passed and was promoted Passed Midshipman, back-dated to August 10, 1847. He is considered a member of the U.S. Naval Academy Class of 1847, but spent very little time at the academy. He received most of his education at sea by the chaplains and officers aboard between 1841 and 1848.

He was next assigned to the store ship USS *Relief*, and went off on another cruise in the Mediterranean Squadron from the fall of 1848 until November 1850. After this cruise he worked at the Naval Observatory in Washington on his first of four tours of duty (1851, 1855-56, 1858, and 1859-60) under Lieutenant Matthew Fontaine Maury, a brilliant man who became the first Superintendent. He was promoted to Master on September 14, 1855, and to Lieutenant the next day.

In between these shore assignments, Van Zandt had sea duties aboard USS *Cyane*, Home Squadron, sailing the Atlantic Coast and in the Caribbean protecting merchant shipping; aboard USS *Vixen*, Home Squadron, moving the ship from Pensacola to New York for repairs; on USS *Dolphin* in the African Squadron from May 1855 to June 28, 1857, patrolling against the slave trade; and on *Steamer Caledonia*, Brazil Station until May 1859. He was off in the Pacific Squadron, again on the USS *Cyane*, when the Civil War broke out; and as a result and despite his southern sympathies, he was unable to depart Union service until December 1861, eight months into the war.

Van Zandt resigned from the U.S. Navy in 1861 and was officially dismissed by the Navy Department on December 24, 1861. He had become a First Lieutenant in the Confederate States Navy on December 7, 1861. After a brief time at the Gosport (Norfolk) Navy Yard, he spent much of the war on duty with the Confederate squadron at Charleston, South Carolina as an ordnance expert. He was at the Confederate ordnance works in Selma, Alabama, in early 1864; before being reassigned to Wilmington, North Carolina. At some point he was captured by Union forces and sent to the POW camp on Johnson's Island in Ohio. He was promoted to Captain in the Confederate States Navy before the end of the war. He took the necessary oath of allegiance to the union in June 1865 and was released from Johnson's Island.

Figure 49: The cottage on the lot first purchased by Jennie Van Zandt O'Neill in 1897 at 1356 Hollywood Ave. Mrs. O'Neill was a descendant of the family of Revolutionary pamphleteer Patrick Henry. Her father, Capt. Nicholas Biddle Van Zandt, was a member of the first graduating class of the U.S. Naval Academy. ***Photo by Bill Semenuk, May 2016.***

The cottage on the O'Neill lot, 1356 Hollywood Ave., is one of the most charming properties at Arundel-on-the-Bay.[104]

Others who owned at Arundel-on-the-Bay in these early years were Henry C. Rothrock of 1345 Girard St. NW in the District, a clerk in the Post Office Department and the Reunion Convention Committee Chair of Public Order for the D.C. Division of the Sons of Confederate Veterans, and Lily B. Spaulding, whose address in the city was listed as c/o of Harvey Spaulding and Sons, lawyers who handled Civil War pension papers.

Frank R. Weller and Michael I. Weller of Pressley and Weller of the District, constructors of waterworks and electric lighting, were active long-term residents. Michael Weller (1846-1915) was president of the Capital City Savings Bank and chairman of the Inaugural Committees of 1905 and 1913. Born in England, he came to the United States in 1867 and lived at 408 Seward Square SE. Charles A. McCarthy (1870-1931), a banker married to Michael Weller's daughter Mary, lived with the Weller family and also was active in life at Arundel-on-the-Bay.[105]

Figure 50: Arundel-on-the-Bay resident Michael Ignatius Weller (1846-1916) was president of the Capital City Savings Bank and chairman of the Inaugural Committees of 1905 and 1913. ***Historical Society of Washington, D.C.***

Selected Early Landmarks at Arundel-on-the-Bay, c. 1904

Figure 51: These Bay frontage owners lived on Chesapeake Avenue which no longer exists.

Selected early landmarks gleaned from a variety of sources and superimposed on a contemporary map of the community.

Cottages along the Bay were on the then existing Chesapeake Avenue.

Endnotes

1. National Historic Landmark Nomination prepared by Ralph Eshelman, under the U.S. Lighthouse Society Cooperative Agreement with the National Park Service's National Maritime Initiative, June 1996, 24p.

2. The Ruth Ann Overbeck Capitol Hill History Project, sponsored by the Capitol Hill Community Foundation.

3. Anne Arundel County Circuit Court, Anne Arundel County Md., Grantor Index to Land Records from Jan. 1, 1838-Dec. 31, 1908, p.37.

4. John Moses, resident of Arundel on the Bay.

5. Madill, Edwin J., *Arundel on the Bay*, 1988, 46p. P2504, Pamphlet Collection of the Kiplinger Library of the Historical Society of Washington, D.C.

6. Papenfuse, Edw. C. et al, *Biographical Dictionary of the Maryland Legislature 1635-1789* ,Volume 426,1985 Archives of Maryland.

7. It appears from the "Bulletin of St. John's College" of 1898 that Chase was a member of the Board since 1887. Several entries in the *Proceedings and Acts of the General Assembly* reference Chase, including in 1868 (Vol. 142, p.2971) where he was reimbursed $30.25 for plumbing work in the Statehouse. He is also mentioned in connection with a dispute over property in Baltimore.

8. The Historical Society of Washington, D.C., MS 401, Arundel-on-the-Bay, Maryland, Records, 1898-1938.

9. This meeting was held on Aug. 27, 1890 at Dr. Hazen's home.

10. John Duvall was born in 1819. It appears he never married, living with his mother and various siblings according to the 1870 and 1880 federal census. He laid out Horn Point in 1868 for the Mutual Building Association, the first platted suburb of Annapolis located across Spa Creek from the town. See Jane McWilliams *A History of Annapolis*, p. 205. He also surveyed Lockwoodville in 1873, an area close to the Naval Academy ultimately annexed to it.

11. Kathryn Schneider Smith, *Port Town to Urban Neighborhood: The Georgetown Waterfront of Washington, D.C. 1880-1920*, The Center for Washington Area Studies of the George Washington University, 1989, p.26.

12. Smith's farm was surveyed for the Maryland Historical Trust State Historic Sites Inventory by Architectural Historian Howard S. Berger in 1990. *Maryland Historical Trust Survey #68-71* describes Smith's Mt. Rainier property: "The Thomas W. Smith Farmhouse is a well-preserved 2½ story cross-gabled frame dwelling with German siding and a wraparound porch with late Queen Anne style decorative detail. It is the only surviving rural agricultural structure representing the pre-subdivision rural agricultural character of Mount Rainier MD." Photographs by Arthur Garroway show the home and its interior details of wood paneling, French doors, and bookcases. Smith left the farm to his brothers Henry W. and Clifford U. Clifford devolved his interest to Henry and in 1922 Henry began the process of platting the ten acres for the subdivision Hariclif. The farmhouse, which burned in 1900 and was rebuilt by Smith, still stands.

13. Proctor, John Clagett, ed., *Washington Past and Present: A History*, 1930. Other source materials used to compile Smith's biography were *American Biographical Directories: District of Columbia*, 1908 and *The Washington Post*, *History of the City of Washington: Its Men and Institutions*, Washington, D.C., 1903. Photographs of Smith's apartment house at 676-4th St. NE are at the Kiplinger Library, CHS 13646 and 00350. Photographs of his row houses in the 200 block of Indiana Ave. NW are CHS 04130. Smith's death was reported in *The Washington Herald* of March 8, 1919. The article details the will of Smith and his survivors; his wife and four daughters. Then married were daughters Mrs. Maj. Charles Sanderson, Mrs. Maj. D.W. Morton. The other daughters were Caroline A. and Maude Smith. Caroline later married Lieut. James Edw. Abbott, son of the publisher of *The Evening Capital* of Annapolis. The Abbotts also owned a cottage at Arundel-on-the-Bay.

14. Hazen is listed in *The 1921 Directory of the Washington Academy of Sciences.* His apartment building at 8th and F Sts. NE, designed by architect F. Allison, was valued at $200,000 according to *The Evening Star*, June 6, 1893. In 1918, he was a stock holder in the Washington Railway and Electric Co. with 50 shares; Thomas W. Smith owned 500 shares. Source: Google search by Bill Semenuk, 2012.

15. Madill history, p. v and the *1900 Census of the United States.* The Shea children were Mary born in 1877, Margaret born in 1878, Rose born in 1881, Helen Louise born in 1883, John J. born in 1885, William born in 1888, and Bernadette born in 1890.

16. *The Journal of the Irish Historical Society*, July 5, 1902 reports Timothy D. Keleher as a paymaster. *The Burlington Weekly Free Press* reported on May 18, 1905 that Keleher was to handle pay for Fort Ethan Allen, Plattsburgh barracks, and installations around Buffalo NY and Portland ME. His son came with him, to serve as his clerk, according to a Google search performed by Bill Semenuk in 2012.

17. Cavanaugh's wife, Annie, was born in 1851. Lawrence Jr., his son from the second marriage, died in 1951.

18. Ancestry.com. Much of the Cavanaugh biographical material was gathered by Bill Semenuk.

19. Ancestry.com: Brad R. Pruden Collection.

20. Madill op.cit.p.iii.

21. Jane McWilliams and Carol Patterson, *Bay Ridge on the Chesapeake: An Illustrated History*, Annapolis, Md.: Brighton Editions, 1986, pp. 114-115.

22. Ann Arundell County Historical Society, Historical and Genealogical Research Center, Kuethe Library, Glen Burnie Md., Subject File: Beaches.

23. *The Sunday Herald and Weekly National Intelligencer*, May 31, 1891, p.24.

24. Ibid.

25. Two properties at Arundel-on-the-Bay have been adjudged by Anne Arundel County preservation planners as meeting the eligibility definition for the County Inventory of Historic Resources; 1365 Chestnut Avenue, Idle Wild, one of the original cottages, and 1363 Myrtle Avenue, the Thomas Somerville property, later built upon by Jack Harris, and occupied by brewery owner Christian Heurich Jr. in 1939.

26. That this club house was located at Arundel-on-the-Bay is confirmed by an advertisement for its sale which appeared in the *Baltimore Sun* on April 13, 1898. It was described as being on Fishing Creek at Arundel-on-the-Bay and partially furnished with accommodations for a club of 20.

27. Stone reported that the cottages being built would cost $3,500 for Smith; for Shea, Hazen, Keleher and himself $2,500; and for Rannells and Cavanaugh $2,000.

28. Deed, October 3, 1891.

29. Deed, October 3, 1891.

30. The excursion was reported in the Washington, D.C. paper, *The Sunday Herald & Weekly National Intelligencer* of June 14, 1891, p.5. The group included F. H. Noyes of the *Star*, A. Walmsey of the *Post*, J. L. Johnson of the *Hatchet*, W. Koch of the *Journal*, S. C. Abbott and W. H. Guthridge of the *Republic*, Louis Schade of the *Sentinel*, C. M. Gedmus and C. A. Bates of the *National View*, W. H. Lepley and Milton E. Smith of the *Church News*, and a representative of the *Sunday Herald*.

31. Anne Arundel County Circuit Court, Land Records Grantor Index, MSA CE 260-367, ca-cn, p.0038. Thomas W. Smith bought lots E & F of block 7 south of Linden Ave. Secretary Timothy Keleher bought lots E & F of block 6 south of Redwood Ave. Agent David D. Stone bought lot F of block 5 south of Sycamore Ave. Parson's lot M was on block 6; Hazen's lots were A & B of block 6. The Bleifus lot was E on block 4. The Gelstons purchased lot E on block 5. Drury's lot was K on block 12. James N. Gray purchased lots E & F of block 29, on the western side of Cohasset Ave. between Sycamore and Redwood Aves. Rannells purchased lot A on block 5.

32. Peter McIntyre purchased lot F on block 21.

33. Margaret Taylor Randall (1861-1959), an accomplished photographer of Annapolis, married Joseph Muse Worthington, a physician. The marriage produced five children.

34. Listed in the 1899 *Directory of the American Academy of Sciences*, Dr. George Burton Heinecke, born in 1871, was described as a prominent physician and past Master of the Stansbury Lodge #24 of the Fraternal Order of the Masons. He married Julia Perry and had one son, Oliver, born in 1896. His home was in the Brightwood Park section of Washington, D.C.

35. *Washington Post*, August 15, 1893.

36. *Baltimore Sun*, August 20, 1893: "Earlier in the summer, her father had been involved in a sailing accident. Messrs. Medford and Heinecke met with an accident while on one of their sailing trips to Kent Island last week. They started for the Island early in the evening and succeeded in reaching it in safety but while returning they were caught in a heavy sea about ten miles from Arundel. The boat would have capsized but for their excellent skill in handling the sails, yet they lost their rudder, and not being able to row against the

strong sea, they were compelled to drift around until morning, when the bay was much calmer and they were enabled to make Arundel in safety."

37. Reynolds purchased lots A&B of block 14. The Heineckes second purchase was lot F of block 4. The National Capital Brewing Company (Albert Carry trustee) purchased lots K, L, and M on block 35 for $600 (SH 42, p.322.)

38. *Evening Star,* May 27, 1893, p.19.

39. *Ibid,* June 24, 1893 p. 9.

40. Born in Ohio in 1841, Medford graduated from the George Washington University law school in 1871 and began his career as a law clerk in the Treasury Department. His wife Laura was born in Connecticut in 1844. Their children were Janet–or "Nettie" as she was called–born in 1871, Homer Sanford born in 1873, and Jessie born in 1879. Medford was a veteran of the Civil War having served in Company E of the Ohio 51st Regiment from December 1864 to March 1865. Sources: Census of the United States 1870, 1880, 1900, and 1920 and the Official Roster of Soldiers of the State of Ohio.

41. According to Ancestry.com, Barr married Ida Stewart (1862-1893) in 1882. Their children were Ida May born in 1883, Margaret born in 1886, John Lester (1887-1969), Almeda born in 1889, and Stewart (1893-1970.), Ida died in November 1893; Barr married her younger sister Almeda (1867-1935) in 1895. The two retired to Gloucester, Mass. and lived with his son John at "Casa del Mar." Barr died in 1937. The family is buried at Glenwood Cemetery in the District of Columbia.

42. The Barr and Sanner purchase was block 38, lots K & L.

43. National Register of Historic Places, District of Columbia, Barr Building, nomination form, Section 8, p.4cc.

44. Sanner married Laura Josephine King (1861-1933) and they had three daughters– Bertha born in1877, Edna born in1878, and Laura Josephine born in 1879.

45. *Washington Herald,* October 29, 1910.

46. Sources: Census of the United States: 1850, 1860, 1870, and 1880 and the Ruth Ann Overbeck Capital Hill History Project. Gessford married in 1852 and lived in Baltimore until 1860 when he moved to Washington. The 1870 census shows the family again in Baltimore. Their children were Ida born in 1856, George W. born in 1858, Carrie born in 1863, Laura born in 1865, William C. born in 1867, and Oliver C. born in 1870. Gessford, whose father emigrated from England, was born in Baltimore. He died at the age of 63 and is buried in the Congressional Cemetery. His son George W. continued as a builder from offices at 1117 G St., S.E.

47. The Murray purchase was lot D of block 10, SH 44-264. The Thomas Somerville purchase was lots E & F of block 9. The James Somerville purchase was lot C of block 6.

48. Sources: City Directories of the District of Columbia: 1889, 1890, 1891, and 1896 and Census of the United States: 1900, 1910, and 1920. James Somerville's wife was Marie and their children were Thomas S., Elinor S. born in 1887, Christiana born in 1887, and James W. born in 1895. James Somerville's home in the District of Columbia was 3306-16th St., N.W.

49. *Washington Herald,* July 27, 1913. The Matthews' property was lot G of block 12.

50. *Washington Post,* August 12, 1893. Cavanaugh's cottage was at Redwood and Narragansett avenues, according to the *Post* of August 2, 1891. Keleher's boat and bath house were completed in August 1893, according to the *Post* of August 15, 1893, "making a very neat and handsome improvement to the bay front."

51. *The Evening Star,* July 8, 1905.

52. *Washington Post,* August 16, 1893.

53. *Ibid,* August 28, 1893.

54. *Washington Post,* August 29, 1893, p.7.

55. McMillan op. cit. p. 92.

56. Calvin Farnsworth, a Clerk in the Registrar's Office of the Treasury Department, was born in Maine in 1887. He married his wife Julie in 1886; their daughter Almena was born in 1887. A veteran of the Civil War, Farnsworth enlisted in Company H of the Maine 18th Infantry, serving from August to December 1862, when he joined the Heavy Artillery Regiment of Company H of the Maine 1st. He was promoted to Corporal in April 1864 and left the service in January 1865. Their address in Washington, D.C. was 2131-1st St., N.W.

57. *Washington Herald,* Sept. 3, 1893.

58. *Washington Post,* December 12, 1893.

59. Anne Arundel County Circuit Court, MSA CE 59-60, SH45, pp. 0061-2.

60. Newspaper reports in 1912 speak of Mrs. Douglass and Mrs. Colbert as chaperones of a young person's theater party.

61. Douglas, Joseph L. Jr. *Frederick Douglass: A Family Biography: 1733-1936.* Winterlight Books, Shelbyville, Ky., 2011, p.369. While serving as Recorder of Deeds in the District of Columbia, to which he'd been appointed in 1881, Douglass and his second wife Helen Pitts Douglass were invited to receptions at the White House of President Glover Cleveland. Helen Pitts, a white feminist from Honeoye, N.Y., and a graduate of Mount Holyoke College, was a daughter of Gideon Pitts Jr., an abolitionist. She married Douglass in 1884.

62. In 1886 and 1887, Frederick Douglass and his wife again took an extended trip to Great Britain and other European sites.

63. Douglas op. cit., p. 447.

64. Nelson, Jack E., Raymond L. Langston, and Margo Dean Pinson, *Highland Beach on the Chesapeake Bay: Maryland's First African American Incorporated Town,* Highland Beach Historical Commission, 2008, p.17.

65. Highland Beach Historical Commission, *Highland Beach: The First100 Years.* Highland Beach, Md.1993, p.2.

66. *The Springfield Republican.*

67. *The Colored American,* Sept. 8, 1900.

68. *Ibid,* July 27, 1901, p.4. Among the other guests at this dance and whist party were Dr.& Mrs. Francis, Mr. & Mrs. H. C. Tyson, Mr. & Mrs. R. R. Colbert, Mr. & Mrs. A. F. Hilyer, Congressman & Mrs. George H. White, and Mr. & Mrs. Henry Baker.

69. Merrill, Walter M., ed. *The Letters of William Lloyd Garrison-Vol. III: No Union with Slave- Holders, 1841-1849.* Cambridge Mass.: Belknap Press of Harvard University Press, 1973, p.273. Michele Gordon Jackson in her book, *Light, Bright and Damn Near White: Black Leaders Created by the One-Drop Rule,* published by the Jackson Scribe Publishing Co. in 2013, cites Charles Lenox Remond's activism against the *Dred Scott* decision on p.307.

70. *The Washington Post,* May 28, 1894.

71. *Ibid,* May 26, 1894.

72. *The Washington Post,* May 28-29, 1894.

73. Born in 1866, Depue married Alice Virginia Church. They had two children, Marguerite, born in1893, and Stanley. Depue's home was 306 11th St. SW, Washington, D.C. in 1934. He died in 1963.

74. Before his marriage, Colford lived with his brother Edward M. Colford and family at various addresses in the Mt. Pleasant section of Washington, the last being 1667 Monroe St. NW. He died in March 1921. Source: *Age of Steel, Iron and Machinery World, Volume 86, p.24.*

75. Offterdinger was born in Lynchburg Va. in 1865 to parents who were native to Germany. He came to the District at the age of 14 in 1880. He married Alice M. Templeton, who was born in Vermont in 1867, in 1890, and they had five children–Theodore born in1893, Fred born in 1897, Harold P. born in 1898, Mildred born in 1910, and Anita. The family home was 1627 Kennedy St. NW in the District. Offterdinger died in June 1940 at Sibley Hospital. His wife, a member of the Dolly Madison Chapter of the Daughters of the American Revolution, the 16th Street Women's Literary Club, and the Vermont State Association, died in 1941.

76. Norwood, Irving C. *The Evening Star,* Dec. 25, 1909.

77. *Evening Star,* April 1910.

78. December 1, 1909, p.2

79. *Evening Star,* July 24, 1913, p.13.

80. Census of the United States 1900, 1910, and 1940 and the *Washington Post,* May 7, 1949. Mr. Towers died in 1949 at the age of 84.

81. June 11, 1910.

82. Deed, GW 107, 403-405, March 3, 1914 and Flanagan, Deirdre "Thomas Point Lighthouse…Then and Now," *Inside Annapolis Magazine,* December/January 2005/06, p. 19. More detail on the history of the

lighthouse can be obtained from Eschelman, Ralph & Candace Clifford, *National Historic Landmark Nomination for the Thomas Point Light Station,* 1984.

83. *Evening Star,* June 15, 1895.

84. *Washington Post,* July 26, 1896.

85. *Ibid,* August 9, 1896.

86. *Washington Post,* August 16, 1896.

87. *Ibid,* July 12, 1896.

88. *Washington Post.* July 12, 1896.

89. *Ibid,* July 26, 1896.

90. *Washington Post,* August 16, 1896.

91. *Ibid,* August 2, 1896.

92. *Washington Post,* July 19, 1896.

93. *Ibid*, August 30, 1896.

94. *Washington Post*, September 2, 1896.

95. *Ibid,* July 5, 1896.

96. *New York Tribune*, October 7, 1909, p.7. Payson's estate was revealed in the *Washington Herald*, November 4, 1909, p.8. His widow Louise Kent Payson died at the age of 79 in 1915 as reported in the *Washington Herald*, September 17, 1915, p.3.

97. Census of the United States: 1870, 1900, 1920. 1903 City Directory.

98. Census of the United States: 1880 and 1910. City Directories of the District of Columbia: 1873, 1879, 1887, 1890, 1891, 1895, 1896, 1907, 1909, 1914, and 1916.

99. *The Washington Post*, February 24, 1905. City Directory 1885. Census of the United States: 1880, 1890, and 1900.

100. *Ibid,* July 19, 1896.

101. *Washington Post*, August 9, 1896.

102. *Ibid,* July 12, 1896.

103. Ancestry.com. The Van Zandts had five children only two of whom survived to adulthood, Mary Garland Morgan (1860-1940) and Jean (Jennie) Cabell O'Neill Herbert (1866-1950.) Jennie, the owner of record of the Arundel property, was married to Francis J. O'Neill, an Associated Press correspondent posted to London and a member of the Board of Governors of the National Press Club. Their home was in Rockland Lake, N.Y. He died in 1907. Jennie married Joseph St. Germain Herbert, an army officer, in 1916.

104. The other children were William Cabell Van Zandt (1855-1872), Henry Meredith Van Zandt (1858-1858), and Elvira Bruce Van Zandt (1869-1872). As a widow Jane Van Zandt lived at 1436 Meridian Pl. N.W. in Washington, D.C.

105. 1910 Census: Weller's wife was Rita Gremina Repette (1849-1927). Their children were Francis R., Michael Angelo, and Mary. City directories of 1920 and 1926 show Michael A. Weller was President of a construction company in his own name; his son Joseph Ignatius, a civil engineer, became Vice President.

Chapter Three

The Chesapeake and Columbia Street Railway, "The Blackberry Train"

Bill Semenuk

Introduction

Local legend has it that out in the Chesapeake between Tolly Point and Thomas Point under less than 10 feet of water lie the remains of a railroad that used to run along the beach. It is said that whenever you have a "blowout" and the shore is exposed, you can still see the timbers and the rails. Local resident David Delia has spoken to neighbors who have seen the remains. Arend Thomas has swum down to them. It's thought that the remains of the rails ended up out in the bay because the sea level has risen and what was originally on the shore is now out in the Bay, or that hurricanes washed them out depositing them offshore. This chapter is the story behind that legend.

During the hot summer of 1892, life in the cities of Washington, Baltimore, and Annapolis was unbearable without air conditioning, but for less than $1 you could get on a train, travel for an hour and a half, and arrive at the beach resort at Bay Ridge that had swimming, a Ferris wheel, casino, zoo animals, electric train rides, and a food pavilion that seated over 1,000 people. For an additional 20 cents you could ride a coal-driven open car steam-train along the beach to a forested overlook above the Chesapeake Bay, a place where you could pick more blackberries than you could carry home. This place was called Arundel-on-the-Bay, and the 20-cent open car train, which was operated by the Chesapeake and Columbia Street Railway, was known locally as the "Blackberry Train" or "The Arundel-on-the-Bay Railroad."

Figure 1: Bay Ridge, Queen Resort of the Chesapeake circa 1890. ***Courtesy of Bill Williams Collection.***

Arundel-on-the-Bay, however, was more than just a delightful place to pick berries. It was a point of land being developed and marketed by a group of Washington, D.C.

Figure 2: This 1895 photograph shows passengers at the Bladen Street station in Annapolis boarding and leaving the Short Line Railroad. Arundel-on-the-Bay developers encouraged these trips to lure prospective buyers to the community. *The Annapolis I Remember Collection, Maryland State Archives.*

businessman under a banner titled the Chesapeake & Columbia Investment Co. As the investors were crafting and publishing their first newspaper advertisements, it was clear that a crucial part of the sales campaign would be to get customers to their newly purchased property, to transport building materials and furniture for their cottages, and to link the "cottagers," as they were called, to the Bay Ridge resort for concerts and social events. The solution was the building of a rail line from Bay Ridge to Arundel-on-the-Bay; thus "The Blackberry Train."

The line had a few other names in regular use and in print " the Arundel-on-the-Bay RR," "Summer Cars," and on the Highland Beach plat, "the Arundel & Bay Ridge Short Line." Readers should note that, whichever name is used in this chapter, that name refers to the vital rail link between Tolley Point in Bay Ridge and a station at the foot of Narragansett Avenue – the link that made development of Arundel-on-the-Bay possible.

Bayside excursion resorts had begun along the Chesapeake Bay in the late 1870s. Tolchester Beach near Rock Hall, Md, a popular amusement park on the eastern shore of the bay favored by Baltimoreans on day-trips, opened in 1877. In Annapolis in 1879, entrepreneur James H. Vansant, chairman of the Bay Ridge Co. and owner of the Annapolis-Bay Ridge Hiring and Livery Stables on West Street across from the B &O Railroad Station, purchased land at Tolley Point for the Bay Ridge resort, opening it in 1880.[1] A pier was constructed there as a port of call for the steamboat *Theodore Weems,* and Vansant bought additional acreage in 1885 and 1886 to expand the resort and acquire right-of way for the Annapolis & Bay Ridge Railroad, which he developed and opened in July 1886.

At this time, it was only through transportation by rail that a summer community like Arundel-on-the-Bay might be successfully developed. An 1896 *Baltimore Sun* story entitled "The New Annapolis" suggested that Arundel-on-the-Bay had a special relationship to Bay Ridge through its railroad developers:

> Arundel-on-the-Bay is an off-shoot of Washington enterprise, and as an annex to Bay Ridge an objective point for the proposed direct railroad to Washington, the only remaining link in rapid transit to insure the rapid development of this beautiful region of Maryland.[2]

Vansant's Baltimore & Ohio Excursion Resort of Bay Ridge was a key first step toward the creation of the "Blackberry Train," which in turn would make visits to and development of the beachfront community of Arundel-on-the-Bay both feasible and enjoyable. In fact, train travel not only figured in the logistics; it was cited as one of the "beauties of Arundel-on-the-Bay" in an advertisement appearing in the *Washington Post* in August 1891:

> Beautifully located on Chesapeake Bay, just south of Bay Ridge. High ground, and thickly wooded with some of the grandest shade trees.

> "Buy a lot from $150 to $400, easy payments, and build a cottage. Only one hour-and-a-half's ride from Washington. You can take the 4:28 p.m. train from the B. & O. station and at 6:15 be on your veranda, enjoying the cool, salty breezes and see large ocean steamers passing up and down the bay. At flood tide take a bath, from as sandy a beach and bottom as at older and more famous resorts. An hour's fishing and crabbing will give you the most exhilarating sport and furnish the table for a day or more.
>
> A drive or walk on the plank road to Bay Ridge will afford you there a musical entertainment enjoyable to all.[3]

In today's market, real estate agents quote the time it takes to drive to the nearest Metro station or the nearest interstate highway. In 1890 there were no highways or automobiles, only horse-drawn carriages, railroads, and ferries. The developers challenge was to build a railroad or run a steamship to their new development in much the same way that today developers pave connecting roads from their property to the main highway, and they are prepared to make the same kind of travel quotes.

In one of the first Arundel-on-the-Bay newspaper ads, the time quoted from the B & O station in Washington to Arundel-on-the-Bay (and–truth in advertising–actually to Bay Ridge) was one hour and 45 minutes. This was the time for the trip published in the Bay Ridge railroad schedule. The total route to Arundel-on-the-Bay included travel using the B&O, Annapolis and Elkridge, and Bay Ridge railroads with a final leg aboard the C&C Railway, the "Blackberry Train."[4]

It can be seen that rail service to the nearby beach resort of Bay Ridge was key to development of and travel to Arundel-on-the-Bay. In 1890 Bay Ridge was a major rail and steamship destination, especially during the summer season. Trains departed Bay Ridge bound for Washington, Baltimore, Wilmington, and even Ocean City Md., by way of a ferry, which carried rail cars over the Chesapeake to Bay City, or Claiborne, as it was known then, thence overland to the ocean.

Figure 3: A train ride to Arundel-on-the-Bay began at the B&O Railroad Station at 3rd & C Streets SE, shown here looking east across New Jersey Avenue, Washington, D.C. in 1893. The station was demolished in 1907 after Union Station opened. *Kiplinger Library of the Historical Society of Washington, D.C.*

Ferries also provided daily service connecting Baltimore with points along the bay; thus, a day-tripper could leave Baltimore's Pier 10 on Light Street in the morning and return from Bay Ridge in the evening. Rail service was equally convenient, offering "businessman's specials" that departed in the morning and returned in the evening. For Arundel-on-the-Bay, the last leg of rail service was the most important link, and the C&C Railway service began on July 1, 1892, and on summers thereafter it ran from June 15 to Sept 15. The *Evening Star* in an article on July 7, 1893, noted that the train from Bay Ridge to Arundel-on-the-Bay ran hourly.

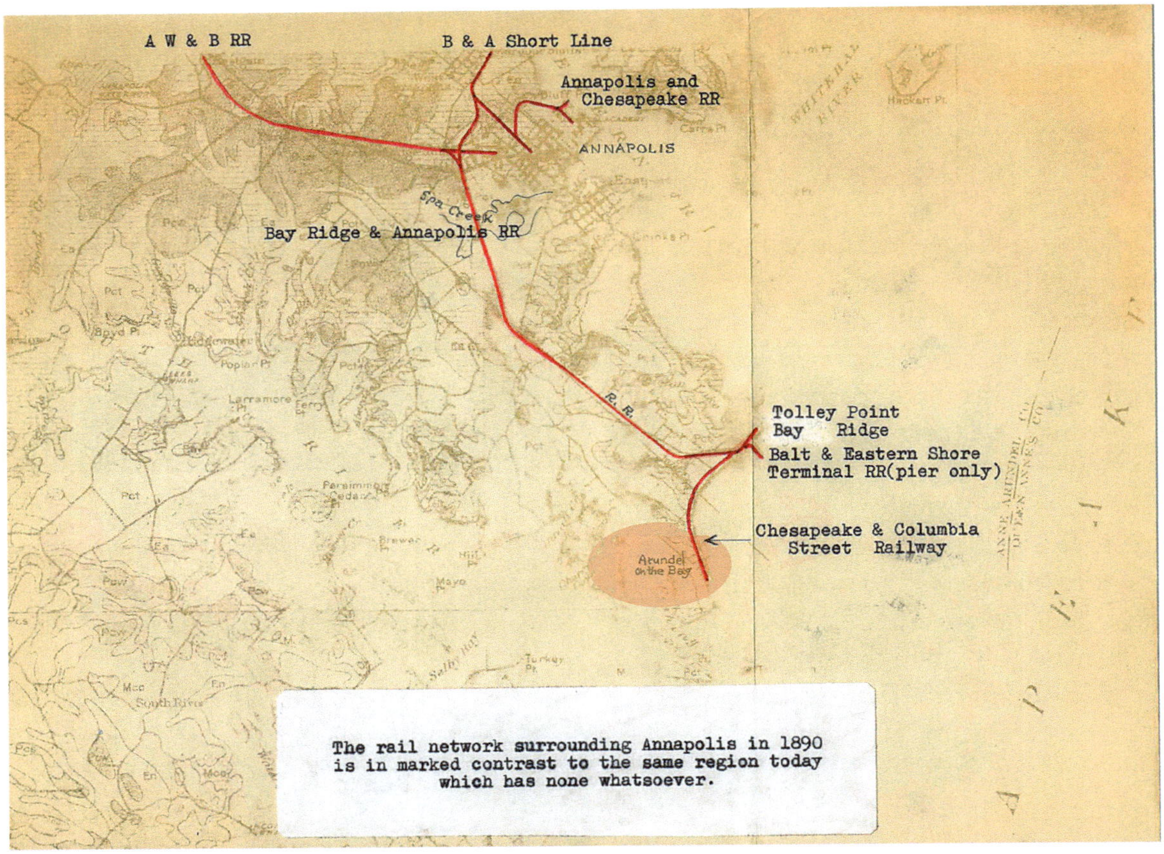

Figure 4: Rail network surrounding Annapolis in 1890 with line ending at Arundel-on-the-Bay. ***Reprinted with permission of the Merriken Collection, National Capital Trolley Museum.***

Noted rail historian John E. Merriken Jr., as part of his manuscript "This Was Bay Ridge," prepared a diagram showing the Annapolis-area rail connections, reprinted above.

To Build a Railroad

The straight-line distance from Bay Ridge's Tolly Point to Arundel-on-the-Bay's Thomas Point was a short few miles across the water. Following the shoreline added some distance and a few obstacles. The most dependable all-weather route was a few hundred yards inland, following the shoreline, but this route would have required several hundred feet of trestle bridge across both Oyster Creek and Black Walnut Creek as shown in the 1892 U.S. Geological Survey map, Figure 5.

A bridge across Black Walnut Creek presented additional challenges because of the steep banks on each side except at its opening to the bay. The route that was eventually selected departed from the rear of the Bay Ridge Hotel on a single track starting parallel to the Bay Ridge railroad's platform and curving south across the fields following the terrain until it arrived at the shore near the current location of the Chesapeake Bay Foundation. From there it followed along the beach until it reached Black Walnut Creek. At this point Black Walnut Creek narrows from several hundred feet to a mere ten feet or so. This simplified the bridge-building considerably but it also located the rail line along the beach, making it more vulnerable to summer storms. Approximately 300 yards down the beach a second bridge was required over the narrow mouth of Oyster Creek, sometimes referred to as the "Cavanaugh Canal."

Cavanaugh Canal is referenced several times in the Arundel-on-the-Bay community minutes. Its location is determined by analysis of the invoices for repair of the canal and the

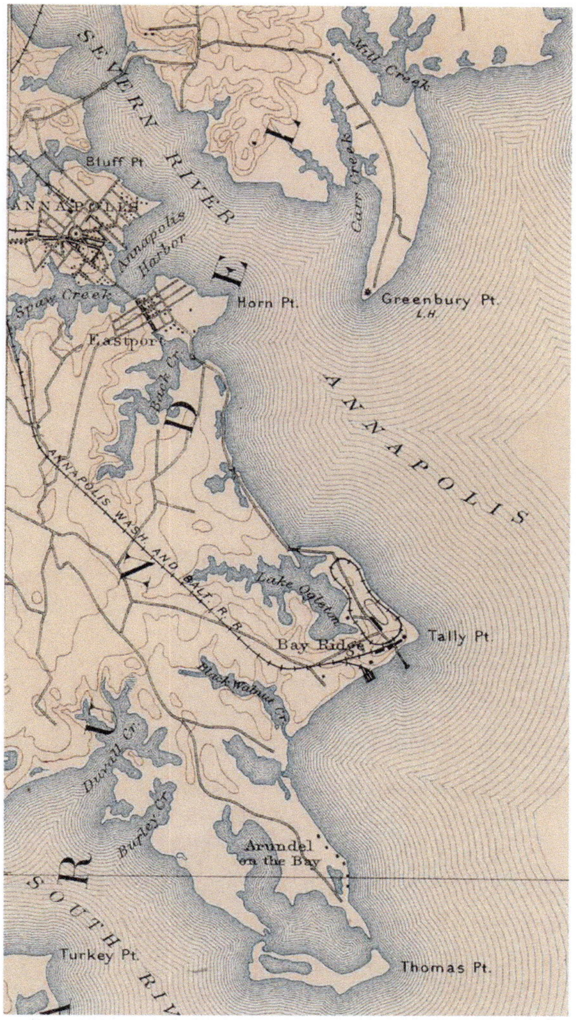

Figure 5: Railroads to Bay Ridge in July 1892. *U.S. Geological Survey*. The six structures shown as dots along the shore in Arundel-on-the-Bay are the cottages of the officers of the Investment Company along the bay front shell road known as Chesapeake Avenue. Tolly Pt. was labeled as "Tally Pt" on this Survey.

accompanying bridge at that location, and as not being the bridge across Black Walnut Creek, the only other bridge crossing.

The reason for the canal's construction at Oyster Creek's entrance to the Bay may have been related to the habit of local waterman to store their oysters in the headwater while they waited for a favorable price in Annapolis. The canal was dug in order to lower the level of Oyster Creek at the point where it passed under the railroad bridge and the plank road bridge. Thus watermen had unfettered access into and out of Oyster Creek by boat under the two bridges. Taking this into consideration in building the bridges, it was probably less expensive to dig the creek lower for the 80-foot distance between the railroad and plank road bridges than to construct higher bridges. Either way, the goal was to keep the peace with the notoriously independent watermen.

The photograph at Figure 7 shows the portion of the tracks just south of Oyster Creek around 1892. It was taken from a point that is now the location of the Oyster Harbor Community Beach.

From here the tracks followed the shoreline and turned inward onto Narragansett Avenue, as shown in the Highland Beach Plat, at Figure 8. They followed this street all the way to its intersection with Magnolia Avenue near the end of the peninsula, passing along the way the rear of the proposed Hotel Arundel-on-the-Bay, which was to be located at the intersection of Narragansett and Linden Avenues. The rail line runs along the bottom of the plat and is denoted by the tiny engine and the car steaming toward Bay Ridge to the right.

Figure 6: Site of "The Blackberry Train" bridge over Oyster Creek. *Photo by Bill Semenuk, October 2012.*

In 2006 Erich Keyes, resident of Arundel-on-the-Bay, related a conversation he had with Walter Tyler, long-time community resident and general handyman. Tyler said that at the southern end of Narragansett Avenue there was a railroad turnaround on

Figure 7: "The Blackberry Train" tracks on the shoreline of Arundel-on-the-Bay across from the Bay Ridge Resort, ca. 1892. A steamboat can be seen at the resort's long pier. Margaret Taylor Randall, a photographer and resident of Annapolis, and a little boy are shown on the beach. ***Henry Shaefer, photographer. Robert G. Merrick, Archives of Maryland Historical Photographs, Collection of the Maryland State Archives.***

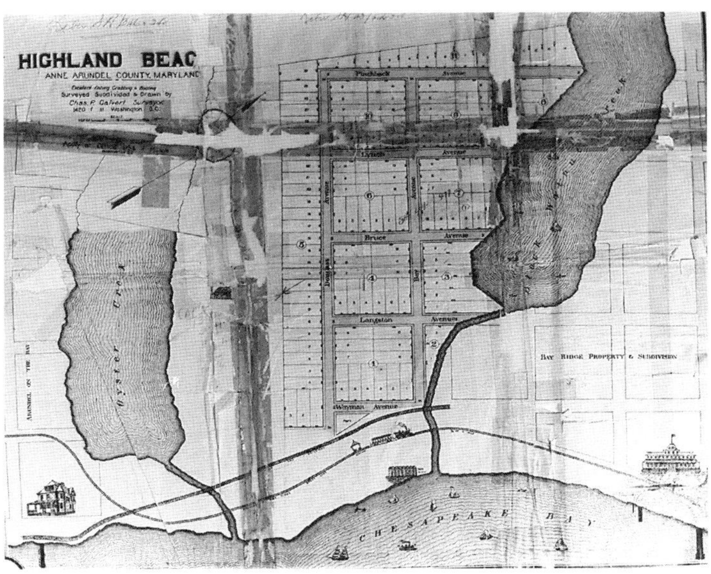

Figure 8: Three Blackberry Train stations (Left to Right), Arundel-on-the-Bay, Highland Beach, and Bay Ridge are shown on the plat of Highland Beach. ***Photo courtesy of Jane McWilliams and Carol Patterson, "Bay Ridge on the Chesapeake," 1986.***

land that is now the Arundel-on-the-Bay community beach. Thomas Worthington, resident of Arundel-on-the-Bay between 1929 and the late 1940s, attests that there was a well and a hand pump located on the opposite side of the street from the Heintz house at the northwest corner of Cohasset and Magnolia avenues. The well and pump were used to replenish the water reservoir of the locomotive to make steam.[5] Arundel resident John Moses adds that the house at the northwest corner of Magnolia and Narragansett avenues was once the train station.

Some of these route details can be seen in the 1904 U.S. Geological Survey map, Figure 9. Although the map doesn't show the railroad tracks, it does show the plank road along the shoreline from the end of the Arundel-on-the-Bay boardwalk to Bay Ridge, which was parallel to and inland of the railroad tracks and within the 80-foot right-of-way the company officers had purchased from the Brashears family who owned the farm that lay between the two beach communities. It also shows the Bay

Figure 9: The Plank road from Arundel-on-the-Bay to Bay Ridge, 1904. ***U.S. Geological Survey.***

Ridge railroad platform at the rear of the Bay Ridge Hotel.

The rail route along the beach between Black Walnut and Oyster creeks avoided costly trestle bridges over the widest portion of the two creeks and successfully connected the community of Arundel-on-the-Bay to the Bay Ridge resort. The plank road directly connected the Arundel-on-the-Bay boardwalk to Bay Ridge and joined what is now Wayman Avenue through Highland Beach (as shown on the Highland Beach plat.) This necessitated a second set of bridges but also allowed horse and buggy traffic and eventually automobile traffic to reach the two communities.[6]

> *"...at the southern end of Narragansett Avenue there was a railroad turnaround on land that is now the Arundel-on-the-Bay community beach."*

When the Bay Ridge Railroad ceased operations in 1903, all hope of connecting service from Arundel-on-the-Bay into Washington and Baltimore was lost. Although the 1899 edition of the *American Street Railway Investments* lists the Chesapeake & Columbia Street Railway Company as "no longer in operation," we know from the Arundel-on-the-Bay community records that the railroad bridges were maintained well into the 1900s in the hope that the electrified Washington-Baltimore and Annapolis (WB&A) Railroad would be extended to Bay Ridge, allowing a route all the way to Arundel-on-the-Bay.

A Sept. 21, 1910 letter from the attorney for the Bay Ridge and Annapolis Railroad Co. to the town documents Arundel-on-the-Bay's unsuccessful request for connecting service to be resumed for the benefit of the community. The death knoll for the railroad was probably the 1920 hurricane "that destroyed the railroad tracks along the beach"[7] and the bankruptcy of the Chesapeake and Columbia Investment Co. Arundel-on-the-Bay resident Arend Thomas tells us that as a teenager in the 1950s he and his swimming companions discovered portions of the old tracks out in the bay about 100 feet beyond the McMurdock pier adjacent to the end of Hollywood Avenue and the Bay.

About the Arundel-on-the-Bay Railroad: The Locomotive

According to Colonel John E. Merriken in his article "This Was Bay Ridge," printed in the bulletin of the *National Railway Historical Society* of 1987, the Arundel-on-the-Bay Railroad had a Rhode Island-built locomotive that was obtained from the Manhattan Elevated Co. in New York City.

A search of the online records for the Manhattan Elevated, the parent company for the New York Elevated, reveals Rhode Island-built locomotives used prior to the 1892 start date of the Arundel-on-the-Bay Railroad. One of these, built in 1879, was recently found in North Carolina. It was a Forney-built 0/4/4T. A fully-restored similar locomotive from the Chicago "L" is on display in the Saint Louis, Mo., railroad museum.

These models look remarkably similar to the locomotive depicted on the Highland Beach plat in Figure 8. In 1891 the Manhattan Elevated was in the process of converting from steam to electric and many of its older steam locomotives were available for sale. A search of the New York Elevated's disposed equipment prior to the 1892 start of the C&C Street Railway by railroad historian Richard Fleischer reveals that there are eight possible serial-numbered steam locomotives which may have been sold to the Arundel-on-the-Bay Railroad: serial numbers 31, 33, 34, 35, 41, 42, 43, and 44, (alternately described with Rhode Island Locomotive Co. construction numbers as 716, 718, 719, 715, and 711-714). These are listed on page 63 of *The Railway and Locomotive Historical Society's Spring 1990 Bulletin 162*. Additional research will be needed to determine which one of these eight possibles may have become *the* Arundel-on-the-Bay locomotive.

Figure 10: "The Blackberry Train" locomotive was identical to that of the Lake Street Elevated Railway as shown in 1893, a Forney 0/4/4T Locomotive and passenger car. ***Chicago Transit Authority, February 15, 1957.***

There are several possible ways the locomotive may have traveled from New York to Arundel-on-the-Bay. First, because the Arundel-on-the-Bay Railroad was of standard gauge, it could ride the rails from New York City to Bay Ridge by paying tolls to the New York Central and Pennsylvania railroads and then to the B&O, which owned the Bay Ridge railroad at the time. The passenger car(s) could then just tag along behind. At Bay Ridge the train could be lifted onto the

Figure 11: "The Blackberry Train" locomotive was identical to this locomotive from the Chicago "L" 1890. ***The National Muesum of Transportation, Saint Louis, Mo.***

Figure 12: "The Blackberry Train" locomotive, Forney 0/4/4T, as a working HOn3 scale steam model in Manhattan Elevated colors. ***MTS Imports.***

Arundel-on-the-Bay track with a rented steam crane, or driven onto the Arundel-on-the-Bay track using temporary tracking.

Alternately, the locomotive could be driven to Washington's B&O station and into the lumberyard of Arundel-on-the-Bay President Smith, whose business was across the street, and later moved to Bay Ridge using the same right-of-way as the Bay Ridge railroad. A third option to bring the locomotive and cars down from New York City might have been by water ferry using the railroad pier-terminal at Bay Ridge, which had served previously as a point of entry for the building materials for the Short Line railroad from Baltimore to Annapolis along the shores of the Severn River. It also served as the ferry-pier for the Ocean City to Baltimore railroad.

The model (Figure 12) shows the maroon and black colors of the Manhattan Elevated locomotive as it would have appeared on the beach chugging between Bay Ridge and Arundel-on-the-Bay.

About the Arundel-on-the-Bay Railroad: Passenger Cars

Figure 13: "The Blackberry Train" passenger car was the same as this Restored Brill Summer Car (electrified) of 1902. ***Baltimore Trolley Museum.***

The Railway Builders List of 1897 included the listed Brill Co. as the manufacturer of the C&C Railroad cars. Figure 13 is a fully restored Brill "Summer Car" from 1902, now in the Baltimore Trolley Museum. It resembles the sketch of the C&C Railway car at the bottom of Figure 8. Merriken's research located a reference to the Arundel-on-the-Bay Railroad in the Brill order book for 1893. Brill's Order #5092, dated March 31, 1893, reads "8 Loose WH Reprs Ord" for Chesapeake & Columbia Investment Co. for Annapolis. Delivery: "Quickly." Merriken's notes go on to say,

"Compared with other entries in the same book, this is interpreted to mean: 8 Wheels only, to be repaired as ordered. This might be the Brill summer car operated by Thos. W. Smith on his small line to Arundel-on-the-Bay."

About the Arundel-on-the-Bay Railroad: Nuts and Bolts

The 1898 edition of *American Street Railway Investments* lists the Chesapeake and Columbia Street Railway as having $100,000 in capital stock authorized and $75,900 issued. It further lists the plant and equipment as consisting of "miles of track (steam), 1.75; gauge, 4 ft. 8½ in.; 30 lb. T rail; 1 car, 1 engine; Rhode Island Locomotive, Brill car." This was industry shorthand to mean that the Arundel-on-the-Bay railroad was 1.75 miles long; used standard gauge (4 ft. 8½ in between the tracks) rails with a "T" cross-section that weighed 30 pounds per foot; had one passenger car and one engine per train; a locomotive built by the Rhode Island Co (known today as the American Locomotive Co., or ALCO); and a passenger car built by the Brill company of Philadelphia.

The officers and directors of the Arundel-on-the-Bay Railroad were also officers of the Chesapeake and Columbia Investment Co., which owned the Arundel-on-the-Bay property. As listed in the 1898 publication, the rail officers were Thomas W. Smith, president; W.P.C. Hazen, vice president; T. (Timothy) D. Keleher, secretary; and Nicholas Henry Shea, treasurer. The board of directors was comprised of Smith, Hazen, Keleher, Shea, and Lawrence Cavanaugh. The general office of the corporation was located at 1st Street and Indiana Avenue N. W., Washington, D.C., as of April, 1897.

From a *Washington Post* newspaper account of Aug. 12, 1893, we know the names of at least two ticket agents: Scott Towers, who was replaced by William Banks.

Reminiscences about the Railroad

Kenneth H. Rucker, President of the National Capital Trolley Museum and close friend of author Merriken, cited earlier in this chapter, has provided copies of all the author's notes that pertain to the Arundel-on-the-Bay Railroad. Among these papers is a text entitled "Some Reminiscences of the Bay Bridge Railroad in the Mid-90s." It describes an 1890s trip from Washington, D.C., to Bay Ridge, the portion of the journey to Arundel-on-the-Bay, minus the ride on the Arundel-on-the-Bay Railroad, and is reproduced here to allow us to experience the trip to the beach.

> The morning excursion train for Bay Ridge left the old B&O station at the north-east corner of New Jersey Avenue and C Street, N.W., at 9.10 AM. The locomotive, No. 812, a conventional 4-4-0 of the period, powered a train of as many as 12 coaches and the round trip fare was $1.50. The route was B&O to Annapolis Junction, later Fort Meade Junction, and then AW&B to a point very near Annapolis and finally the Bay Ridge & Annapolis to destination, where it arrived at 10.55 AM. There was a late afternoon train for office people staying at the shore and an early morning one to return them to the city in time for office.
>
> The excursion train returning left Bay Ridge at 7.45 PM. If there were 2 sections, as there sometimes were, the 2nd was powered by a camel-back, No 753, which did not appear quite so powerful as the 812 as it had more difficulty in getting the heavy train rolling on the slight up-grade away from the Bay Ridge platform. An outstanding feature of the return to town in the dark was the wait at Annapolis Junction for the Royal Blue from New York to clear the Junction ahead of the excursion train. Would it hit us? (*Trains at the time were not closely time-synchronized and the danger of a local Bay Ridge Annapolis train entering onto the main North-South rail line from New York to Washington required caution.*)
>
> Going down in the morning, the train always stopped at a point in the woods (Cedar Park, currently Taylor Avenue) about 15 or 20 minutes before reaching Bay

> Ridge and for no apparent reason. Looking out the car window on the blind side, the dome of the State House could be seen thru a gap in the trees and it only seemed 2 or 3 city blocks away. How was it that the train was in the woods and yet so near a big city. The point was that Annapolis had no suburbs and the city stopped short at the end of each outgoing street. This view of the State House was just about the same as that which appears now-a-days in so many pictures of the B&A yard leading to Bladen Street Station, only it was from the south instead of the west. Looking back, it seems that this mysterious stop might have been at the point where the Annapolis & Bay Ridge diverged from the AW&B and the connection came in from Bladen St.

Arundel-on-the-Bay residents Bill Semenuk and Marian Kratage have visited the Cedar Park site (now Taylor Avenue) and verified the view; although partially blocked in 2012 by newer buildings, you can get the same view from the parking lot of Annapolis Police Station just south of the old roadbed, now a bike trail.

A sketch (Figure 15) of the Cedar Park railroad intersection known as Bay Ridge Junction in Annapolis is shown on the next page. It was provided by railroad historian Bill Williams.

From Cedar Park, the Bay Ridge railroad followed what is now Amos Garret Boulevard down to Spa Creek crossing to Truxtun Park.

A postcard depicting the Spa Creek Bridge (Figure 16) is also shown followed by an aerial view of the Spa Creek crossing.

Merriken's narrative continues:

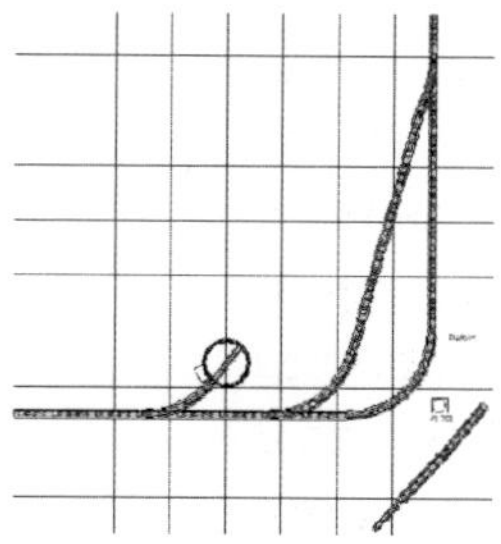

Figure 14: The Bay Ridge track layout and "Blackberry Train" spur at the Bay Ridge terminus. ***Track layout by Walkersville Southern Railroad Engineer John C. Lotz.***

> The approach to Bay Ridge was on a slight down grade. A facing point switch (a switch that allowed the train to turn off on a siding) to the left lead to the turn-table, and a little further along another facing point switch to the left led to a passing track (a siding that allowed one train to stand and wait while another went by) which paralled the main line on the blind side (the side opposite the side where the engineer sat) to a point well beyond the other end of a platform, where it again joined the main and connected with the loop around the grounds of Bay Ridge Electric Railway (see Figure 5). There was no station, but a wide platform, longer than the longest train, and this platform was on a slight angle so that the approaching train turned a little to the left to come along side. The water tank was at the near end of the platform. On arrival of the train (between switch 2 and switch 3 shown in Figure 18), the locomotive was uncoupled, run forward past the (3rd) switch, then backed along the passing track to the turn-table, where it was reversed and stood there until time to couple to the 7.45 train.

The track layout at Bay Ridge described in the last sentence above is shown in Figure 14 and in both Figure 5 and Figure 9.

Merriken's narrative description of the trip goes on to describe the approach to the rear of the Bay Ridge Hotel:

> On the other side of the (Bay Ridge) train platform, toward the water tank end, a single track, having no connection with any other, and starting from a stub end, wandered off across the fields to the west and reached Arundel-on-the-Bay, a distance of 2 miles. A locomotive from Manhattan Elevated of New York and one of their open cars of early vintage, both painted red, was the only rolling stock I ever saw. The local name for this outfit was "The Blackberry Train."

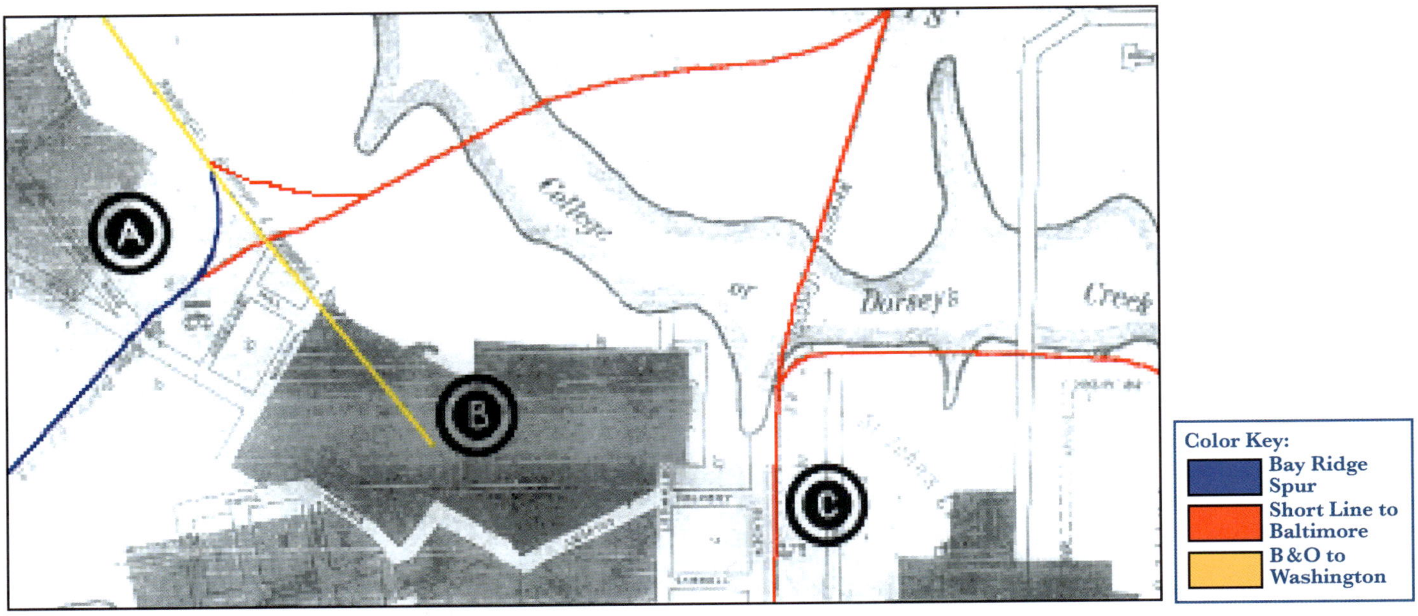

Figure 15: Annapolis railroad stations and the Cedar Park Intersection. "A" is Cedar Park, "B" is the West St. station, and "C" is the Bladen St. Station. *Bill Williams Collection.*

Figure 16: The Bay Ridge railroad bridge over Spa Creek. *Courtesy of Bill Williams Collection.*

Figure 17: The Railroad from Annapolis to Bay Ridge. shown in an aerial view of the Spa Creek Crossing in 1938. ***The Annapolis I Remember Collection, Maryland State Archives, SC2140-547. Courtesy of the Bill Williams Collection.***

Arundel-on-the-Bay History Project

Endnotes

1. McWilliams, Jane and Carol Patterson, *Bay Ridge on the Chesapeake*; Brighton Publications: 1986.

2. *The Baltimore Sun*, April 19, 1896.

3. *The Washington Post*, August 14, 1891.

4. An Annapolis, Washington & Baltimore railroad timetable of Dec 10, 1892, contained in *The Travelers' Official Guide of the Railway and Steam Navigation Lines in the United States and Canada*, published by the National Railway Publication Company in June 1893, shows this to be optimistic as the trip from Annapolis Junction to Annapolis was one hour in itself. By 1904, that trip had shortened to 43 minutes, according to John E. Merriken in an article entitled "The Elk Ridge and Annapolis Railroad" in *The National Railroad Historical Society Bulletin*, Volume 38, Number 6, 1973.

5. 2012 interview of Thomas Worthington by Pamela Duncan. William Semenuk's interview with Erich Keyes in 2006 revealed that as a youngster, Mr. Keyes would dig in the sand at today's community beach for old bottles and junk. Mr. Tyler, who lived at the corner of Rockaway and Chestnut avenues, told Erich Keyes that he was the caretaker of the old hotel that sat at the Bay end of Narragansett Avenue. Tyler was a waterman and in the winter he was the only resident of the community.

6. Photographs from ca. 1892 and 1920 of the plank road bridge across the Black Walnut Creek are shown on page 10 and 14 of Nelson, Jack et al, *Highland Beach on the Chesapeake Bay: Maryland's First African American Incorporated Town*, Virginia Beach, VA. Doring Co, 2008.

7. See Nelson, Jack E., *Highland Beach on the Chesapeake Bay*, pp. 19, 22, and 44 for additional photographs of the Arundel-on-the-Bay railroad tracks.

Acknowledgement

Historians Carol Patterson and Jane McWilliams shared their wealth of knowledge enabling us to understand and portray accurately the history described in Chapters 2, 3, and 4.

Photograph by Marc Grigsby

Chapter Four

Cottage Life in the Town of Arundel-on-the-Bay: 1898-1919

Pamela Duncan

Introduction

Society page writers in local newspapers chronicled a lively social scene at Arundel-on-the-Bay during the 1890s and the early years of the 20th century. This genteel gossip covered the opening and closing of cottages, visitors, parties and entertainments, and the annual elections. Washingtonians were encouraged to provide the *Evening Star* with their summer addresses, which were then mentioned in the social columns, often in a special section of the paper called "Summer Resorts." The "Star Resort Bureau" in this section also provided consumers with information on hotels, railroad and steamship fares, and schedules.

Many who bought lots or vacationed at Arundel-on-the-Bay were connected in building, banking, real estate, or civic life of the District of Columbia and, to a lesser extent, that of Baltimore. In this chapter, continuing the detailed social chronicle begun in Chapter Two, we will learn more about the residents and their activities in the two decades after Arundel-on-the-Bay was designated as a town.

Incorporation of the Town of Arundel-on-the-Bay in 1898

On February 22, 1898, the Maryland House of Delegates gave approval on first reading to a bill to incorporate Arundel-on-the-Bay. Second reading and final vote was held on February 26.[1] Seven commissioners with broad authority to shape the community would govern the town and were named in the statute, with the first community election to be held in July 1899. They could regulate the look of the cottages, including doors, windows, steps, and the architectural ornamentation on the street side of homes. They could establish the type of wood used for the cottages, and they were given the authority to construct public facilities and protect and preserve the waterfront.

The legislation contained a formula for sharing the cost of community facilities–piers, docks, seawalls, and dikes–based on the proximity of the lot owner to the water. Fifty percent of expenses were to be borne by frontage owners along the Bay between Cedar and Magnolia avenues on the eastern half of the blocks. Another 25 percent would be paid by owners along Narragansett Avenue in the western portion of those blocks. The remaining 25 percent share would be contributed by owners of all other lots on Narragansett Avenue from Cedar to Magnolia avenues.

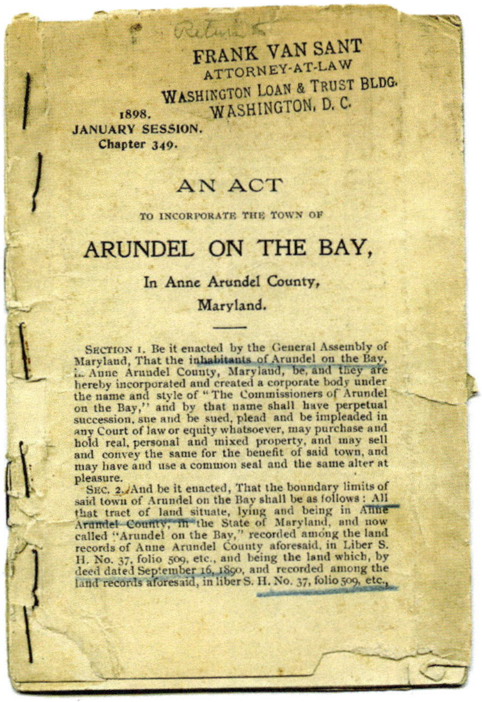

FRANK VAN SANT
ATTORNEY-AT-LAW
WASHINGTON LOAN & TRUST BLDG.
WASHINGTON, D. C.

1898.
JANUARY SESSION.
Chapter 349.

AN ACT

TO INCORPORATE THE TOWN OF

ARUNDEL ON THE BAY,

In Anne Arundel County,
Maryland.

SECTION 1. Be it enacted by the General Assembly of Maryland, That the inhabitants of Arundel on the Bay, in Anne Arundel County, Maryland, be, and they are hereby incorporated and created a corporate body under the name and style of "The Commissioners of Arundel on the Bay," and by that name shall have perpetual succession, sue and be sued, plead and be impleaded in any Court of law or equity whatsoever, may purchase and hold real, personal and mixed property, and may sell and convey the same for the benefit of said town, and may have and use a common seal and the same alter at pleasure.

SEC. 2. And be it enacted, That the boundary limits of said town of Arundel on the Bay shall be as follows: All that tract of land situate, lying and being in Anne Arundel County, in the State of Maryland, and now called "Arundel on the Bay," recorded among the land records of Anne Arundel County aforesaid, in Liber S. H. No. 37, folio 509, etc., and being the land which, by deed dated September 16, 1890, and recorded among the land records aforesaid, in liber S. H. No. 37, folio 509, etc.,

Figure 1: Frank Van Sant's 4 x 6 inch copy of the act incorporating the Town of Arundel-on-the-Bay in 1898. Van Sant, an attorney, was active in the early years of the community and served as a town commissioner and town secretary through the 1940s. *Historical Society of Washington, D.C.*

Former U.S. Rep. Lewis E. Payson was among those designated as a town commissioner. Thomas W. Smith and the others named by the legislature to lead the new town were previously officers of the Chesapeake & Columbia Investment Co. and the Chesapeake & Columbia Street Railway. They included Timothy D. Keleher, who owned a cottage, boat, and boathouse on the Bay front; Nicholas H. Shea, who built the family cottage Idle Wild on Chestnut Avenue at the Bay; and Lawrence C. Cavanaugh, who built two cottages at Redwood and Narragansett avenues. James C. Courts, an influential congressional official who built a cottage on Chesapeake Avenue in 1900, and James W. Somerville, son of Thomas Somerville, the plumbing magnate, also were appointed commissioners.

At their first meeting as officials of the town on May 7, 1898 at Cavanaugh's home, 608 East Capitol Street in the District of Columbia, Smith was elected to serve as temporary president, a position from which he would act as mayor and chief executive officer. James Courts was elected temporary secretary, Somerville was elected treasurer, and R. T. Jones was appointed to the position of bailiff. In August, meeting at Smith's cottage at Arundel-on-the-Bay, Smith, Payson, and Courts were named as a committee to formulate a code of laws for the town.

The statute required the commissioners to meet four times a year for specific purposes. In February they were to decide the annual real estate tax rate, in May to authorize repairs to property needed for the season, and on the Fourth of July weekend to prepare for the annual election later in the month. After community voting, a fourth meeting was to be held by the commissioners to elect officers.

In keeping with the new designation as a town, a large party was reported in the August 6, 1898 edition of the *Washington Post*:

> The entertainment given last night by the guests of the Bay Ridge Hotel to citizens of Arundel-on-the-Bay was attended by 75 persons. The programme embraced vocal and instrumental music...recitations...song and dance, and mind reading by Mme. Euleika, the palmist.[2]

Fishing and Gunning Clubhouses

The Fishing Creek side of the community served as the location for several clubhouses, although little is known about them beyond newspaper references. A clubhouse had been among the first facilities planned for Arundel-on-the-Bay by the Chesapeake & Columbia Investment Company and, in 1891, two lots on the northern side of Hollywood Avenue at Fishing Creek were sold for that purpose to the partnership of William L. White as treasurer, William H. Otterback, and Conrad Zeller. We only know a little about two of the three. Otterback was born in 1865, son of a keeper of a livery stable in the District.

Figure 2: A hunting rifle mounted on the fireplace of a cottage at Arundel-on-the-Bay. ***Pamela Duncan, October 2017.***

Sometime after 1892 he became a clerk in the Post Office Department and his residence for many years was on Seward Square at 513 C Street SE. He also bought three lots in Arundel-on-the-Bay at the corner of Magnolia and Rockaway avenues in 1900. Conrad Zeller (1863-1932), the son of German immigrants, was listed in the 1880 U.S. Federal Census as a cigar maker. According to the 1900 census he was a Laborer in the Post Office Department; in the 1910 census his occupation was as a Dynamo Tender in the government.

Construction on the Hollywood Avenue lots was completed in short order, and a clubhouse for fishing and hunting, or "gunning" as it was called, and an engine storage building, were assessed at $500 in the county tax records of 1892.[3] The building, engine, and a horse were listed and appraised at $900 in 1894. Taxes for this property were paid by the investment company.

From the early advertising of the Chesapeake & Columbia Investment Co., we also know that a South River Gunning and Fishing Club located at Arundel-on-the-Bay. Two lots were sold to the Club on the same block containing the lots of the Otterback partnership and marked paid in company records, but the deed was never recorded.[4] In any event, in 1898, the "famous" South River Gunning and Fishing Club House, described as being "a very short distance from the South River on Arundel-on-the-Bay,"was offered "for sale–cheap." The advertisement in the *Baltimore Sun* of April 13, 1898, read, "The House is partly furnished and has accommodations for a club of twenty...Taxes and insurance paid up for one year... Fishing and oystering in season excellent..." Prospective purchasers were referred to Charles Schafer, trustee, at 804 E St. NW, Washington, D.C.[5]

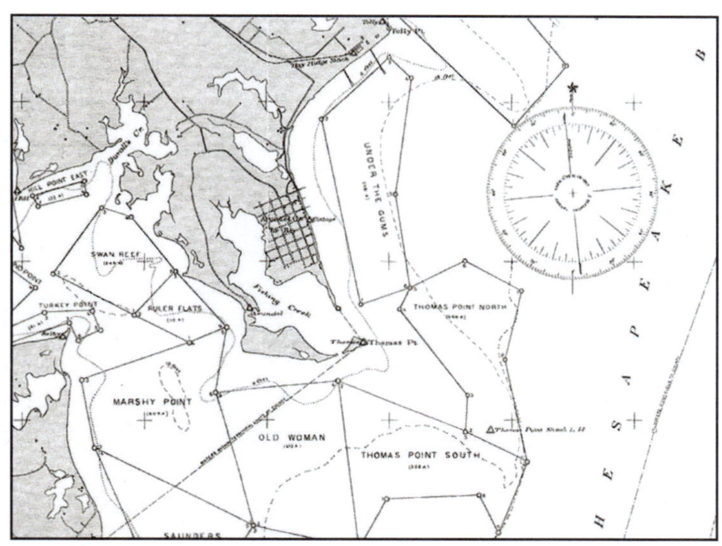

Figure 3: Maryland Natural Oyster Bars, 1906-07. Areas around Arundel-on-the-Bay are named Under the Cove, Thomas Point North and South, Old Woman, Marshy Point, Ruler Flats, and Swan Reef. ***Maryland Shellfish Commission, U.S. Coastal and Geodetic Survey, U.S. Bureau of Fisheries.***

An Annapolis Gun Club, in 1901, included at least one member from Arundel-on-the-Bay, William H. Thomas. Thomas operated a clothing store in Annapolis and was grandfather to Thomas Carroll

Figure 4: The Annapolis Gun Club, 1901. Top row standing (L-R) Dan Thompson, Chas. Crandall, Medford Roe, Weinie Kauffman, Jack Boucher, Nick Killman, Erasmus Clausen, Rudolph Smith, Jack Swallenberg, Louis Boessel; middle row sitting Edgar Basil, Dick Lookyear, Patty Brooks, Oliver Knackstedt; front row sitting Flora Cantler, Will Armiger, Will Thomas, Tom Strange, Louis Heintz, John Levay, Tom Tydings. ***Courtesy of Thomas Carroll Worthington.***

Worthington whose adventures are documented in Chapter Five. Whether this club used a clubhouse at Arundel-on-the-Bay is unknown.

William Thomas also was a member of the Thomas Point Gunning Club, shown below in 1903, and is seated on the front row far left.

Reference to an Arundel Fish and Gun Club is found in the county tax records for Arundel-on-the-Bay in 1904. This club located its clubhouse on Saratoga Avenue, a block inland of Fishing Creek, on the southeastern corner of the intersection with Myrtle Avenue. The deed of purchase for the lot was dated April 3, 1896, but it was never recorded.[6]

A final reference to a clubhouse at Arundel-on-the-Bay is that found in the African American newspaper, the *Washington Bee* of April 15, 1921, reporting that the building had been destroyed by fire. It was said that a defective flue caused the destruction of the property, then owned by John Walter Galloway (1873-1945) of Forest Park, Baltimore. Described as a popular resort for gunners on the Chesapeake, the clubhouse was then a fully furnished 10-room frame building. A number of hunting trophies and pelts were lost because fire departments from Annapolis

Figure 5: The Thomas Point Gunning Club in 1903. ***The Annapolis I Remember Collection, Maryland State Archives.***

and Eastport arrived too late to save the building.[7] Galloway bought the three blocks on which the earlier clubhouses were located from the Investment Co. in 1918.[8]

Galloway, who began his career as a messenger at the Weaver Coal Co. in Jersey City, N.J., was president of the Maryland Coal Co. and two of its affiliates. He and his wife, Elizabeth Mercer, lived on Park Heights Avenue Extended.[9]

The Hotel Cavanaugh, the Arundel, the Arundel Hotel, and the Arundel Inn

There were several places for the public to stay overnight either operating simultaneously or possibly following one another using differing names and perhaps the same building. The large hotel for 500 guests envisioned by the founders was never built. It was to have been in block seven, along the Bay between Chestnut and Linden avenues, but that block was platted and sold. Then it was to be along Narragansett Avenue, behind and west of the pavilion constructed in 1895 on the northern side of Chestnut Avenue between Narragansett and Chesapeake avenues. On the other hand, the plat for Highland Beach (see Chapter 3) shows a hotel at the first stop of the "Blackberry Train" at Arundel-on-the-Bay. This would locate it just south of the bathing beach adjacent to the Cavanaugh Canal and Oyster Creek.

We do know that guest houses – variously named the Hotel Cavanaugh, the Arundel Hotel, the Arundel Inn, and the Hotel Arundel on the Bay – operated here. Ads for the Hotel Cavanaugh appeared during the summer of 1898. This facility could have been near the bathing beach, or located on lots Commissioner Lawrence Cavanaugh owned on the northwest corner of Narragansett and Redwood avenues.

In June 1899, an Arundel Hotel was advertised as opening for the season by proprietor S. G. Swain: "Fishing, Crabbing, bathing. Home comforts and good taste."[10] In 1901, the Arundel Hotel was advertised in the July 6th edition of the *Washington Evening Star* by Miss Mary Vandersall: "Arundel Hotel, Arundel-on-the-Bay…take B. and O. trains: 2 hours from city; fishing; crabbing; salt water bathing; shady grove; cool nights; table 1st class; terms mod."

In June 1902, an advertisement in the *Annapolis Evening Capital* announced that the hotel was under new management. R.H. Cuthbert of 729 East Pratt Street in Baltimore was to be contacted for a circular. In June 1903 it was reported in the *Evening Capital* that the gunning clubhouse had been moved from Fishing Cove to the Bay front at the end of Magnolia Avenue. Could the clubhouse have been a hotel? That would locate the facility at the terminus of the "Blackberry Train" at Narragansett and Magnolia avenues.

Mr. Cuthbert managed the hotel, then called the Arundel Inn, again in the summer of 1903, and the July 11th edition of the *Evening Capital* named ten guests registered at the Inn including two married couples, a single woman, and five single men. On July 16, the advertisement for the Inn noted that the Arundel Athletic Association was to hold an event there. On August 8, the *Evening Star* reported a euchre card party at the Inn: "The porches were brilliantly illuminated with Japanese lanterns and presented a gala appearance. Besides the guests of the inn a large number of cottagers enjoyed the game."

Guests also were reported as registered at the Country Club, including the Superintendent of the *US Capitol* and the fire marshal of the District of Columbia, making this cottage another location for overnight accommodations. The Arundel Country Club, later called the Wahoo Club, was a cottage built by Smith.

No other references to a hotel appeared in the press until May 1908 when President Smith advertised in the *Evening Star* that a 20 room furnished cottage was available as a "fine opportunity for a summer boarding house keeper." Prospective proprietors were instructed to contact Smith or Cavanaugh. In July, the hotel was advertised as available for rent at

$200 for the remainder of the season. In August, Smith replied to an inquiry from persons wishing to stay at the hotel by referring them to Annie Tyler, wife of the caretaker.[11]

Figure 6: At 15 Massachusetts Ave. N.W. next to the Government Printing Office, the Hotel Harris operated by Arundel-on-the-Bay residents, served tourists visiting the city. ***Original vintage postcard.***

The first reference to a Hotel Arundel on the Bay appears in the *Baltimore Sun* of December 16, 1908, when it was reported that the next run of the R.S. Motorcycle Club would be to Annapolis, and "Dinner arrangements have been made at Hotel Arundel on the Bay." No additional references to a hotel have been found, other than one in March, 1910 when Smith and Cavanaugh offered the building for sale or rent.[12]

Another location for the hotel has been offered anecdotally. Erich Keyes, a current resident and a curious and inquisitive child when his family moved to the community in the 1960s, was told by Walter Tyler, (1901-1986), son of the bailiff George N. Tyler appointed in 1904, that he was the caretaker of the hotel. Tyler, who lived in a house at Saratoga Avenue between Oak and Hollywood avenues, pointed to a house on the Point as the site and talked of the train turn-around and a water tank nearby at the intersection of Cohasset and Magnolia avenues and the convenience to guests coming to the hotel. Erich remembers playing on the beach alongside Magnolia Avenue and finding old bottles and pieces of coal. Coal would have been needed for the summer cars.

However, neither Louise Linkins Seely nor Thomas Carroll Worthington, whose family houses were on Point Pleasant, remembered a hotel. The house identified by Walter Tyler as the hotel was then owned by Vernon Wilkerson M.D., the grandfather of Board Chair Lori Strum. It was built and owned since 1914 by John (Jack) and Mary Kate Harris and later their son-in-law, Philip Maley, president of the Arundel Commissioners in the 1930s, all proprietors of the Hotel Harris at 15 Massachusetts Avenue, N.W. in the District.

The house in question was larger but very similar in style to the extant 1363 Myrtle Avenue which Harris built for his sisters in 1916; the house on Narragansett Avenue on the Point is no longer standing. Lori Strum and Erich Keyes played in the house as young people and describe it as having a quite large living room and porch. Lori notes that the sleeping rooms were connected by doors that could be locked as connecting hotel rooms do, and there was an attached two-story shed with old bottles in it, and had been a water tower on the site. Erich noted that an entry path was lined by cedar trees.

Figure 7: The Wilkerson house at Arundel-on-the-Bay, shown here in the 1960s, was built by Washington, D.C. hotelier Jack Harris, ca. 1914. Anecdotal evidence suggests it was once a hotel. ***Photograph courtesy of Lori Strum.***

There is, however, no documentary evidence to confirm a hotel after 1910, although it can be surmised that one could have operated after Mr. Maley's death in 1934 by his wife Ada Harris Maley, at a time when both Louise Seely and Tommy Worthington were not paying close attention to Arundel-on-the-Bay, and when Walter Tyler would have been old enough to have been the caretaker.

Shoreline Erosion and Infrastructure Tackled by the Commissioners in 1899

Moving ahead on community business as mandated by the formative legislation, Commissioner Cavanaugh proposed the adoption of a tax rate of 1 cent on the dollar value of property at a town commissioners meeting of Feb. 25, 1899, held at Smith's home in the District. This rate was reauthorized annually for many years thereafter. Addressing their primary concern, Smith and Payson were constituted as a Committee of Ways and Means, whose task was to preserve the shoreline from erosion. Building a protective wall of riprap was discussed, and the two were urged by their fellow commissioners to consult with Col. McKenzie of the Army Corps of Engineers on this and other possibilities for shoreline protection. At a meeting in March held at Courts' residence in the District, the commissioners discussed the proposal to build a stone wall along the Bay front made by the Mcclenahan Brothers of Port Deposit, Md. After discussion of the plans at meetings throughout the summer, in August Commissioners Smith and Baughman were given authority to contract for the wall.

In September, Commissioners Payson and Courts were asked to prepare an ordinance for the project, which would require amending the 1898 legislation incorporating the town. These changes were developed and presented at two subsequent meetings, and adopted by the commissioners on October 14, 1899. On March 29, 1900, the Maryland General Assembly enacted the amendments which refined the powers of the commissioners to issue bonds and to determine assessment and collection of taxes. The community treasurer was now to prepare the tax list of eligible residents for Anne Arundel County.[13]

As to funds for roads and bridges it was announced, at a commissioners meeting on April 15, 1899 at Smith's home in the District, that Anne Arundel County would begin to make appropriations for repairing the bridges and roads at Arundel-on-the-Bay.

In July, the commissioners discussed the role of the bailiff and set the salary for the position at $100 per year, with $15 being paid in the summer months and $5 per month for the months of October through May. Chapter 2 of the town ordinance, imposing a $5 charge for visiting tent campers who were not property owners, was enacted. Chapter 3 – prohibiting a variety of offenses: intoxication, loud talk and profane language, weapons, leaving any smelly or dead thing in an alley, trespassing, bathing naked, gambling, liquor sales, any unsupervised burning or burning in an open or public place, and allowing pigs or any infected animal within 100 feet of water – also was approved, as was Chapter 6 on the subject of vagrancy. The Mayor and bailiff were given arrest authority and the bailiff was to receive an additional $1 in salary for each arrest made.

> *"...prohibiting a variety of offenses, intoxication, trespassing, bathing naked, gambling... and allowing pigs or any infected animal within 100 feet of water."*
> *Arundel-on-the-Bay Town Ordinance, 1899*

The role of the bailiff was further expanded to include authority to impound any horse, cattle, swine, or sheep found running at large, and to charge the errant owner 75 cents as an impoundment penalty and an additional 50 cents for any feed given to the animal. A resolution passed by the commissioners on July 1, 1899, at their meeting at Payson's house at Arundel-on-the-Bay, required the bailiff to visit each hotel, cottage, or camp twice a week from June through September. This was to ensure compliance with the town ordinance on the removal and disposal of garbage. Also at that session, the commissioners established an account for repairs and scheduled an election for July 29 – the first to be held after the incorporation of the town.

By statute, the commissioners were required to give three weeks running notice to the public of the date and location of the election, in a paper published in Anne Arundel County and one published in Washington, D.C. Announcements of the balloting also were to be posted at three locations in Arundel-on-the-Bay ten days before the election; at the summer house – a small open gazebo-like structure – at Point Pleasant, on the bulletin-board at the pavilion, and at the post office. Eligible voters were defined as persons over the age of 21, either residing within Arundel-on-the-Bay for six months before the election or having interest in real property in the town. Three election judges appointed by the commissioners supervised the process.

With the exception of Cavanaugh, and of Keleher who was away, the town commissioners appointed by the legislation – Smith, Payson, Shea, Courts, and Somerville – were elected in the summer of 1899 by 22 voters. Two new commissioners, R. C. Baughman of Baltimore and Franklin T. Sanner, the builder from Washington, D.C., also were elected.

Figure 8: Main Street in Annapolis as viewed from Church Circle, shown in a postcard, ca. 1900-1908, which residents of Arundel-on-the-Bay visited by boat, horse drawn carriage, or rail for shopping or tourism. A crowd has been attracted to an event on the sidewalk. ***The Annapolis I Remember Collection, Maryland State Archives.***

At the meeting held afterward, the Commissioners voted to retain the officers as elected the previous year.

In August 1899, Alice Mary Oulahan (1853-1925) was gifted a lot on the south side of Sycamore Avenue between Chesapeake and Narragansett avenues. She was a daughter of Irish immigrant Richard Oulahan (1829-1895), a poet who wrote an ode to Arundel-on-the-Bay in 1891. A copyist at the Division of the Census and later the Pension Office, Alice Mary became a teacher. She married John William Sanderson.

Her father was a member of the 164th N.Y. Infantry from 1862-1863 and an aide-de-camp to Gen. Michael Corcoran, the commander of what was called "Corcoran's Irish Legion" in the U.S. Civil War. After the war in 1864, Oulahan was appointed by President Lincoln to the 3rd Auditors Office of the Department of the Treasury. He lived at 618 A Street S.E., near a number of the founders of Arundel-on-the-Bay.

Alice Mary's brother, Richard V. Oulahan Jr., was the Washington correspondent for *The Sun* in New York City, and listed in the "*Who's Who of 1921*". According to David Greenberg in his book on political press manipulation, *"The Republic of Spin,"* as a young reporter Richard Oulahan Jr. coined the phrase "Rough Riders" in describing President Theodore Roosevelt's wartime excursion into Cuba.[14] Oulahan Jr. was considered the dean of the Washington D.C. press corps at his death in 1931. In uniting Arundel-on-the-Bay families, a grandchild of Richard Oulahan Sr. married Susan Courts, daughter of James Courts. Their son was named Courts G. Oulahan.

The New Century: Standing Committees for Town Management

Real estate activity by the Chesapeake & Columbia Investment Co. lessened in the first decade of the new century. Eight lots at Arundel-on-the-Bay were recorded as sold between 1900 and 1907. The final transaction, in July 1907, was a grant of right-of-way to the C & P Telephone Co. for telephone service.

The town commissioners continued to focus on improvements and maintenance of the community. In June 1900, at a meeting of the commissioners held in his District of Columbia office, Smith announced a contract to haul and dump clay on Chesapeake Avenue between the pier and the Cavanaugh Canal at 10 cents per load and between the Canal and the Bay Ridge line at 15 cents per load. In July, the commissioners approved expenses for lamps on the boardwalk and payments to the bailiff for work on roads and bridges and his salary and to James Gantt for digging a well.[15]

Commissioners Payson, Courts, Shea, Somerville, Sanner, and Smith were re-elected that summer and Ames Furbee Medford of Washington, D.C. was newly elected. Medford was Chief of Auditors at the War Department. His home at Arundel-on-the-Bay called The Gables, located on the bay front south of Magnolia Avenue next to that of Payson, included an extensive pier and the family entertained often.

In August 1900, the commissioners established four standing committees on the key issues of town management. Shea was named committee chair for water supply, Payson for grounds, roads and bridges; Sanner for lights and waterfront; and Medford for sanitation, law and order. In November, meeting at Shea's home in the District to review accounts, commissioners Smith and Sanner were asked to contract for hauling and placing additional clay on Chesapeake Avenue. Clay, being impervious to water, was a sought-after material for road building.

Residents and their guests continued an active calendar of pleasurable bayside entertainments. The *Washington Post* reported in July:

> The newest thing out is a crab bake. This form of entertainment is becoming quite popular, a number being held the past week. The invited guests assemble on the beach, where a large fire is made out of drift wood and other debris, and the crabs are put on to cook. In the interim, games are enjoyed until the shelled delicacy is ready to be served. The gentlemen do the honors and wait upon the fair summer maidens.[16]

On Aug. 20, 1900, the *Baltimore Sun* reported that a chaperoned group of young people summering in the community had been caught in a squall while sailing:

> Their boat was tossed by the wind and every moment was expected to capsize. Several of the ladies fainted. The vessel finally put in at Whitehall and the party … entertained by Mrs. Morse. The steam yacht Mystery was sent in search of the party, who returned to Arundel the next morning.

A New Pier and Other Improvements: 1901 to 1904

Preparing for the coming summer, the commissioners met in February 1901 in the District of Columbia. Commissioner Somerville moved to authorize the president "to appoint a committee of two Commissioners to select and mark as useless trees standing in the streets and between streets and building lines and to contract for felling and cutting same into cord wood and with the power to dispose of same." At a June meeting held at Payson's residence in the District, Commissioners Smith and Courts were authorized to "put in good and proper condition the pier, bridges, ditches, board walks, lamps, summer houses and wells of the town." Fees for tent campers were increased. As noted in the minutes:

> …no camping party to erect a tent, temporary shed or building on any lot in the Town of Arundel-on-the-Bay not owned by the head of the family or other person composing said camping party until he or they shall have paid to him (the bailiff) the sum of $10 as required by town ordinance.[17]

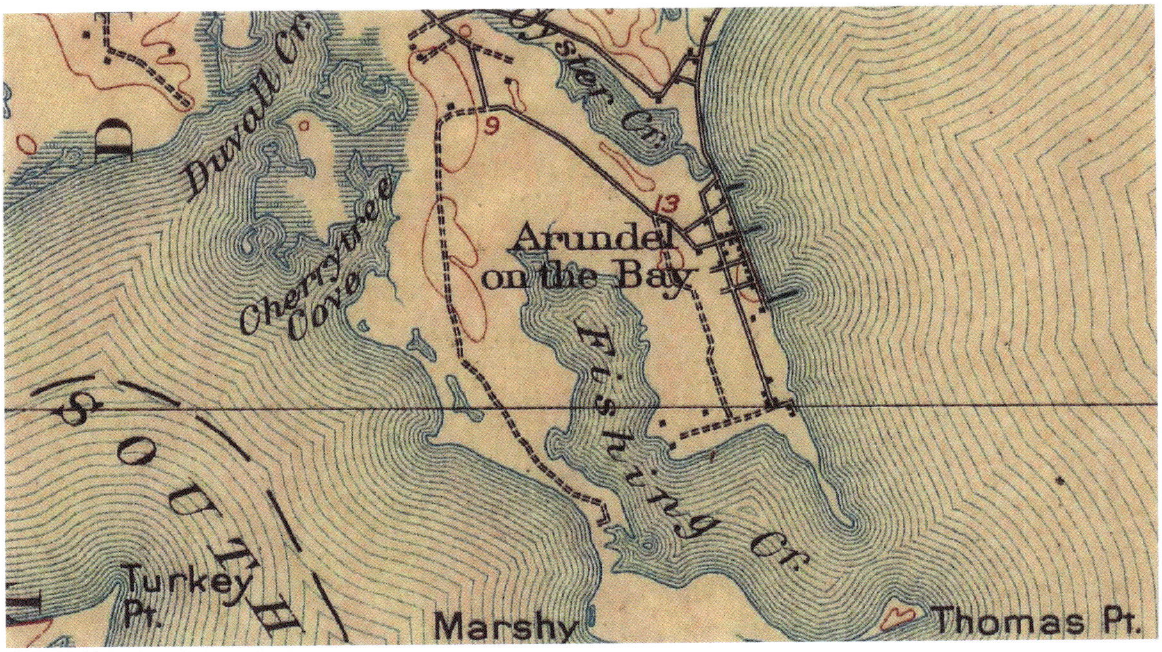

Figure 9: A detail of the 1904 U.S. Geological Service map of the Chesapeake Bay region, based on survey data of 1902, shows the cottages and piers constructed at Arundel-on-the-Bay. The dots represent cottages. It appears that north-south streets of Chesapeake, Narragansett, and Newport Avenues, and Magnolia Avenue running east-west along Fishing Creek were in existence at the time, as were portions of Cedar, Walnut, Sycamore, Redwood, and Linden Avenues.

In September 1901 the commissioners, all having been re-elected that summer, voted to construct a new pier. It was to be built into the Bay from the shore below the community pavilion on Chestnut Avenue, located just north of Idle Wild, the Shea family cottage. The Chesapeake & Columbia Investment Co. would pay for the construction. As planned, the pier would be at least four feet wide, more than 250 feet long, and would end at a 12 foot by 30 foot platform with a roof and seats on three sides. Builders would keep costs down by using old wood from other projects. In other action on the Chesapeake Bay shore that September, the commissioners authorized the purchase of 100 boatloads of stone to be placed along the shoreline, and they approved rebuilding the boardwalk from the public pier at Walnut Avenue to the end of the peninsula at Point Pleasant.

Accounts were reviewed at a commissioner's meeting of Oct. 30, 1901, and Smith was given the authority "to contract for resurfacing with clay the roadway from the old Bay Ridge Gate along Chesapeake Avenue to Point Pleasant and for all necessary repairs to bridges."

In March 1902, Commissioner Medford was elected to be treasurer as James Somerville was moving to California. President Smith directed the bailiff to purchase a new pump for one of the public wells and to contract for repairs to the road to Bay Ridge. In May, Smith reported that the improvements underway, including the new pier, would cost $1,250. These expenses were now to be shared by the town and the Chesapeake & Columbia Investment Co.

During the summer of 1902, the commissioners arranged the hauling of coal oil for the lamps along the boardwalk and oversaw an extension of the existing breakwater along the Bay front, improvements to the road to Bay Ridge and to Chesapeake Avenue, and repair of the canal and boardwalk. The canal in question was the connection between Oyster Harbor and the Bay, known as the "Cavanaugh Canal." This feature was at that time part of Arundel-on-the-Bay.

The eight voters of 1902 re-elected commissioners Smith, Medford, Courts, Payson, Sanner, and Shea. Arthur Lee Bosley of 219 North Calvert St. in Baltimore was newly

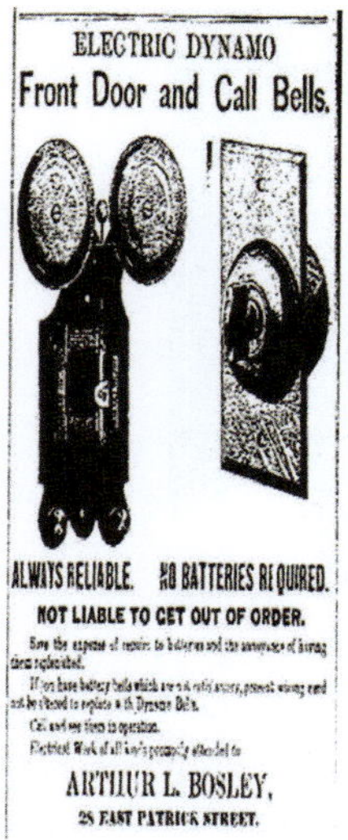

Figure 10: The company advertisement of Arthur L. Bosley of Baltimore, Md., elected a commissioner of Arundel-on-the-Bay in 1902. Bosley was in the electric power industry. *The News, Frederick, Md., Feb.22, 1894.*

elected. Bosley and his partners formed companies to bring electric power to Frederick and later Cumberland, Md. The family maintained two cottages in the community–Liberty Cottage for their daughters, Beatrice and Marguerite, and Deer Lodge for themselves. Mrs. Bosley became Grand Regent of the Daughters of the American Revolution in the State of Maryland in 1914.[18]

Grocer Jeremiah J. Brosnan and his wife Ellen purchased a lot on Chesapeake Avenue in 1902. His store was located at 732 Second St. in southwest Washington. Edward S. York, a real estate broker, bought a lot on Narragansett Avenue at Linden Avenue in January 1903. At the time York lived at 509 East Capitol St. in the home of his in-laws Warren and Flora Orcutt, next door to Arundel-on-the-Bay founder William Hazen. Born in Vermont in 1862, York came to the District of Columbia as a child in 1870.

In July 1903, the commissioners voted to construct public stairs "giving access for the public to the beach" and to reimburse Miss Gelston for the construction of stairs from Sycamore Avenue to the beach at her property. It was reported on July 30, "At Arundel on the Bay delightful dances are held every Saturday night." The Bay Ridge Orchestra furnished music for dances at Arundel-on-the-Bay.[19] Thirteen voters participated in the election of 1903.[20]

An Arundel Athletic Association meet, to be held on August 13, was reported on in the August 4 edition of the *Washington Evening Star.* Running, high jump, 50 and 100 yard dashes, wheelbarrow race, broad jump, and a quarter mile run were among the 14 events planned.

A Crisis in Transportation to Arundel-on-the-Bay: 1904-1907

In 1904, Arundel-on-the-Bay residents learned that the Bay Ridge resort was not to open for the summer and train service from Annapolis to Bay Ridge would be abandoned. A meeting was held at the home of Commissioner Courts in the District in March to discuss the options. Upset at the prospect of losing rapid access to the community, the commissioners urged Smith to communicate with Baltimore & Annapolis Railroad Co. officials to advocate for transportation for the coming season. This effort was to no avail as it turned out; hiring a horse and carriage at the rail station in Annapolis was to be the only option for rail travelers to access their cottages at Arundel-on-the-Bay. This impediment overshadowed community life for several years.

In August 1904, the commissioners appointed a new bailiff, George N. Tyler, to begin work in October, and adopted an ordinance more clearly defining the duties of the position. Specified were keeping plank walks and breakwaters in repair, cleaning the wells in May, mowing weeds and bushes along sidewalks and in streets, and lighting street lamps at early dusk and extinguishing them at 11 p.m. After lighting the lamps, the bailiff was to stay near to or on the pier "to perform any needed service." During the off-season months of October through May, the bailiff was to keep an eye on all cottages, report any damages, and make repairs necessary. In late fall and early winter, the bailiff was to "carefully burn" leaves and grass on vacant lots in inhabited blocks, and burn the grass on the salt marshes. Commissioner Cavanaugh leased a cottage to Tyler and his family, and a contract was signed initiating a long period of Tyler family involvement at Arundel-on-the-Bay (see Chapter Five). According to an accounting in 1919, Anne S. Tyler, Tyler's wife, bought a lot on the southwestern corner of Cohasset Avenue at Linden Avenue.

In February 1905, the commissioners reauthorized the property tax levy; however, the remainder of the meetings for the year lacked a quorum. The *Washington Evening Star* on June 12, 1905 predicted a general downturn in activity: "It is thought but few of the cottages at Arundel will be open this year, owing to the lack of railroad facilities." In 1906, the tax rate again was reauthorized. Again, there was no quorum for three remaining meetings of the year.

In the spring of 1906, an eight-room cottage at Arundel-on-the-Bay was listed for sale in the *Washington Evening Star* classified advertisements. Facing the bay on a corner lot, the asking price was $1,200. The Booth's Farm Agency advertisement read, "Why not buy this nice home and summer there with your family? Finest fishing, boating and bathing..."[21] Another cottage was offered for rent for the three- month summer period for $60 and a second with six rooms was offered for $50 for the season.

The *Washington Evening Star's* "Arundel" column continued to track community events through the summer of 1906, reporting on July 6 that the Fourth of July "was celebrated with a magnificent display of fireworks at the pier." A bridge club had been formed, the *Star* reported on Aug. 5, and John Shea was out on his boat, *The Island Bud*, it was noted on Aug. 20. The paper also broke the news that a party for a three-year old was held at a cottage called Umph's Villa.

In September, the commissioners met to inspect breakwaters under construction on the waterfront, made plans for repairing the pier and cutting trees and undergrowth for the next season, and reviewed two years of treasurer's reports for 1905 and 1906.[22] *The Annapolis Sunday Evening Capital* of Sept. 3, 1906, reported:

> Arundel on the Bay 'colony' is described as 'more or less inaccessible, (due to) roads often over plowed fields, through mudholes, uphill and down dale and across a canal 15 to 20 feet wide at low tide.

Newspaper Leaders at Arundel-on-the-Bay

According to the *Baltimore American*, reporting on the July 1907 annual contest for Commissioners at Arundel-on-the-Bay, "...the election aroused no little interest. Even the ladies who are cottagers and taxpayers there exercised their right of franchise under the charter of the village." Although women voted, they did not yet hold office; Thomas Smith, James Courts, Nicholas Shea, Ames Medford, and Arthur Bosley were re-elected. The community elected two new commissioners, both newspapermen – William M. Abbott and Philander C. Johnson.[23] Telephone service became available in July.

Abbott (1839-1912) was the founder and civic-minded activist editor of the *Annapolis Evening Capital.* He came from the Eastern Shore to work at another paper and established the *Capital* in May 1884. His home at Arundel-on-the-Bay was called Gloucester Cottage, and later in 1917 in the *Washington Evening Star* was referred to as Wilfanem Lodge. Long time Arundel-on-the-Bay resident, Rick Hutzell, is currently the Editor of the *Annapolis Capital.*

Philander Chase Johnson (1866-1939) was a newspaper columnist, editor, humorist, and critic, writing the columns "Postscripts" in the *Washington Post* and "Shooting Stars" at the *Washington Evening Star.* His books included "*The Sayings of Uncle Eben*," published in 1896, and "*Now-A-Day Poems*" and "*Songs of the GOP,*" both published in 1900. His "*Senator Sorghum's Primer of Politics,*" published in 1906, contained such clever adages as: "It is a fortunate thing for society that the courts do not get the same chance at the Ten Commandments that they do at the Constitution of the United States." Johnson also penned, "Politics is the art of turning influence into affluence," and "Every man who has attained to high position is a sincere believer in the survival of the fittest." Johnson purchased former Rep. Payson's Chelsea Cottage on Chesapeake Avenue south of Magnolia Avenue.[24]

Miss Gelston's musicale was featured in the *Washington Sunday Star* of Aug. 20, 1907:

Figure 11: Arundel-on-the-Bay residents made a picnic trip to the West River in July 1907 on the steamer *Emma Giles,* shown here at the Tolchester Wharf, ca. 1915-1925. *The Annapolis I Remember Collection, Maryland State Archives.*

> A very pretty musicale was given Thursday evening by Miss E. H. Gelston at her cottage at Arundel-on-the-Bay in honor of her house guest…The cottage was beautifully illuminated with Chinese lanterns and soft tapers. Miss Gelston gave selections from the opera of the "Mikado."… Miss Blanche Calvert presenting Nanikipoo [sic]. Recitations were rendered…Selections from the graphophone [sic] were thoroughly enjoyed. A butterfly dance by Mariam Beebe, a little tot of two summers, was gracefully rendered.

Figure 12: William Martin Abbott, editor and publisher of the *Annapolis Evening Capital* and a resident of Arundel-on-the-Bay. *Evening Capital, Historical and Industrial Edition, 1908.*

On Aug. 27 the *Star's* "Arundel" column noted that "bridge whist" had become a popular morning pastime. A fishing party organized by Carl DuBois, a tent camper, had "caught 100 rock and taylors" on Saturday, the column stated. A taylor, or tailor, is a bluefish.

Some relief to the crisis in transportation was given in August 1907 when Anne Arundel County approved providing road tax revenues directly to the treasurer of Arundel-on-the-Bay. The *Baltimore American* reported that the town commissioners wanted a shell road constructed to Annapolis because the roads were in a miserable condition. At the same time, the Commissioners argued before the county that declining property values were no longer reflective of the assessments on record, and requested a "horizontal reduction" in the rates.[25] No action was taken on the town's request for reduced assessment of real and personal property, which was sent to a county committee for review. Advocating further for transportation options, Arundel-on-the-Bay commissioners appeared before the State

Figure 13: The Eastport Bridge in 1907, used by Arundel-on-the- Bay residents traveling by horse drawn carriage or car between the community and Annapolis. ***The Annapolis I Remember Collection, Maryland State Archives.***

WINS WOMEN

MAYOR THOMAS W. SMITH,
Who Sitteth Upon the Throne at Arundel-on-the-Bay.

OUR BELOVED SMITH TURNS SUFFRAGETTE

Mayor Thomas W. Gives 'Em Down in Maryland Villagette.

Figure 14: A tongue -in-cheek article reporting on the ability of women to vote in town elections at Arundel-on-the-Bay. ***Washington Times, Aug. 2, 1908.***

Roads Commission in the fall of 1907 to urge improvement in the roads linking Arundel-on-the-Bay to Annapolis.

Typhoid Fever at Arundel-on-the-Bay

In 1908, the season began with the normal issues faced in previous years: it was necessary to reconstruct the pier and the pavilion, purchase new covers for the wells, and repair the boardwalk and breakwaters for the coming summer. At the elections in July, 15 voters re-elected the commissioners of 1907.[26]

The duties of the town bailiff were further expanded. The minutes of a meeting of the commissioners held in the summer of 1908 note:

> …the bailiff was urged to patrol the entire waterfront along Chesapeake Avenue each night and to leave public lamps burning until between 5 and 6 o'clock each morning except the first one at the north end and the last one at the south end of Chesapeake Avenue to be extinguished at 11 each night.

However, the most important concern that summer was the matter of public health. At the commissioners' meeting of Aug. 1, 1908, an ordinance titled "Regulation of Privies" was adopted as Chapter 9 of the Town Regulations. In October, these rules were expanded to include a Chapter 9½, "The Regulation of Privies and Stables." The facilities, which were to be cleaned only between midnight and 5:00 a.m., were to be equipped with moveable galvanized iron or metal cans. Any pits under the privies were to be lined with concrete. All refuse was to be burned, and all stables were to be cleaned on Mondays and Thursdays.

The need for these specific regulations was reported by the *Baltimore Sun* in September:

Figure 15: Thomas Smith's business interests in the District continued to expand. This apartment house at 676 4th St. NE was built in 1908 for the president of the Arundel-on-the-Bay commissioners. ***Pepco News, December 1908, Historical Society of Washington, D.C.***

> Arundel-on-the-Bay, a small summer resort on Chesapeake Bay, five miles from Annapolis, is having a typhoid fever epidemic. Five cases have developed there within the last few weeks, although all the patients have been removed to hospitals for treatment and steps have been taken by those in charge of the place to locate the cause for the prevalence of the disease. [27]

James Courts, son of the chief clerk to the U.S. House of Representatives Committee on Appropriations, and two women in the Calvert family of Washington were among those who had been taken ill.

As part of the effort to combat the outbreak, the position of Town Scavenger was established at a salary of $1 per month. John Booth was appointed to the job and given the authority "to charge not to exceed 50 cents for the removal from privies of each can and disposal of the contents."

In early October, the commissioners received a report from John F. Anderson, M.D., Assistant Surgeon of the Public Health and Marine Hospital Service, on the recent cases of typhoid fever. This was sent to the owners of each cottage, along with a letter containing instructions for health and a copy of the new regulations. [28]

The commisioners sought an abatement of county taxes in 1908 on the holdings of the Chesapeake and Columbia Improvement Co., which were valued at $7,875. The assessment comprised 300 acres of land at $20 per acre for a total of $6,000; a farm house and barn at $200, a corn house at $200, the pavilion at $600, the wharf at $100, an engine at $750, and a horse at $25.

Waterfront Projects and Other Community Development: 1909-1911

Preparations for the summer season of 1909 began in May with the commissioners expressing continuing concern about disease. The minutes of May 2 cite their resolve as a health measure "to gather up and haul away all broken crockery, tin cans, bottles, and other rubbish in the rear of the cottages that may be calculated to afford breeding places for mosquitos" and to purchase "a barrel of crude petroleum…to be poured on ponds and stagnant pools in and near the town." At this session, they also approved the action of President Smith sending "a sailing vessel from Washington with material including lumber and nails for repair of the board walk and pier and terra cotta tile for drains and street culverts." It was noted that there had been some discussion in the press about a proposed extension of the Washington, Baltimore & Annapolis railroad as a trolley line from Annapolis, through Eastport and to Arundel-on-the-Bay.[29] This did not materialize.

In June, several advertisements listing summer rentals at Arundel-on-the-Bay appeared in the Washington papers. A seven-room cottage facing the bay was offered for $25 for the season; another advertisement offered a house for $50 for the season. Still another described a rental as:

Figure 16: The Annapolis Harbor in 1910, today's "Ego Alley," as viewed from City Dock. The Meredith Lumber Co., property of the family who owned a cottage on the Point at Arundel-on-the-Bay, and later a significant share of the community, is the building at the top left. ***The Annapolis I Remember Collection, Maryland State Archives.***

> ...delightfully located 2-story 5-room cottage: use of telephone: completely furnished; near the beach; commodious verandas; beautiful lawns; always cool breezes...an ideal cottage in perfect order.[30]

In August, the *Washington Bee* reported that a group of African-American campers from Washington, D.C., and their friends from Annapolis, met at a campsite off Adams Street in Annapolis. They later traveled by boat to Arundel-on the-Bay, where they visited Mrs. Francis, Mrs. Curtis, Mrs. Lewis, and the Douglass family. The Wormley, Ridgely, and Bennett families were among those participating.[31]

The commissioners continued to make improvements in community infrastructure. At a meeting in August it was determined to place an additional street lamp on Chesapeake Avenue between Sycamore and Redwood Avenues and to erect hand rails at points along the boardwalk next to the waterside. Robert Leatherberry of Shady Side, Md. was contracted with to dig an artesian well to a depth of 150 feet on the center of the beach in front of Block 7 (between Linden and Chestnut Avenues) The exact location of the well was to be marked "at a point indicated by a stake, the stake being a piece of yellow pine board from the board walk driven into the sand near an old scow which lies against the bank." President Smith warned that the contractor's fee of $150 would not be paid until the flow of water resulting reached four gallons per minute.[32] In October 1909, the Investment Co. sold Thomas Point Island to T. Clifton Bosley, and used the funds to retire a $1,000 loan and make other payments.

Town commissioners, at meetings in May and July 1910, continued the prior years' focus on infrastructure. The work list included constructing a landing pier at the existing recreational pier located at Chestnut Avenue, and repairs to boardwalks, the pier, pavilion, and "roadways near the canal and to all bridges." In July, the commissioners moved the street lamps away from the edge of the Bay to a position between the boardwalk and

Chesapeake Avenue, and placed new lamps on the pier, at the front of the pier steps, and on Chesapeake Avenue. The railway line, which reportedly dropped from regular use in 1906, was now being maintained. The commissioners directed that "trees and bushes overhanging the road to Annapolis be trimmed and crossing of the railroad to Bay Ridge... repaired." Breakwater work near Cavanaugh Canal also was continued.[33]

"Crabs are so abundant that even the dogs catch them."

The Douglass and Curtis families were in residence at Arundel-on-the-Bay in the summer of 1911 according to the *Washington Bee*. That summer, continuing to be quoted in the newspapers as a humorist, Commissioner James Courts complained that the new air-conditioning system at the Capitol was causing him to shiver. He made clear that he would be attending the Fourth of July fireworks at Arundel-on-the-Bay, pronouncing them far preferable to the District of Columbia's show with its crowds and political speeches.

Commissioners Johnson and Medford called attention to the unfavorable condition of the breakwater in front of their residences at a meeting in July. As a result, the minutes noted "Commissioner Johnson was authorized, at his own expense, to remove the summer house in front of his residence and relocate the same over the public well at the north of his residence."

The *Washington Herald* reported that, as August was the month of greatest activity at Arundel-on-the-Bay, the pavilion floor was being put in order. Card parties were being held, it said, and "crabs are so abundant that even the dogs catch them."[34]

Town commissioners were elected for two year terms in 1911. As to the voting that summer, the *Sunday Star* reported on August 6:

> A town meeting was held last night, at which the election of the seven commissioners of Arundel, held a week ago, was confirmed. The commissioners are Messrs. M. I. Weller, Thomas W. Smith, E. C. Graham, Amos [sic] Medford, J. C. Courts, all of Washington, A. L. Bosley of North Baltimore and W. M. Abbott of Annapolis. At this election the women property owners at Arundel had the right of franchise as well as the men.
>
> Probably the most unique feature of the election was the voting of a woman aged eighty-five, who cast her first ballot, and walked a half mile for the privilege. She is Mrs. Frank Jones of Washington.

Sixty-four property owners, men and women alike, were certified for voting at Arundel-on-the-Bay in 1911. The list included the names of five African-Americans: Austin M. Curtis M.D., Charles R. and William H. Douglass, Mrs. A. J. Colbert, and Mrs. M. E. Harrison. In addition to the lot owners previously mentioned, a druggist, William H. Bradford of 801 C St. NE in the District of Columbia, and John J. Brosnan of 504 4½ St. SW, Washington, D.C, a lawyer and president of the Provident Relief Association, were on the rolls.

Capital publisher William Abbott and his wife celebrated their 50th wedding anniversary at Arundel-on-the-Bay that summer. A surprise party was given by their daughters, Mrs. Emma A. Gage, now the editor of the paper, and Mrs. A. B. McManus, who owned an adjacent cottage. E. C. Graham, it was reported, took several "flash light pictures" of the guests.[35] Graham was to become president of the commissioners of the town in 1918.

The Second President of the Town of Arundel-on-the-Bay: Edwin C. Graham

Edwin C. Graham was born in Warren County, Ill., in 1872. He married Annie L. Barron of Virginia in 1894 and by 1900 had become president of the District of Columbia electric company. Later he was president of the Hamilton National Bank at 619 14th Street N.W. Their daughter Lorraine was born in 1896, son Edwin Mirick in 1902, and daughter Anna in 1904. The family cottage at Arundel-on-the-Bay was named Nedanna after the two younger children. In 1910 the Grahams lived at 1426 Columbia Rd. NW; in 1930 they lived at 2921 44th Pl. NW, where the household included a grandson, Graham Callahan, a private duty nurse, and a household assistant.

Graham served as president of the D.C. Board of Education in 1925. He continued to be a commissioner of Arundel-on-the Bay, and served again as president of the Commissioners after the death of Philip M. Maley in December 1934. Around 1934, the Grahams established a second residence in Miami, Fla. He died there in May 1953.[36]

Graham's son Edwin Mirick was a midshipman at the Naval Academy in the Class of 1923.

Figure 17: Edwin C. Graham, president of the Arundel-on-the-Bay commissioners beginning in 1918 and of the District's electric company. He later became President of the Hamilton National Bank. *Library of Congress.*

In December 1911 the *Washington Times* reported that the Bay Ridge resort had been purchased for subdivision and that the new owners, Baltimore hoteliers, the Rennetts, planned to construct a large hotel. The restart of rail service from Annapolis to Bay Ridge had been arranged, leading the commissioners to hope for renewed interest in Arundel-on-the-Bay. As the article stated, the development of Arundel-on-the-Bay had been "halted when Bay Ridge closed, about five years ago." Because rail service had been suspended from Annapolis to Bay Ridge, Arundel-on-the-Bay property owners were made to drive five miles overland from Annapolis.[37]

Figure 18: Son of Edwin C. Graham, president of the town commissioners of Arundel-on-the-Bay, Edwin M. Graham was a midshipman in the Class of 1923 at the U.S. Naval Academy. He died in Florida in 1971 after a career in real estate in the Washington, D.C. area. *Lucky Bag Yearbook, 1923, U.S. Naval Academy.*

"Bill the Avenger" Inherits a Cottage at Arundel on-the-Bay and other issues of 1912

As an odd historical footnote, an item relating to Arundel-on-the-Bay appeared in the *Washington Evening Star* on March 7, 1912. It was reported that William Jones – known as "Bill the Avenger" because of his attempt to kill Charles J. Guiteau, the assassin of President Garfield in 1881 – had been awarded the bulk of the estate of his wife, Catharine M. B. Jones. The estate included a cottage valued at $600 at Arundel-on-the-Bay, located on the south side of Hollywood Avenue midway between Newport and Rockaway avenues.

In an article entitled "Where MD Women Vote," the *Baltimore Sun*, reporting on the 1912 election of Arundel-on-the-Bay Commissioners, wrote:

> While the question of women's suffrage is being agitated throughout the country, this little incorporated township on the bay shore is probably the only bailiwick in Maryland where women have the right of franchise…the women eagerly await the coming of the day when they march up to the polls and exercise their right to cast a ballot.[38]

On September 30, 1912, James W. Owens, an attorney in Annapolis, wrote Frank Weller of Arundel-on-the-Bay concerning the assessment list in general, and the tax sale of a property in the community which was in default. Owens warned: "It would be well for you or some of your Company to take over this property as Adams is a colored man and knows that you don't want any colored people in your settlement." This letter is the only written evidence of the practice of racial segregation found while investigating the history of the community between 1890 and 1919.

Adams may well have been Annapolis councilman J. Albert Adams, the only African American member of that body, who in August 1908 met Booker T. Washington and took him to the George Bowen guesthouse at Highland Beach. The next day Washington was to be the guest of honor at a launch party.[39] In 1909, the *Washington Bee* reported that Al Adams was host to a large party of visitors from Washington, D.C., and that he transported guests to Arundel-on-the-Bay in his boat; at the time he was a bachelor and described as a great catch for some young lady.[40] There is no evidence that Adams occupied property at Arundel-on-the-Bay.

The Idyllic Summer of 1913

In 1913 the *Washington Herald* reported successful lobbying by the commissioners resulting in "the new shell road between Annapolis and Arundel on the Bay which has conquered the sands, so motors are a pleasure instead of the painful progress of last season." In addition, it was noted, "just now all are rejoicing in the erection from end to end of the town of a wooden boardwalk." The *Herald* also described an unusual incident at Arundel-on-the-Bay:

> A different sort of rapid transit visitor was the Naval Hydroaeroplane which skimmed by so near the water…with such an unholy buzz on the recent trip to Old Point Comfort, it brought out practically every resident, in all manner of early morning costume. It was a sight worth waking for, but gone before the sleepy eyes were fairly open.[41]

"For Washingtonians who can vote nowhere else the suffrage liberty of Arundel is not its least attraction."
Washington Herald, July 27, 1913.

Figure 19: Oyster Boats, native Chesapeake Bay vessels, in 1910 at the foot of Prince George Street in Annapolis. *The Annapolis I Remember Collection, Maryland State Archives.*

As had been noted in the past, the *Baltimore Sun's* report on the election of commissioners in 1913 emphasized that the Town of Arundel-on-the-Bay had the distinction of being the only place in Anne Arundel County, and in the State of Maryland, where women were allowed to vote. Elected commissioners that summer were Arthur Bosley of Baltimore, and James Courts, Edwin Graham, Ames Medford, Nicholas Shea, Thomas Smith, and Michael Weller of the District of Columbia. The *Sun* noted, "There are about 30 cottages at Arundel, which means about 100 voters and the number of women voters is nearly equal to the men." The *Washington Herald* proclaimed "For Washingtonians who can vote nowhere else the suffrage liberty of Arundel is not its least attraction."

At the post-election meeting held in the pavilion, the commissioners described plans for next season, better transportation and the formation of athletic groups being among them. They cited securing good drinking water and improved sanitation as accomplishments of previous years.

The *Washington Herald* also reported on the improvements to life at Arundel-on-the-Bay made by its Women's Civic League. They leased the pavilion – described as being in a "tottering" condition – and restored it and installed screens. They also opened a circulating library in the post office, still located in the cottage owned by Commissioner Cavanaugh and leased to the Tyler family, where residents could borrow current magazines for two cents a day. The Civic League raised funds for these community projects in a variety of ways, including a "cake carnival" at which ladies competed in the culinary arts, a "pantry sale," a debating society, and card games like auction bridge and Five Hundred, both popular games at the time. The league sponsored a Bible story hour, whose chief narrator in the summer of 1913 was the head of the primary department of St. Paul's Chapel in New York City. The *Herald* reported:

> August is supposed to be the big month in this resort of sand and wood. It is then that the many government officials who own cottages at this popular Chesapeake Bay town take their vacation, bathing in the surf and sitting under the shade trees which make Arundel-on-the-Bay unique among seaside resorts. Many of us carry memories of blinding stretches of dazzling sands and torrid heat devoid of trees. Here it is different. The woods overlap the bathing beach and sunshades are carried for artistic effect rather than from necessity. Though it lacks five days to the most "popular" month, events are crowded into every hour of the waking time and there is not a dull moment and not a case of sickness in the entire community.[42]

"The oyster ridge running parallel with the shore road, about a thousand feet off shore, is already dotted with the oyster fleet, which adds much to the picturesque features of the autumn landscape."

In August the *Herald* further reported that motor boat service was available from Annapolis to Bay Ridge, making the round trip three times a day. This gave another option to Arundel-on-the-Bay residents for travel to connect with the "Blackberry Train." "Arundel-on-the-Bay is filled almost to capacity…and the cool nights and sparkling days make it an ideal vacation home," the *Herald* noted. The Wahoo Club, or Arundel Country Club as it was referred to, was open as were numerous other homes including the Magnolia Cottage of the Van Vleets, The Anchorage of the Van Zandts, Lucie's Cottage, and the Belmont Cottage, and tents were pitched by campers. "The good roads and cool days tempt owners of motors and coaches to drop in on Arundelites frequently." It was a beautiful place in the fall of 1913, according to the *Herald:*

> Brilliant weather of almost midsummer heat marks the post holiday season. The Labor Day celebration had a splendid background of smiling skies and placid seas, nature seeming to chide the vacationists who are turning their backs on the village on the homing flight, just as the time life seems most worth living here.
>
> The population can certainly be termed 'floating' not only for the part out in the boats, but those who are 'up anchor' for Washington, and the large incoming parties for the hunting and oysters. The oyster ridge running parallel with the shore road, about a thousand feet off shore, is already dotted with the oyster fleet, which adds much to the picturesque features of the autumn landscape. The bivalves are said to be fat and are selling for less than $1 per bushel. The nap and crack of rifles indicate rabbit shooting has begun. There has been a prohibition against promiscuous hunting here for the last five years, so the woods are now well stocked. In fact, the pet dogs go on their own personally conducted rabbit hunts, and come home with bulging sides.[43]

Less than a week later a turn in the weather was reported:

> Post-vacation days here are chiefly notable for a weather mixup–after summer nights when blankets were always necessary now comes a period when the lightest of clothing seemed too heavy–a veritable flare-back of summer, that made the oyster craft question the arrival of the month with "R" in it and sent the tongers back to their truck farms–that being the alternate occupation of many of the natives. On the heels of the returned dogdays came a dry nor'easter which made the bay a thing to be admired and carefully avoided by both bathers and boats. Now all is peace and the weather and water conditions ideal–cottagers with children to be placed in school are regretfully closing up their homes, but the happy hunters are coming in daily, though it is a long time before frost is due when the hunting begins to be at the best.[44]

A Photograph Album of the Linkins Family at Arundel-on-the-Bay from 1914

Louise Linkins Bezdek Seely–whose clear memories of Arundel-on-the-Bay as it was more than one hundred years ago have informed this history–was born in February 1913 in Washington, D.C. Bill Semenuk, Arundel-on-the-Bay resident and a researcher and writer for this community history project, traveled to Florida to collect Louise's memories and family photographs of summers in the community dating back to 1914.

The family's summer home was Chelsea Cottage, built by former U.S. Rep. Lewis E. Payson and his wife Louise in 1895 and located on Magnolia Avenue at the Bay front. Payson was the uncle of Louise Seely's mother, Mabel Kent. In 1895, after the deaths of their parents, Mable and her younger brother Sidney lived with the Paysons in Washington, D.C. at 1229 Massachusetts Ave. NW.

"Louise reports that there was no electricity in 1914. Oil lamps and candles were used, as were outdoor privies."

Louise Seely's father, William H. Linkins, or Bill as he was known, also summered at Arundel-on-the-Bay with the Weller family and in 1909 met Payson's niece Mabel, whom he later married. Born in 1881, Bill Linkins was a lawyer and real estate investor. His father, George, owned the 20th Street market in the District under the name of his business, "G.W. Linkins Real Estate Co." In 1914, Bill Linkins, also known as "Captain Bill," bought the former Payson cottage from newspaperman Philander Johnson.[45] Linkins' first boat was the *Dorothy Louise*; he later owned a cabin cruiser called *Toadfish* and was an avid fisherman with a reputedly wild sense of humor.

Louise reports that there was no electricity in 1914. Oil lamps and candles were used, as were outdoor privies. A story passed down by her family relates that around the turn of the century a small section of the porch at the Payson house had been screened off and came to be called "Judge Payson's Mosquito Parlor" by the neighbors, who had to sit outside at their own cottages swatting mosquitoes for the lack of screens.

(See images on following pages.)

Figure 20: Louise Linkins playing on the family pier at Arundel-on-the-Bay in 1915. ***Courtesy of Louise Linkins Seely.***

Figure 21: Louise in front of the Jack Harris house on the Point, on the Bay front south of Magnolia Avenue, 1915. Harris, owned the Hotel Harris in Washington, D.C. Board Member Lori Strum played in this house as a child when it was owned by her grandfather, Vernon Wilkerson, M.D., from 1957 to 1980. John H. (Jack) Harris also built 1363 Myrtle Avenue. ***Courtesy of Louise Linkins Seely.***

Figure 22: Louise Seely's mother, Mabel Kent Linkins, in full swimsuit at Arundel-on-the-Bay, c. 1915. ***Courtesy of Louise Linkins Seely.***

Figure 23: Bill Linkins, father of Louise Linkins Seely, in 1909. ***Chain and Sprocket Club photo, Historical Society of Washington, D.C.***

Figure 24: Facing the camera is Louise's older brother, also named Bill Linkins, at Arundel-on-the-Bay, c.1915. ***Courtesy of Louise Linkins Seely.***

Figure 25: Big brother Bill and Louise in period bathing attire at Arundel-on-the-Bay in 1915. ***Courtesy of Louise Linkins Seely.***

Figures 26 and 27: A Model T Ford on the left and Bill Linkins' Scripps-Booth on the far right are parked alongside the Linkins' home at Arundel- on-the-Bay, c.1915. ***Photo courtesy of Louise Linkins Seely.***

Figure 28: Mable Kent Linkins in the foreground, her daughter Louise Linkins, and Aunt Esther Linkins on the porch of the family summer home at Arundel-on-the-Bay, c. 1918. *Courtesy of Louise Linkins Seely.*

Figure 29: Louise's brothers, Kent and Bill Linkins, out in a canoe at Arundel-on-the-Bay. c. 1925. *Courtesy of Louise Linkins Seely.*

Figure 30: Louise and her brother Bill in front of the bulkhead on a sandy beach at Arundel-on-the-Bay in 1918. *Courtesy of Louise Linkins Seely.*

Figure 31: Dorothy Biggins and Louise at Arundel-on-the-Bay, c. 1922. ***Courtesy of Louise Linkins Seely.***

Figure 32: Louise and her brother Kent on a swing at Arundel-on-the-Bay, c. 1922. ***Courtesy of Louise Linkins Seely.***

The Van Sant Family

One of Louise's playmates at the Bay was Jack Van Sant. Born in 1917, Jack was a son of Frank Van Sant, an attorney who was Secretary of the commissioners throughout the 1930s and into the 1940s. As such he played a crucial role coordinating meetings and decision making for the community, then dominated by two groups owning a significant number of lots.

Figure 33: Jack Van Sant at Arundel-on-the-Bay, c. 1922. He donated the papers of his father, Frank Van Sant, to the then Columbia Historical Society in 1988. ***Courtesy of Louise Linkins Seely.***

Frank Van Sant was born in the District in 1877. He served in the U.S. Navy in the Spanish-American War, after which he became a lawyer and practiced from offices in the Southern Building at 15th & H Streets NW in Washington, D.C. Van Sant and a neighbor at Arundel-on-the-Bay, Michael I. Weller, served together on the Committee of Public Comfort of the Inaugural Committee following the election of President Woodrow Wilson.

The Van Sant cottage at Arundel-on-the-Bay was on Magnolia Avenue west of Narragansett Avenue. An active member of the Chain and Sprocket bicycle club, Frank Van Sant enjoyed cycling activities in and around Annapolis and Arundel-on-the-Bay. The family, including his wife Eva and their two sons, John and Frank Jr., lived at 3925 Livingston St. NW in the District.[46]

The Chain and Sprocket Club

Recalling the homes of families like the Galloways, the Wellers, and the Bosleys who lived along the shore north of the community pavilion on Chestnut Avenue. Louise Linkins Seely also remembered that the clubhouse of the Chain and Sprocket Club was located in that same stretch of Chesapeake Avenue. President Smith donated his Geneva Cottage for the purpose. One of the original bicycle clubs in Washington, Chain and Sprocket was founded at Western High School in the District in 1895. Reorganized in 1897, the club was then limited to 25 members. By 1901, the club had become a social fraternity and held social events for its members at Arundel-on-the-Bay, who included Frank Jones, Joseph Milans, Frank Weller, Bill Linkins, and Frank Van Sant.[47] A number of Arundel-on-the-Bay young people were members of the Junior Chain and Sprocket and of its female Junior Auxiliary.[48]

Figure 34: In addition to this March, the Chain and Sprocket Club also had two Club Yells. The lyrics of one began "Chick-a-dee-pop." ***Historical Society of Washington, D.C.***

Figure 37: The menus for the weekend meeting of the Chain and Sprocket Club held at Arundel-on-the-Bay in 1911. ***Historical Society of Washington, D.C.***

Figure 35: Frank Van Sant, wearing the Chain and Sprocket Club beanie and his trademark turtleneck shirt, sketched in 1912. He was a commissioner of Arundel-on-the-Bay. ***From the Washington Daily News, November 30, 1956, p.47. Historical Society of Washington, D.C.***

Figure 36: The Chain and Sprocket Club in 1922. Frank Van Sant is shown in the middle of those seated; Bill Linkins, with a hat on, is seated to his left. ***Courtesy of Louise Linkins Seely.***

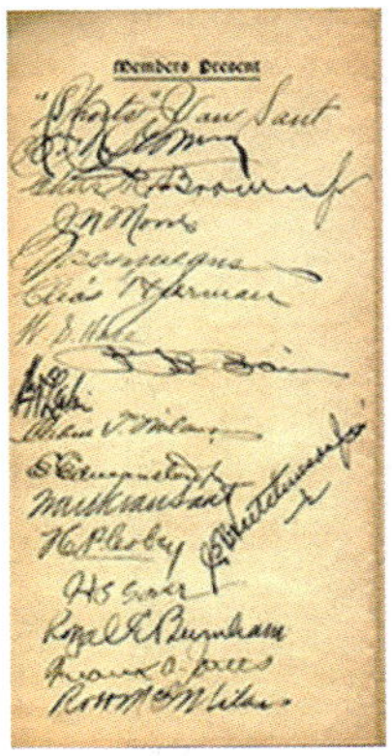

Figure 38: Those in attendance signed the back of this copy of the program and included William Linkins and "Shorts" Van Sant. Frank Van Sant was 5'4" tall.

Conditions in 1914

The shoreline road from Arundel-on-the-Bay to Bay Ridge, shown angling off to the right at the top of Figure 9, was closed to automobiles during the summer of 1914, although it was deemed safe for horse and buggy travel. Community automobiles traveling to and from Annapolis were now required to use the inland network of shell-covered farm roads. An example of the rudimentary condition of area roads at the time is shown below.

The *Baltimore Sun* reported on the election of town commissioners in the summer of 1914. In an article entitled "Women Vote Tomorrow," the paper noted that the community was unique in giving women the right to vote. The story featured the oldest woman voter in the town, Mrs. Nicholas Biddle Van Zandt, widow of the former Navy captain. Jane Van Zandt, 88 years of age, no relation to the Van Sant family described above, had lived in Arundel-on-the-Bay for more than 20 years.[49] (See Chapter Two for more about the Van Zandt family.)

Figure 39: West Street at Route 2 looking toward Annapolis in 1915. a route residents of Arundel-on-the-Bay would have used to get to the community. ***The Annapolis I Remember Collection, Maryland State Archives.***

The July 25, 1914 edition of the *Baltimore Sun* made clear the challenges of this shoreline community, reporting that Arundel-on-the-Bay was contemplating constructing a bulkhead and moving the boardwalk farther inshore because the beach was washing away.

A 1914 press reference to Arundel-on-the-Bay was among many referring to activities at Highland Beach as being located at Arundel-on-the-Bay in the early years. For the purposes of real estate tax assessment, Highland Beach was the recognized name of the community founded in 1893. The confusion most likely originated from the way mail was addressed, as mail for the community was received at Arundel-on-the-Bay until the opening of the Highland Beach post office in 1917. The *Washington Bee* noted on September 15, 1917, "Highland Beach formerly known as Arundel-on-the-Bay – has now a well-established Post Office and takes the name its founders gave it." Raymond Langston, co-author of the 2008 Highland Beach history, adds that the whole area, including Highland Beach and south to Thomas Point, was commonly referred to as Arundel-on-the-Bay. It was not until Highland Beach received its town charter in 1922 that references became more specific and accurate, he said.[50]

Life continued to be pleasant at the town, although corporate financial matters were under scrutiny in 1914. In a statement of May 5, President Smith acknowledged that not all of the 2,000 authorized shares of the Chesapeake & Columbia Investment Co. designed to raise $100,000 had been issued. The seven founders, or "originators" as they were called, had received 200 shares each at no cost beyond their initial payment of $2 per share into the company. Fifty shares had been sold to outsiders at the $50 set share price. The commissioners agreed at the annual business meeting of 1914 that they needed to raise some cash, and on Sept. 10, letters were sent to each share owner, requesting prompt payment of an assessment of 25 cents per share. "These funds are absolutely required to pay the annual tax levy against the property and other obligations already due," the letter read.[51]

The Roar of a Hurricane in 1915

The *Annapolis Evening Capital* described a destructive storm which hit the Annapolis area, including Arundel-on-the-Bay, in early August. Although designated a tropical storm, reports suggest that winds reached hurricane force, and it was viewed at the time as the worst storm to strike the city within memory. In Annapolis, houses lost their roofs, walls collapsed, power lines went down, boats were smashed, and graves at St. Anne's Church were ripped open by the roots of falling trees. The highest tides in more than 50 years flooded Eastport and downtown Market Square in Annapolis and nearby streets. The paper reported that every pier at Arundel-on-the-Bay was destroyed. In addition, the bridge over the Cavanaugh Canal at Oyster Creek was washed out.[52]

Paradise Lost in 1916

Based on public records and newspaper articles, we can estimate that in the spring of 1916, there were at least 33 cottages in the Town of Arundel-on-the-Bay. On April 18, 1916, a fire swept through the community, leaving only six cottages standing. The remainder, furnished and unfurnished, lay in smoking ruins, along with the associated boathouses and piers and a community boardwalk and clubhouse. The *Baltimore Sun* detailed the breakout and spread of the blaze:

> *"Arundel-on-the-Bay, a small summer resort, nine miles below Annapolis, on the Chesapeake Bay, was almost completely wiped out by fire this afternoon."*
> *Baltimore Sun, April 18, 1916.*

> Arundel-on-the-Bay, a small summer resort, nine miles below Annapolis, on the Chesapeake Bay, was almost completely wiped out by fire this afternoon.
>
> The blaze, which started in the brush back of the resort, was swept by a 30 mile-an-hour gale from the northwest and rapidly licked toward the 30 odd cottages on the bluff above the beach. The fire raged throughout the afternoon and tonight only half a dozen of the dwellings remain, the others being a mass of smoldering embers.
>
> Some of the cottages were completely furnished, others only partially. In a few instances the furniture was saved. The loss is estimated at between $25,000 and $30,000, and it is understood that only a few of the dwellings were insured.
>
> The brush fire started early this morning on a small farm half a mile distant from the resort, but when the high wind sprang up the flames began to spread rapidly and soon got beyond control. Residents of the neighborhood put up a determined fight,

> but it was soon realized that their efforts would be of no avail. Then a call was sent to the city volunteer fire department, which caused Capt. Philip E. Porter, fire marshal, to dispatch the automobile engine and a combination hose and chemical truck.
>
> The fire laddies made a quick trip over the county roads, and although greatly handicapped in their work by local conditions managed to save several of the cottages. The boardwalk, pier and clubhouse, upon which several hundred dollars was being expended for improvements, were among the property destroyed.
>
> Arundel-on-the-Bay is colonized almost exclusively by Baltimore and Washington people who own cottages there and who would spend the summers from June to September there. It is the only place in the State where women have the right of suffrage, the Mayor and Board of Commissioners being elected every summer and all of the women cottagers having a vote as well as the men.
>
> Thomas W. Smith, a merchant of Washington, has filled the office of Mayor for a number of years. He is one of the largest property owners at the resort, and practically all of his cottages were destroyed in the conflagration today.
>
> The Gloucester cottage, owned by Mrs. Abbott, widow of William M. Abbott, editor of the Evening Capital, the daily paper of Annapolis, was among the first to fall a prey to the flames.[53]

The *Annapolis Evening Capital* reported that three cottages owned by Thomas Smith, including his Geneva and Concord Cottages, were destroyed and a fourth was heavily damaged. The *Capital* also reported as destroyed Peter J. McIntyre's Rose Cottage; the cottages of Mrs. Michael I. Weller, Mrs. Annie Tallerday, Mrs. Emma Abbott Gage, and Louis Boeckstyne; T. Lincoln Townsend's Lincolnhurst, Dr. George Heinecke's Cedar Cottage, Arthur Lee Bosley's Deer Lodge, Edwin C. Graham's Nedanna, and two cottages owned by Dr. J. T. Hopkins of Washington, D.C. The newly-constructed Wahoo Club, which had just been furnished the Friday before, also burned.[54]

Mayor Smith and his colleagues moved immediately to act in the face of this loss. As reported on May 3, 1916, in the *Washington Herald*, the commissioners met at the Ebbitt House Hotel in Washington, D.C., to discuss rebuilding the community, and a subsequent meeting had been scheduled. In July, the *Evening Star* reported that two of 15 cottages destroyed by the fire had been rebuilt and four were in the course of construction. Richard Galloway purchased the Boeckstyne property and completed a "handsome bungalow," and Mrs. Michael Weller purchased the Oulahan lot which was adjacent to her cottage, the article noted.[55]

Louise Linkins Seely, who had recently turned three when the fire broke out, recalls being told that sailors from a U.S. Navy ship anchored at Tolley Point came ashore to help fight the fire, and put out the fire which had started on the roof of her family cottage, formerly the Chelsea Cottage but now known as the Linkins Cottage. In her opinion, the newspaper reports of the extent of the fire were exaggerated.

After the Fire at the Town of Arundel-on-the-Bay

In its report on the 1917 election of town commissioners, the *Baltimore Sun* reported on the community's unique display of women's suffrage, noting, "(the fact that) women may vote there is due entirely to the property-ownership qualifications and seldom, if ever, in the history of the place has it transpired that all of the women taxpayers did not cast their ballots."[56]

Voting took place at the pavilion on the pier and was followed by fireworks. Thomas Smith, Nicholas Shea, Edwin Graham, Charles McCarthy, William Linkins, and Lincoln Townsend were elected as commissioners. Edwin Graham agreed to serve as president during the illness of Thomas Smith. It was reported in the *Star* that the Grahams were occupying their new cottage.[57] Townsend was elected treasurer, and McCarthy secretary. The focus of the commissioners' attention after the election was to be on achieving improvements to the roads between Arundel-on-the-Bay and Annapolis.

Thomas Lincoln Townsend, vice president of the National Electric Supply Co., was active in the Republican Party affairs, serving as a delegate to the Republican National Convention in 1928, as vice-president and treasurer of Republican State Clubs, and as president of the President Harding and Coolidge Club. He was a vice-president of the Keystone State Society and treasurer of the City Club of which fellow Arundelites Edwin Graham was president and Charles Semmes vice-president. Born in Pennsylvania in 1865, Townsend died suddenly in 1929 at his home in the District, 4601 17 St. NW.[58]

Figure 40: Elected a commissioner of Arundel – on-the-Bay in 1917, T. Lincoln Townsend, vice-president of the National Electric Supply Co. and active in the Republican Party, was among those who would successfully urge the first use of electric lights on the national Christmas tree lit by President Calvin Coolidge in 1924. *Library of Congress.*

Impact of the Fire of 1916 on Arundel-on-the-Bay
Partial Listing

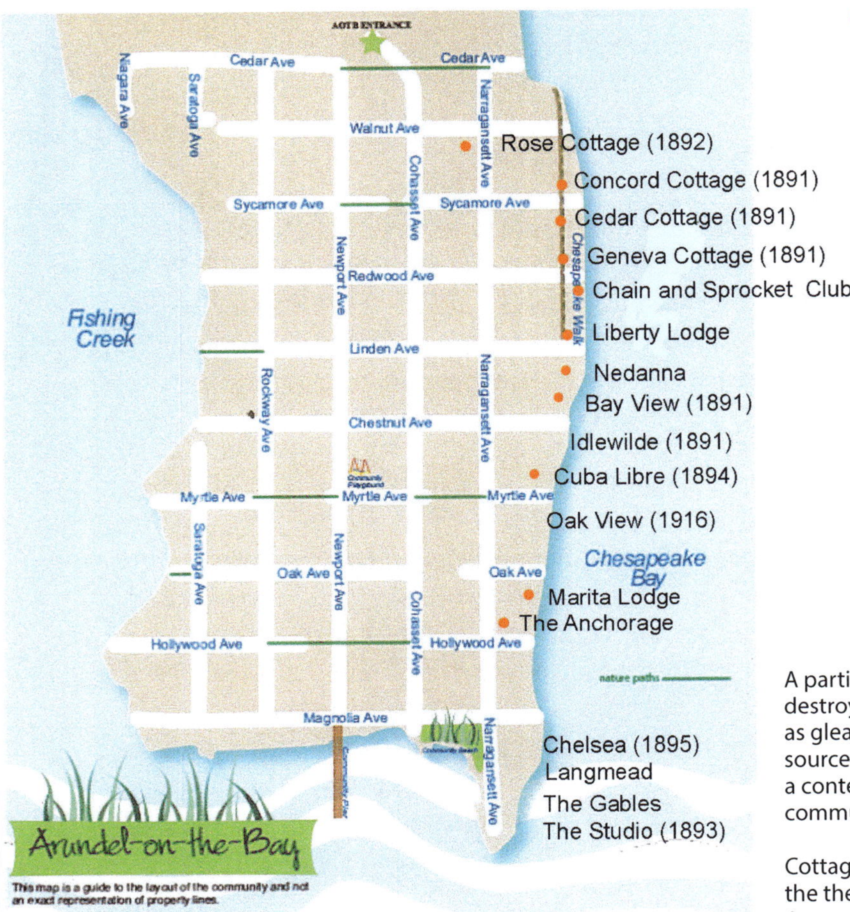

● Cottages Destroyed

Named Cottages Locations unknown:

Umph's Villa
● Gloucester Cottage
Magnolia Cottage
Lucie's Cottage
Belmont Cottage
● Lincolnhurst
Two View Cottage
Chicago Cottage

A partial list of cottages destroyed by the fire of 1916, as gleaned from a variety of sources and superimposed on a contemporary map of the community.

Cottages along the Bay were on the then existing Chesapeake Avenue.

Arundel-on-the-Bay co-founder Nicholas H. Shea, vice-president of the Federal National Bank, died in September 1917. *The Evening Star* reported that he had been a grocer for 50 years in the District of Columbia and left an estate valued at $560,000. His daughters Margaret, Rose, Helen, and Bernice inherited Idle Wild Cottage.[59]

During the summer season of 1918, according to reports in the *Annapolis Evening Capital*, the family of Walter W. Waltermeyer of Forest Park in Baltimore was "making extensive improvements to the breakwater in front of their home" and George Galloway "who owns one of the handsomest and most attractive homes at Arundel-on-the-Bay" also had a launch for fishing parties. The Galloway cottage was on the site of one of the original cottages at Arundel-on-the-Bay, that built for founder William Rannells, the present 1356 Redwood Avenue. The Waltermeyer cottage, also on the site of an original cottage built for a founder, Timothy Keleher, is today's 3440 Chesapeake Walk. The *Capital* reported:

Figure 41: 4601 17th St. NW, the home of Arundel-on-the-Bay Commissioner T. Lincoln Townsend in Washington D.C.'s Crestwood neighborhood. *Google Earth.*

> ...Galloway...arrived here today with a party of friends for a week-end fishing trip on the bay.
>
> The party will make their headquarters at the Galloway cottage during the trip, using Mr. Galloway's fine launch to go on the fishing trip, during the several days' outing. Fish are said to be biting off Tolley's Reef and good catches are being made.[60]

In 1918, Edwin Graham took over the duties of president of the town due to the declining health of Thomas W. Smith. The *Capital* reported that Smith motored for a two week stay in October, accompanied by a nurse and an attendant.[61] Elected town commissioners that summer were John Walter Galloway and George Saulsbury of Baltimore and Edwin C. Graham, William H. Linkins, Charles A. McCarthy, and William T. Shea of Washington, D.C., a son of founder Nicholas Shea. The bailiff was Elijah Wells. (See Chapter Five for a profile of this interesting man.)

Rita Weller, widow of Michael I. Weller, chair of the Executive Committee of the Women's Civic League of Arundel-on-the-Bay, gave a party for 25 servicemen on September 8. The event was held in the pavilion. The *Capital* reported:

> A spread will be provided...by other ladies whose summer homes are there, and who linger these beautiful September days.
>
> The menu will consist of ham, bread and butter, Maryland biscuits, salads, pickle, jellies, hot coffee, ice cream and cake.
>
> There will be piano and Victrola music, and patriotic songs will be sung.
>
> Bathing and boating will afford diversion for the men.[62]

The homes of Lincoln Townsend, Edwin Graham, and the Colberts were broken into in late December 1918; the incidents were reported in the *Evening Capital* in an article entitled "AOTB Depredations Have Mysterious Motives."[63] Nothing was missing from any of the cottages, whose owners were notified of the break-ins by the caretaker, Mrs. Tyler. The Townsend and Colbert cottages were entered through windows left open; the Graham cottage was broken into through glass at the back door and ransacked:

> ...buffet drawers and those of dressers being left open and contents scattered about, but nothing is missing. As the cottage was well supplied with all kinds of canned goods, preserves, jams, etc. and none was taken the object of the intruder cannot be surmised. At first it was thought that some fisherman or oysterman sought a night's lodging at these cottages, but beds were undisturbed and everything left intact.

The death of Thomas W. Smith, a founder and long-time president of the town commissioners, brings to an end this story of the early era of life at Arundel-on-the-Bay. Smith died on March 2, 1919, at his home at 1867 Columbia Rd. NW in the District of

Columbia. The cause of death was Bright's disease, a chronic disorder of kidney function; the newspapers noted that he had been in poor health for several years. He was survived by wife Catherine and daughters Carrie, Mable, Maude, and Esther. His son, Linville Smith, died in 1918.

Obituaries in the *Evening Star, Washington Herald,* and the *Baltimore Sun* praised Smith as a self-made man, active and many-faceted. The *Baltimore Sun* wrote, "He was a great believer in the future of Washington D.C. and an optimist in all things as they concerned the city which he loved."[64] We can surmise that his sentiments toward Arundel-on-the-Bay were the same.

Arundel-on-the-Bay Bankrupt?

In late 1919, George E. Emmons, an accountant who handled tax filings for the Chesapeake and Columbia Investment Co., undertook a review of its financial standing. A list of owners of the 1,487 shares of capital stock was prepared and their payments of the periodic assessments on those shares made in 1904, 1908, and again in 1914 were ascertained. A dividend given in August 1892 and land sales block by lot were scrutinized as were company records and treasurer's reports of cash accounts, disbursements, assets, and liabilities. This was to determine the size of any dividends to be made to stockholders upon the sale of the company's land. Emmons concluded "it is important for the Company to reorganize its affairs at once."[65] As only William Hazen remained of the original founders, Emmons recommended that the presidency of the investment company devolve to him, with William T. Shea, son of founder Nicholas Shea, who had been appointed by Smith to fill the role of Secretary and Treasurer in April of 1918, continuing in that capacity.

Endnotes

1. The votes were reported in the February 23 and 26, 1898 editions of the *Baltimore Sun*. The legislation is codified as Chapter 349.

2. *The Washington Post*, August 26, 1898.

3. Maryland State Archives C35-2, Anne Arundel County District #2, Board of County Commissioners Assessment Record 1876-1896. The Otterback partnership purchased lots G&H on block 68, in 1891. The Arundel Fish and Gaming Club located on block 62, lot H.

4. Emmons, George E., "Statement of the Chesapeake and Columbia Investment Company," c. 1919, p. 20.

5. *The Baltimore Sun*, April 13, 1898.

6. Emmons report, p.19.

7. The Galloway residential cottage was on the lot owned by founder William Rannells, now 1356 Redwood Avenue.

8. The Galloway purchase of July 13, 1918 was Blocks 62, 63, and 68. The Otterback partnership clubhouse was in Block 68 and the Arundel Fish and Gun Club clubhouse was in Block 62. Blocks 62 and 63 are between Myrtle and Hollywood Avenues on the north-south and Rockaway and Saratoga Avenues on the east-west. Block 68 is between Oak and Hollywood Avenues and Saratoga Avenue and Fishing Creek.

9. 1900 U.S. Federal Census.

10. *Washington Evening Star*, June 29, 1899, p. 11.

11. *Washington Times*, August 7, 1908.

12. *Washington Evening Star*, March 27, 1910.

13. Laws of Maryland, Chapter 125, An Act to amend an Act, entitled an "Act to incorporate the Town of Arundel-on-the-Bay, in Anne Arundel County Maryland, approved April 8, 1898," approved on March 29, 1900. 4p.

14. Greenberg, David, *The Republic of Spin*, W.W. Norton & Co. Inc. 2016.

15. In addition, Wesley Taylor, William D. Jones, and Eugene Butler were paid for repair of walks, bridges, wells, and hauling at Arundel-on-the-Bay.

16. July 15, 1900.

17. Kiplinger Library, The Historical Society of Washington, D.C., MS 401 Arundel-on-the-Bay, Maryland, Records, 1898-1938, Minutes of the town commissioners, June 1, 1901.

18. *The Baltimore Sun*, July 21, 1912. Bosley and several other partners including his father, Grafton Bosley, a farmer with valuable real estate, formed the Frederick Light and Power Co. and won a 30 year franchise to bring electricity to the city. In 1901, he incorporated the Cumberland Electric Light and Power Co. to serve power there. After his untimely death in 1917 at the age of fifty-two, the family lived at the Preston in Baltimore. Also consulted, 1880 and 1900 Census of the United States and references from the *Frederick Post*.

19. McWilliams, Jane Wilson & Carol Cushard Patterson, *Bay Ridge on the Chesapeake: An Illustrated History*, Annapolis MD: Brighton Editions, 1986, p.100.

20. Others persons paid for work at Arundel-on-the-Bay in 1903 were James Crowdy and Robert H. Parker.

21. *The Evening Star*, April 5, 1906.

22. John Booth and Joseph H. Figg were paid for work at Arundel-on-the-Bay in 1906.

23. July 28, 1907.

24. Johnson was born in West Virginia; his father, Sylvanus Elihu Johnson, also was a journalist. Johnson began his career as a reporter, living at 1512 Q Street NW in 1888. He married Louise Covert (1864-1906) in 1891. In April 1908, Johnson married Mrs. Mary Ann Hagmann of New Orleans and moved from an apartment in The Victoria to 3427 34th Place, N.W. in the Cleveland Park neighborhood where they lived with a cook and a butler. They lived in Rockville, Md. according to the U.S. Federal Census of 1930.

25. *The Baltimore American*, August 28, 1907.

26. *The Baltimore Sun*, August 5, 1908.

27. Ibid, September 2, 1908.

28. Among those paid for work at Arundel-on-the-Bay in 1908 were Thomas Coats, Moses Gross, Charlie Arthur, G. L. Smith, and Joseph Gross for work on the pier and a small wharf.

29. *The Baltimore Sun*, May 1, 1909.

30. *The Evening Star*, June 27, 1909.

31. August 28, 1909.

32. Specifications, August 10, 1909.

33. Others paid for work at Arundel-on-the-Bay in 1910 included Charles Ritter, Henry Meyers, Joseph H. Wheeler of the Eastport Coal Co., W. F. Childs, Noble Carroll, and E. J. Rawlings.

34. *The Washington Herald*, July 30, 1911.

35. *Ibid*, July 16, 1911.

36. Ancestry.com, census reports, and city directories were used to prepare this summary.

37. *The Washington Times*, December 21, 1911, p.20.

38. July 25, 1912.

39. *The Baltimore Sun*, August 23, 1908.

40. August 28, 1909.

41. *The Washington Herald*, July 27, 1913, second news section, p.2.

42. *Ibid*, August 10, 1913, p.3.

43. *The Washington Herald*, September 7, 1913.

44. *Ibid*, Sept. 14, 1913.

45. Payson bought two parcels totaling 2-1/4 acres of land in Middletown, RI according to the *Evening Star*, July 9, 1904, p. 13. He died in October 1909. The funeral was held at his home, 1229 Massachusetts Ave. NW in Washington D.C., according to an account in the *Washington Times*, October 6, 1909, p.2.

46. Frank Van Sant was born on October 16, 1877. Still single in 1900, Van Sant lived in his father Louis Van Sant's home at 2316 M Street NW. He married in 1915. At the 1920 census, the family was living at 2411 M Street NW. A son, Frank Randolph Van Sant born in 1926, died in 2005. The 1930 census lists the Van Sants as resident at 3925 Livingston St. NW in the District. Frank Van Sant was a short man standing 5'4" tall and weighing 130 lbs. at his registration for the draft in 1942. All born after April 28, 1877 were required to register. Frank Van Sant died in 1966. He was buried at Arlington National Cemetery; his wife Eva died in 1969. His son, Ltc. John Edward (Jack) Van Sant served in WWII and the Korean War. He was in the U.S. Army from 1940 to 1960. He died in 2003 and is buried at Arlington National Cemetery.

47. Historical Society of Washington D.C.: Special Collections Finding Aid, Kiplinger Library. The Chain and Sprocket Club disbanded in 1963 and its records were donated to the Society by John E. Van Sant in 1985-86.

48. Members of the Junior Club were John and Frank R. Van Sant Jr., William H. Linkins Jr., and the Wellers: George Harlow, Francis Harlow, and Richard Hartman Weller. Sallie Rita Weller was a member of the Juniors Auxiliary, as was Louise Linkins Bezdek Seely. The Historical Society of Washington, D.C., MS 365, Chain and Sprocket Club folders 1-8.

49. *The Baltimore Sun*, July 24, 1914.

50. Interview, June 11, 2016.

51. The documents are among the papers at the Historical Society of Washington. Smith's statement was dated May 8, 1914. That of the secretary, elected at the rate of $20 per year, was dated August 5, 1914.

52. *The Annapolis Evening Capital*, August 3, 1955.

53. *The Baltimore Sun*, April 18, 1916.

54. *The Annapolis Evening Capital*, April 18, 1916. *The Washington Times* of April 19, 1916, on p.11, reported that 15 cottages were lost.

55. *The Evening Star*, July 9, 1916.

56. *The Baltimore Sun*, July 29, 1917.

57. *Evening Star*, July 15, 1917.

58. D.C. Select Deaths and Burials 1840-1964.

59. *The Evening Star,* September 25, 1917.

60. *Ibid,* September 20, 1918.

61. *The Evening Capital*, October 31, 1918.

62. *Ibid,* September 7, 1918, p.4.

63. *The Evening Capital*, December 31, 1918.

64. *The Baltimore Sun*, March 3, 1919; *Evening Star,* March 2, 1919; and the *Washington Herald*, March 3, 1919. The details of Smith's will, reported in the *Washington Times* of March 7, 1919, indicated that his wife was left a residence at 2334 Columbia Rd. NW. The *Washington Herald* of March 7 and 8, 1919, reported the will included a substantial donation to the Casualty Hospital and bequests to family.

Town commissioners elected to serve in the summer of 1919 were: John Walter Galloway and George Saulisbury of Baltimore, Edwin C. Graham, William H. Linkins, Charles A. McCarthy, William Shea, and Frank R. Weller of Washington, D.C.

65. Emmons, George E. "Statement of The Chesapeake and Columbia Investment Company" p. 23.

Acknowledgments for Chapters 2 and 4

Special credit is given the photograph collection of Louise Linkins Bezdek Seeley, and her memories which enliven Chapters 2 and 4.

Carol Cushard Patterson, who researched the same time period for the landmark study of Bay Ridge, spent a morning with the history group, sharing her knowledge, enthusiasm, and suggestions. We credit our desire to leave no stone unturned to her advice to be persistent. Her colleague, Jane McWilliams, published work was invaluable as was her introduction to Thomas Carroll Worthington.

Each member of the history group contributed comments on this work. Most special assistance was given by Bill Semenuk in research and by Bob Meissner and Philip Allen in writing.

Arundel-on-the-Bay residents' interest spurred the project on. The role of Lori Strum and Erich Keyes in making personal contributions especially stands out.

Finally, thanks are due to Jessica Smith, Research Services Librarian, Kiplinger Library, Historical Society of Washington, D.C. and Megan C. Craynon, Deputy Director, Special Collections, Maryland State Archives who provided great assistance in making information and images from their collections available.

Wintering Swans, the Old Community Pier, and Thomas Point. *Photograph by Marc Grigsby.*

Chapter Five

Arundel-on-the-Bay Between the World Wars

Karen Neale

Between 1919 and 1949, residents of the Town of Arundel-on-the-Bay pursued a lifestyle between the wars that focused on entertaining, swimming, boating, fishing and crabbing. This somewhat laid-back style of living contrasted strongly with the difficult times the nation as a whole suffered following World War I, during the Great Depression and through World War II. This chapter tells some of the community's story in that period.

Three residents of Arundel-on-the-Bay were fortunate in recent years to locate and speak with more than a dozen former residents and visitors to the community in the first half of the 20th century. These included Jim Bezdek, Hugo Bezdek, Florence Clark (since deceased), Sandy Clark, Fred Garrett, William Lofton (since deceased), Ned Madill, Mike Mullen, Pamela Sue Norris, Ruby Kendros Pelecanos, Bill Schumacher, Louise Linkins Bezdek Seely (since deceased), George Tyler III, and Thomas Worthington (since deceased), who helped bring this and other chapters to life.

Figure 1: William Linkins and son Kent under a gas lamp near the south end of Narragansett Avenue on the Bay front, with the Linkins boat *Dorothy Louise* tied to the Linkins pier in the background in early 1920s. *Photo courtesy of Bezdek Linkins collection.*

The 1920s: The Lay of the Land

In the early 1920s, Arundel-on-the-Bay still was lush, green forest, interspersed with occasional houses and ancillary structures, such as wells, chicken houses and horse stables. Oyster shells covered the dirt on Arundel-on-the-Bay Road that dead-ended at the entrance to the small town, and the avenues and lanes leading to each house. Oil lamps lined Chesapeake Avenue along the Chesapeake Bay side of the community, but illuminated the street only during the summer months when the town's commissioners hired someone to maintain them.

Houses at the north and south ends of the Arundel-on-the-Bay peninsula were almost at sea level, while the homes midway on the Bay side had steps leading down brush-and grass-covered cliffs to a pristine, sandy beach along the clear water's edge. No matter where you stood, you had a majestic view of the Chesapeake Bay. The Fishing Creek side of the peninsula also offered sandy beach, with shallow water for easy crabbing, and easy access for boat launches.

During the 1920s, retired Navy CAPT Elijah Wells was known for "keeping an eye on things" during the off-season. He lived in a cottage in Block 67, Lot A (Saratoga and Magnolia Avenues) overlooking Fishing Creek with his dog and cat for company. In an interview with the *Baltimore Sun*, Wells said that the other executives are all commuters they live "out of town." He explained:

> They come down in the summer, though, set up their shore cottages and dispose of all important business that has piled up during the winter. William H. Linkins of Washington is the Mayor, and is assisted by the Board of Commissioners, all of whom live in Washington, except one who lives in Annapolis, about five miles away. But according to census statistics, these officials are not residents of the town. [1]

Wells was known as the sole year-round inhabitant even though, according to the 1920 census, other year-round residents were the George N. Tyler Sr. family that included eleven children. Somehow the Tylers were not counted in the 1930 census.

Elijah Wells, Town's Lone Resident, Has No Trouble With Municipal Problems

ELIJAH WELLS

Veteran Seaman Holds Post Of Sheriff, Fire Chief And Caretaker At Arundel-On-The-Bay

Figure 2: Retired CAPT Elijah Wells, sole year-round resident of Arundel-on-the-Bay for many years, was featured in the *Baltimore Sun* on October 17, 1930. *Permission from the Baltimore Sun.*

Summertime signaled the arrival of horse carriages, Ford Model Ts, and other early cars pulling alongside Arundel-on-the-Bay houses, bringing residents and visiting family members and friends from up and down the East Coast. Residents added porches onto existing homes for greater outdoor comfort. Social comings-and-goings, the activities of the town's board of commissioners, and highlights of recreational and cultural events were reported in newspaper articles and advertisements. These accounts, along with U.S. census records, deeds, phone directories, historical and photo collections and personal memoirs helped create a collage of life in Arundel-on-the-Bay between the World Wars.

The summer population must have been substantial. Phillip Booth of Eastport in Annapolis (son of Julia Booth, whose obituary in the *Annapolis Evening Capital* on January 9, 1919 said, "she belonged to the old race of colored people.") kept a store in Arundel-on-the-Bay. He also engaged in hauling freight between there and Annapolis.[2]

Figure 3: New porches being built onto the Lewis Payson house at Chesapeake and Magnolia Avenues in 1922. *Photo courtesy of Bezdek Linkins collection.*

The former Booth family home that Mr. Booth built still stands at 606 Second St. in Eastport.[3]

Besides supplies for everyday living, Arundel-on-the-Bay residents required a variety of goods and services for entertaining. The *Washington Herald* on August 6, 1922, reported that the Washington Board of Trade's Membership Committee held its first outing at the summer home of Mr. and Mrs. Francis R. Weller. More than 40 committee members attended, and the gathering included boating, swimming and fishing.[4]

Recollections of Louise Linkins Bezdek Seely

Figure 4: Louise Linkins Bezdek Seely at age 100, in Spring 2013. *Photo by Bill Semenuk.*

The most senior of those who provided memoirs is Louise Linkins Bezdek Seely, introduced in Chapter 4.

Beginning in 1914, Louise spent every summer at her family home at Arundel-on-the-Bay throughout her enrollment at George Washington University, and after her marriage in 1934 when she brought her two sons, Hugo and Jim Bezdek, to spend summers. In numerous accounts, Louise recalled people and events in the community through her last stay in 1971.

Louise also recollected African American families who enhanced the daily lives of the summer residents, and John Wesley Harris, generally known as "Wes," was the head of one of those families. Mr. Harris worked as a handyman for Louise's father, and Louise recalled that, among other tasks, he built a baby carriage for her, constructed the family pier, and drove the Harris family's trash wagon. Louise reminisced that her son Hugo "spent many happy hours on the trash wagon flies and all!"

Although Wes did not live at Arundel-on-the-Bay, Louise said everyone knew him, and she even remembered his family's nicknames. The 1920 census lists the family as John, 40, his wife Lulla, 34, and children: John W., 19; Matilda, 18; Theodore C., 13; George W., 12; William J., 9; Luther, 4; and Arthur, 2. The 1940 census indicates that John and his wife lived on Annapolis Neck Road in Eastport.

Figure 5: Louise Linkins Bezdek with son Hugo Bezdek and Luther Harris in the background at Arundel-on-the-Bay in 1938. *Photo courtesy of Bezdek Linkins collection.*

Louise also talked about the George N. Tyler Sr. family. The Tyler children, based upon census data, were born between approximately 1896 and 1916. They are listed as John L., Mary, George N. Jr., Albert A., Bertha B., Walter J., Thomas W., William C., Jessie C., Philip C., and Marjorie A.[5]

Louise recalled about the Tylers:

> Oystering was the family business, all of them (the sons) helped their pop, and

Figure 6: Louise Linkins and Bill Linkins on the boat *Dorothy Louise* in 1922, helping John "Wes" Harris set pilings for their family's pier. ***Photo courtesy of Bezdek Linkins collection.***

occasionally with fishing and other work. Tommy Tyler built his house in 1939 near where his father George used to tie the bugeye that was his oyster boat, along the low-lying shore of Fishing Creek nearest the corner of Rockaway and Chestnut avenues. Pop Tyler also ran freight and fishing parties. Before my dad got his boat, I vaguely remember going on one [fishing party] and my father telling me to watch out for the

Figure 7: John "Wes" Harris, Louise Linkins, Bill Linkins, and William J. Harris alongside the Linkins home, in early 1920s. Louise identified the cars as a Ford Model-T on the left and her father's Scripps-Booth on the right. ***Photo courtesy of Bezdek Linkins collection.***

Figure 8: George Tyler III during an interview in 2013. ***Photo by Karen Neale.***

'headache stick', meaning the boom, when tacking the bugeye. Walter was a good carpenter and got into building boats. His own was 42 feet long, called the *Sea Fox.*[6]

In the fall of 2013, George Tyler III, born in 1940 and namesake of George N. Tyler Jr., joined Karen Neale and Bill Semenuk for breakfast at the Main Ingredient restaurant of Annapolis. His grandfather, George Nelson Tyler 1st, was appointed Arundel-on-the-Bay caretaker in 1904. "Whole family was born down there!" George said, referring to Arundel-on-the-Bay. George spoke with special pride about his grandmother Annie, wife of George Tyler Sr., Mrs. Tyler was named postmaster of the town in July 1906. A rural carrier was named in August 1943.

Figure 9: Arundel-on-the-Bay resident John Frederick Warfield (1882-1957). ***Photo courtesy of Stephanie Reese.***

George said that as an adult he returned to Arundel-on-the-Bay often and stayed with his uncle, Walter [Tyler]. He explained that during the summer, family members would "make a living catching fish with a gill net, and get ducks and fish up to the Lexington Market in Baltimore." He added, "Uncle Walter held the licenses for the duck blinds; had to get permission from Uncle Walter in order to hunt."[7]

Eventually, Walter Tyler bought the entire block of Saratoga Avenue between Hollywood and Oak Avenues in Arundel-on-the-Bay from Carey Meredith and family of the Meredith Lumber Company. [8]

Figure 10: Arundel-on-the-Bay resident Isabel Josephine Edmonds Warfield. ***Photo courtesy of Stephanie Reese.***

Figure 11: The original cottage at 1362 Myrtle Ave. (Bay front) in 1926, after it was moved inland. ***Photo courtesy of Fred Garrett.***

Figure 12:. After final expansion in 1939, the Warfield house at 1362 Myrtle Ave. as viewed from Narragansett Ave. ***Photo courtesy of Fred Garrett.***

Over the years, Louise also remembered the house of John Warfield, an electrical contractor, and his wife Isabel that stood at 1362 Myrtle Ave. Originally, Commissioner Thomas Smith purchased the house in 1904. He later transferred it to his daughter Anita

Figure 13: Lynne Garrett and John Mullen at 1362 Myrtle Ave. in Arundel-on-the-Bay, about 1940. ***Photo courtesy of Fred Garrett.***

and George W. Philips as joint tenants in 1916.[9] In Louise's time, the house became known as the Philip's house. Originally located a reported 100 feet farther out in the Bay, the cottage was moved inland in the 1920s.

Warfield bought the property from Philips in 1939 and renovated it extensively. The extended Warfield family enjoyed it until 1954 when it was sold to Todd and Gladys Duncan. Warfield's company, now known as the Warfield and Sanford Elevator Company, is headquartered in Laurel, Maryland.

Warfield's grandsons Fred Garrett and Mike Mullen, who enjoyed many summers at Arundel-on-the-Bay, confessed that when their grandfather decided to sell the house in the early1950s they would remove the "For Sale" sign from the property Sunday evenings after their grandfather left for Washington and replace it before he returned the following Friday afternoon. It took Grandfather Warfield a while to discover why the property had not been sold.

More on property dealings in the community follows.

Governance, Real Estate, and the Investment Company's Bankruptcy

On July 31, 1922, the *Baltimore Sun* reported: "Arundel on the Bay, an incorporated township and summer resort on the Chesapeake Bay colonized chiefly by Baltimoreans and Washingtonians, held its annual election of Commissioners for the Town Council. There was no contest, and less than a score of votes were cast." The article indicated that in previous elections there had been excitement because the incorporated town was the only place in Maryland where women had the right of suffrage.

Elected commissioners were: Howard Bokee and George Saulsbury of Baltimore and Edwin Graham, William H. Linkins, Charles A. McCarthy, Philip M. Maley, and Frank R. Miller of Washington D.C.[10]

Life seemed to be normal in Arundel-on-the-Bay. Before the crash of 1929, real estate transactions were abounding south of Walnut Avenue. Typical advertisements of houses for sale or rent in the early 1920s were:

- "Cottage, furnished, 7 rooms and bath, garage, stable, poultry house, artesian well water."[11]
- "Furnished cottage, 7 rooms and bath; about 1 acre on waterfront; large shade trees; large assortment fruit; garage, stable, poultry house, etc. excellent artesian well water; immediate possession. Exceptional bargain."[12]
- "Bungalow at AOTB on the Chesapeake Bay; 11 rooms furnished, bath, double garage, beautiful view; sandy beach!"[13]

Figure 14: Displaying the day's catch were (l-r) Charles Linkins, his father George W. Linkins, Philip Maley, and William H. "Big Bill" Linkins, at Arundel-on-the-Bay in early 1920s. ***Photo courtesy of Bezdek Linkins collection.***

Many advertisements for furnished cottages or bungalows in the 1920s, however, included language such as "bargains for quick buyer," suggesting these might be difficult financial times for some. This turned out to be true, particularly for the original developers. The lots were not selling out. (See Chapter 4 for the 1919 review of the financial standing of the Chesapeake and Columbia Investment Company.)

On August 18, 1925, the authorities tacked a notice on the court house door for an auction of "Property was Known as Arundel on the Bay" that had been owned by the Chesapeake and Columbia Investment Company. According to the trustees' notice, the property to be auctioned was:

> All of the unsold portions of the tract of land located on the Chesapeake Bay [including Oyster Creek] and Fishing Creek . . . consisting of 252 acres of land which had been laid off in streets and avenues, blocks and lots, for building site purposes by the Chesapeake and Columbia Investment Company, the former owner of the property . . . . This property offers unusual opportunity for good investment, being one of the most attractive locations on and near the water left in Anne Arundel County. A large part of the property lies on Fishing Creek, a tributary of South River, and all of it is in full view of the Chesapeake Bay, and a large part of it is separated from the beach only by the houses fronting thereon.[14]

On July 23, 1926, the trustees for the defunct Chesapeake and Columbia Investment Company sold the unsold portions of their tract of land at Arundel-on-the-Bay for $32,750 to Carey L. Meredith and William G. Meredith, trading as the Meredith Lumber Company.[15] Carey Meredith owned a cottage at the southern tip of Narragansett Avenue on what was called "The Point."

Figure 15: Arundel-on-the-Bay. ***Revision Plat 492 (1927), Plat Book 9, p.25, Anne Arundel County Circuit Court.***

On March 18, 1926, Joshua F. Johnson, president of the J. F. Johnson Lumber Company, purchased on the company's behalf the Meredith Lumber Company.[16] Johnson Lumber still exists with locations in Millersville and Edgewater, Md. Subsequent real estate transactions between the Merediths and other buyers support the conclusion that the Merediths continued to own and operate the real estate portion of the Meredith Lumber Company. Furthermore, a May 1927 revised plat of Arundel-on-the-Bay – showing it bound by Fishing Cove, the Chesapeake Bay and Oyster Creek – was filed by Anne Arundel County surveyor J. Revell Carr on August 15, 1927 and listed the Meredith Lumber Co. as "Owners" of the unsold lots.[17]

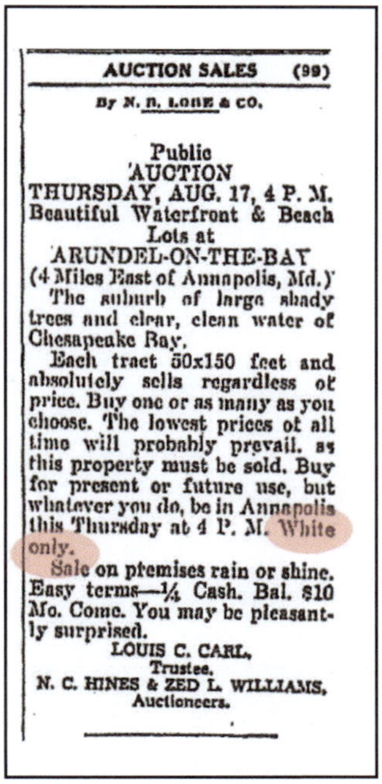

AUCTION SALES (99)

By N. B. LOBE & CO.

Public
AUCTION
THURSDAY, AUG. 17, 4 P. M.
Beautiful Waterfront & Beach
Lots at
ARUNDEL-ON-THE-BAY
(4 Miles East of Annapolis, Md.)

The suburb of large shady trees and clear, clean water of Chesapeake Bay.

Each tract 50x150 feet and absolutely sells regardless of price. Buy one or as many as you choose. The lowest prices of all time will probably prevail, as this property must be sold. Buy for present or future use, but whatever you do, be in Annapolis this Thursday at 4 P. M. White only.

Sale on premises rain or shine. Easy terms—¼ Cash. Bal. $10 Mo. Come. You may be pleasantly surprised.

LOUIS C. CARL,
Trustee.
N. C. HINES & ZED L. WILLIAMS,
Auctioneers.

Figure 16: "White only" notice of public auction of lots in the classified ads of the *Baltimore Sun* on August 15, 1939. *Permission from the Baltimore Sun.*

Two Different Communities Developed in Arundel-on-the-Bay

Interestingly, none of the chronicles that have surfaced regarding the period after World War I explained that there were two, almost separate communities living in the Town of Arundel-on-the-Bay. This incorporated resort town was intended for "whites only," as ads and auction notices advertised even through 1939.

Figure 17: Physician Austin Maurice Curtis was a summer resident of Arundel-on-the-Bay from the 1890's through the 1930's. *Geni.com.*

Yet summer residents who were African American owned property in the northeast section of the town. By 1894 the Chesapeake and Columbia Investment Company had sold lots to families of color in Arundel-on-the-Bay between Walnut and Cedar Avenues (Block 3): Alice J. Colbert on May 10, 1893; Laura A. Douglass on November 4, 1893; and, Mrs. M. E. Harrison on September 17, 1894, who also is believed to have been a person of color. (Mrs. Colbert and Mrs. Douglass were introduced in Chapter Two). The most well-known from a historic standpoint was Mrs. Douglass, the wife of Charles Douglass, whose father was the famous African American author and orator Frederick Douglass.[18] Records do not indicate any development of the property before Mrs. Douglass sold it in 1916 to Dr. Austin M. Curtis for $400.[19]

Figure 18: Swim party including Dr. William Garvin Lofton Jr. 2nd from left, and Dr. Merrill Hargro Curtis far right. All were standing near the Curtis and Lofton houses between Walnut and Cedar Avenues on Chesapeake Walk with the bulkhead and the Bay in the background, mid 1940's. *Photo courtesy of Carol McMahon, granddaughter of Dr. William G. Lofton Sr.*

Both Dr. Curtis and his wife Namahyoka Gertrude Sockum Curtis were distinguished in the field of medicine. Dr. Curtis was described as the youngest of a group of leaders at the turn of the century known as the "Big Four" of Negro medicine.[20] Born in Raleigh, N. C. in 1868, he graduated from Lincoln University in Pennsylvania in 1888. Dr. Curtis earned his medical degree from Northwestern University in Chicago, Ill. in 1891, the same year that he married Miss Sockum of Oakland, CA. He was the first Negro intern at

Provident Hospital in Chicago and later became an attending surgeon there. At that time, such facilities with an all-Negro staff were virtually the only hospitals where people of color could be treated.

In 1896, Dr. Curtis became the first Negro surgeon appointed to the staff of non-segregated Cook County Hospital in Chicago. Two years later, the Curtis family moved to Washington, D.C. where Dr. Curtis had been offered the position of chief surgeon at Freedmen's Hospital. It had been established in 1862 for the treatment of former slaves. Dr. Curtis held that position from 1898-1938, maintained a private practice, served a term as president of the National Medical Association, and was a professor of surgery at Howard University's School of Medicine for 25 years.

All three of the Curtis sons graduated from Howard University's School of Medicine and became physicians: Arthur Leo Curtis in 1912; Austin Maurice Curtis, Jr. in 1914; and, later after practicing dentistry, Merrill Hargro Curtis in 1932. To distinguish the sons from the elder Curtis, he became known as "Dr. A. M." or "Pop" Curtis. Dr. A. M. was described as being "of medium stature, lean and possessed of tremendous energy and dynamic personality. His deep, sonorous voice booming out to associates as he walked along with short, quick strides."[21]

Figure 19: Visitor Dr. Mark DeLeon preparing for an event in front of the Curtis family house with "The Boat House" sign, next door to the Lofton family house in the background between Walnut and Cedar Avenues on Chesapeake Walk in the mid-1940s. ***Photo courtesy of Carol McMahon collection.***

Mrs. Curtis served as a contract nurse and team leader during the Spanish-American War, and as a Red Cross volunteer during the Galveston flood and the San Francisco earthquake. In recognition, Mrs. Curtis received a U.S. government pension, and upon her death in 1935, was buried at Arlington National Cemetery.

Mrs. Curtis was described as:

> ...an outstanding figure in her own right. She was a warm-hearted, forceful [woman] with manifold interests and abilities. Although the latter carried her into public affairs, she was strongly individualistic in her attitudes toward social conventions and loved to retreat to the family summer home at Arundel-on-the-Bay, near Annapolis, Md., where she would completely flaunt them.[22]

In the summertime, Dr. and Mrs. Curtis raised their four children including daughter Gertrude Ellen Curtis at their home in Arundel-on-the-Bay. The eldest son, Austin, bought the Brosnan property, Lot E of Block 3, in 1923.[23] As a result, the Curtis family owned two properties side-by-side on the Bay front, where there probably always was "a doctor in the house" during the summer.

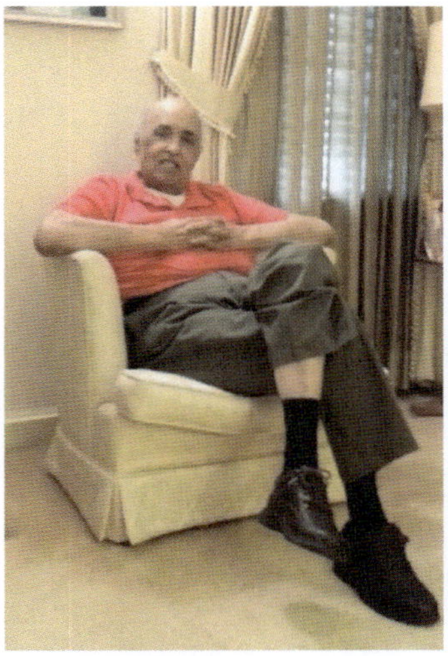

Figure 20: The late Dr. William "Buster" G. Lofton Jr. at home in Washington, D.C., during an interview in August 2013. *Photo by Karen Neale.*

By more than one account, white Arundel-on-the-Bay residents south of Walnut Avenue ventured north when a child needed immediate medical attention like a broken arm or leg, however, colored residents never ventured south.

Dr. A. M. passed away in 1939. Dr. and Mrs. Curtis left their Bay front property to their son Merrill. Dr. and Mrs. Merrill Curtis did not have children, but Merrill had his sister Gertrude's oldest son, Fleming Henry "Buddy" Norris III, as a guest at the house every summer, and years later they also entertained as guests Buddy's wife Henrietta Ellen "Penny" Singleton Norris and their children. Buddy and Penny inherited the house and there they raised their children, Maurice Hatcher Norris and Pamela Sue Norris. Ultimately, members of the Curtis family owned for 65 years the lot that Laura Douglass first purchased in 1893.[24]

In an August 2013 interview, the late Dr. William "Buster" G. Lofton Jr. (died in 2015), whose mother's sister was married to Dr. Merrill Hargro Curtis, reminisced about spending much of his childhood summers at the Curtis family home, because Dr. A. M. wanted him to play with his grandson Buddy Norris even though the boys were four years apart. Dr. Lofton emphasized that he loved the Bay but recalled, "I had to go fishing with Buddy every single day until he decided to come in… even though fishing was not my cup of tea." Dr. Lofton said that he liked to go crabbing at the entrance to Oyster Creek where "you could see crabs coming into the Creek and heading out to the Bay."

In 1944, Dr. Lofton's father bought what is known today as "the yellow house" on "Chesapeake Walk." "We had a lot of good times there all our friends from med school and their families," said Dr. Lofton.

Northernmost Part of Arundel-on-the-Bay

Figure 21: Ruby Kendros Pelecanos, who spent summers at Arundel-on-the-Bay in the mid-1920s, at age 92 in Estero, FL in June 2016. *Photo courtesy of daughter Jeanne Georgelakas.*

In the late 1920s, Ruby Kendros Pelecanos was five years old. She recounted in August 2015 that her father Nicholas Kendros, who owned a sandwich shop near the White House, also owned a food concession. She said that it was located at what was called "Arundel Beach", later known as "Arundel-on-the-Bay."

> *"The Community of Oyster Harbor formerly was the northernmost part of Arundel-on-the-Bay"*

Mrs. Pelecanos recalled going to the lumberyard on West Street with her father and her uncle, Louis Mandris of Annapolis. Then the men built a screened pavilion on the beach, and all three of them slept upstairs in the pavilion at night. Mrs. Pelecanos said that her father also built a bridge across the stream that ran from the Bay into a really marshy area, and added, "You could catch lots of crabs there."

The location of the pavilion probably was the beach bordered on the north by a narrow channel into Oyster Creek. This area of Chesapeake Bay frontage, which is now part of the community of Oyster Harbor, formerly was the northernmost part of Arundel-on-the-Bay. Mrs. Pelecanos said that during the two years when she spent summers on the sandy beach, there were no houses in the area.[25]

Figure 22

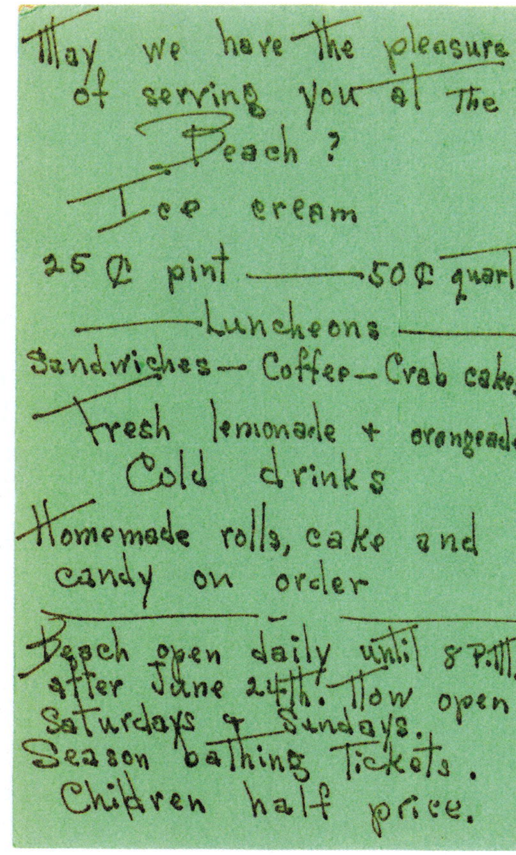

Figure 23

Front and back of cards for bathing and hot luncheon on beach at today's Oyster Harbor, the northern portion of Arundel-on-the-Bay in the mid-late 1920s. ***Van Sant collection, Historical Society of Washington D.C.***

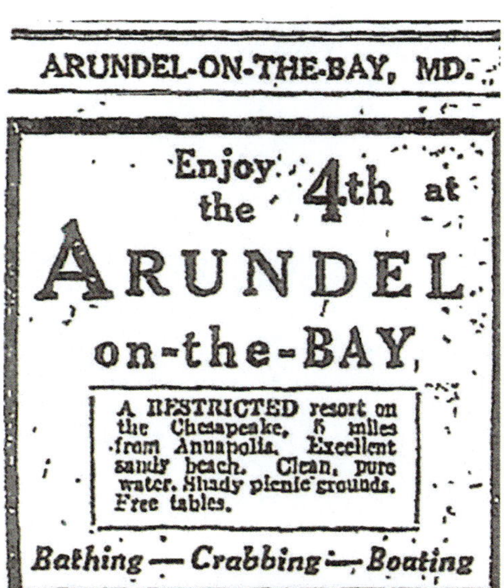

Figure 24: "Enjoy the 4th at Arundel-on-the-Bay, A Restricted Resort..." appeared in the July 1, 1932 ***Baltimore Sun. Permission from the Baltimore Sun.***

Mrs. Pelecanos' account could be reflected on the menu cards advertising a sandy beach called "Arundel-on-the-Bay" overlooking the Chesapeake. The cards even specified "Hot Luncheon served in a Large Screened Pavilion."

The 1930s: The Smallest Incorporated Town?

"He is in Town" – with "town" clearly meaning Arundel-on-the-Bay – was the headline of a March 1931 blurb from *The World's Work*, a monthly magazine that reported on life, business and politics in America. "In 1920, had 12 inhabitants; in 1930, one."

"Believed to be the smallest incorporated town in the U.S." "*This World's Work's*" factoid also was featured in one of *Ripley's Believe It or Not!* syndicated newspaper panels.

That "one" in the 1930 census was Elijah Wells. This made for a clever quip, but in reality the 1920 census had listed the large Tyler family, who lived in the community year-round, and the1940 census listed the same Tyler family at the same address.

Disintegration of Part of Arundel-on-the-Bay's Southernmost Tip and the Creation of Thomas's Island

In the 1930s, the Bay water was lower than today, and the Point (the southernmost tip of the Arundel-on-the-Bay peninsula) extended farther into Fishing Creek than today.

As the Bay water rose and the various hurricanes in 1933 and 1936 attacked the shoreline of the Point it disintegrated slowly and broke into two distinct small islands shown in the 1957 Coast and Geodetic map (Appendix B). Arundel-on-the-Bay playmates

Figure 25

Figure 26

Thomas's Island, now submerged, is shown in Figure 25 on the right in the background of a 1927 photograph of Kent Linkins; and, again in Figure 26 in the upper left in the background of a photograph taken from the Linkins pier in the late 1920s. ***Photos courtesy of Bezdek Linkins collection.***

named these "First Island" and "Second Island". They even built a small shelter/play fort on "First Island" as shown in a Worthington family photograph (See Figure 36).

In addition to the disintegration of the Point, the southernmost tip of the Thomas Point neighborhood off Arundel-on-the-Bay Road extended farther into the Bay as shown in the 1957 C&G map. And what was known as the Thomas Point of the 1920s disintegrated into an island, "Thomas's Island", and farther inland "Thomas Point" that we know today. The now submerged "Thomas's Island" shows clearly in the background of the photos above as well as the 1957 C&G map (See Endnotes). Today's U.S. Geological Survey charts show the former Thomas's Island as a rocky, subsurface "hazard to navigation."

Mini-Neighborhoods of the Smallest Incorporated Town

In the 1930s and 40s, Arundel-on-the-Bay south of Walnut Avenue seemed to have at least five "mini-neighborhoods," where family homes clustered with those of friends, relatives, and neighbors, either because of common interests or because the children got along and played together. Many of the fathers worked in Washington or Baltimore and returned to their summer homes only on the weekends. So the children creatively entertained themselves during the week, and looked forward to the arrival of the iceman, trash man, and local craftsmen.

The first mini-neighborhood was comprised of residents on "the hill", so-called because it was the highest elevation in the community on the Bay front, stretching along Narragansett Avenue from Redwood Avenue south to Hollywood Avenue. Households here included the Galloways, the Waltermeyers, the Chain and Sprocket Clubhouse (a cottage used by a D.C. cycling and fraternal organization), the Bosleys, the Grahams, the Pyles (on site of the old Pavilion), the Shea/Madills, the Warfield/Mullens, the Heurichs, the Wellers, and the McCarthys.

Figure 27: Buddy Gosnell ordered a summertime treat in 1937. ***Photo courtesy of Thomas Worthington collection.***

The second mini-neighborhood consisted of neighbors on the "The Point," that tip of Narragansett Avenue south of Magnolia Avenue that juts into Fishing Creek. Families here included the Payson/Johnson/William Linkins, the Charles Linkins at "Langmead", the Medford/Shaver/McKees, the Maleys, the Thomases/Worthingtons/Schumachers, the Somers, the Gosnells, and the Merediths.

The third mini-neighborhood was made up of folks on "the beach" in the vicinity of the current community beach along Magnolia Avenue, facing Fishing Creek and what was then Thomas's Island. It included the Rudd, the Van Sant, and the Clark/Heintz/Schumacher households.

The fourth included households on "the Creek," namely Captain Wells and Walter Tyler. And the fifth mini-neighborhood encompassed other residents inland of the Bay and the Creek along Narragansett, Cohasset, and Rockaway Avenues. They included the Tyler Sr. family and the Cavanaugh family.

Figure 28: A dozen children from the mini-neighborhoods of Arundel-on-the-Bay south of Walnut Avenue including (l-r, back row) Paul Stomatis and Tom Schumacher; (l-r, front row) the Hicks twins, two unidentified, Bill Schumacher, Buddy Gosnell, Jack Gosnell, Ted Schumacher, Joe Howard, and Tom Worthington in late 1930s. ***Photo Courtesy of Thomas Worthington collection.***

In the late 1930s, a dozen children from the hill, the Point, the beach, the Creek and inland posed with the Arundel-on-the-Bay community pier in the background and today's community beach along Magnolia Avenue in the foreground.[26]

Interesting Property Maneuvers in Arundel-on-the-Bay

On June 15, 1933, Carey L. Meredith and William G. Meredith trading as the Meredith Lumber Company plus other members of the Meredith family sold to Robert S. Tiger and Ben S. Hill of Washington, D.C., a large amount of the lots and parcels of land south of Cedar Avenue in Arundel-on-the-Bay that was part of the Meredith Lumber Company purchase from Chesapeake and Columbia Investment Company in 1926.[27] On June 24, 1933, Mr. Hill and Mr. Tiger and his wife Blanche E. Tiger deeded the same property that they purchased from Meredith Lumber Company to an entity called Arundel-on-the-Bay Properties, Incorporated. [28]

> *"The said lot of land should not be sold, leased, transferred to, or occupied by any person or persons of the African, Asiatic or Mongolian blood or descent..."*

The deeds for both transactions included "conditions and restrictions." Among the nine restrictions was:

> FIFTH: The said lot of land should not be sold, leased, transferred to, or occupied by any persons of the African, Asiatic or Mongolian blood or descent; this provision not to include the occupancy by any servant or employee of any owner or occupant of said property. [Appendix A]

The Town Commissioners at Work

Records from the 1930s, which the estate of Franklin Van Sant deposited at the Kiplinger Research Library of the Historical Society of Washington, D.C., showed that the Arundel-on-the-Bay commissioners in 1933 were H. E. Doyle, J. H. Simpson, Philip M. Maley, E. C. Graham, Fred Vogt, C. L. Meredith, and Franklin Van Sant. According to the meeting agenda of June 30, 1933, a request for $15,000 was to be sent to Gen. Hugh Johnson of the Industrial Recovery Administration, for construction of a seawall around the Bay front.

As Secretary of the Arundel-on-the-Bay Board of Commissioners, Van Sant also sent a rather amusing, albeit serious letter, dated June 13, 1933, to J. Wesley "Wes" Harris, who had become a contractor to the community. The subject of the letter was the purchase of a new horse. Van Sant wrote:

> I am particularly interested in seeing that you do not buy another horse that will drop dead on you shortly after you get him and that you do not buy a horse from someone who does not own him, which happened in the last instance.
>
> If you are satisfied that the horse you are to get is a proper deal and that the horse is a good one, tell whoever you are buying it from that I will see that the money is sent for this from your town contract, but in the meantime let him turn the horse over to you so that you can handle your work. [29]

On June 26, 1933, the town's commissioners approved restrictions regarding building on lots in Arundel-on-the-Bay. The restrictions appear to be based upon the "restrictions" included in recent land transactions relative to the town, including the discriminatory "Fifth" clause.

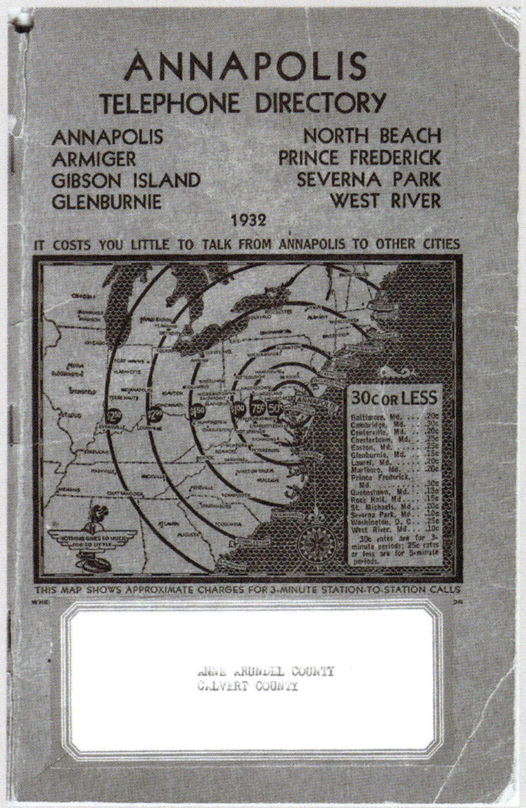

1932 Telephone Listings for Arundel-on-the-Bay Households

"The 1932 Chesapeake and Potomac Telephone Company of Baltimore City" listings for Annapolis provide a snapshot of Arundel-on-the-Bay's mostly summertime households. Many should be familiar including year-round resident, caretaker and bailiff Elijah Wells, Dr. Austin Maurice (A.M.) Curtis and CMM'R William H. Linkins.

J. Herbert Armiger
DeWitt Brown
Edwin M. Conner
John M. Cook
Dr. A. M. Curtis
A. J. Dietrich
J. C. Dietrich
H. E. Doyle
Mrs. Thomas W. Edwards
M. Ehrhardt
J. W. Galloway
E. C. Graham
Charles L. Linkins
Wm. H. Linkins
P. M. Maley
Carl A. McCandless
Fred R. McKee
J. Compton Peach
D. F. Power
Tho. B. Reid
C. E. Skipper
Chas. F. Stock
(Thos. Point Ducking Club, South River)
Wm. H. Thomas
(Wm. H. Thomas & Co. Men's Clothing, 148 Main and 88 Conduit)
Elijah Wells
Wm. A. Woodburn
W. J. Woodbury
T. Carroll Worthington
Fred R. Turbyville
Mrs. Fred Vogt.

Figure 29: Seated on Wes Harris's wagon in the 1930s are Ted Schumacher (rear), Tommy Worthington, Bill Schumacher and Hugo Bezdek. ***Photo courtesy of Thomas Worthington collection.***

The restrictions, among other things, specified that only one dwelling could be erected on any one lot and that the dwelling must be 30 feet from the front property line, of "artistic appearance," and have no flat or tarpaper roof. Furthermore, they specified that sills must be made from long-leaf pine or fir; all porch floors were to be fir or heart

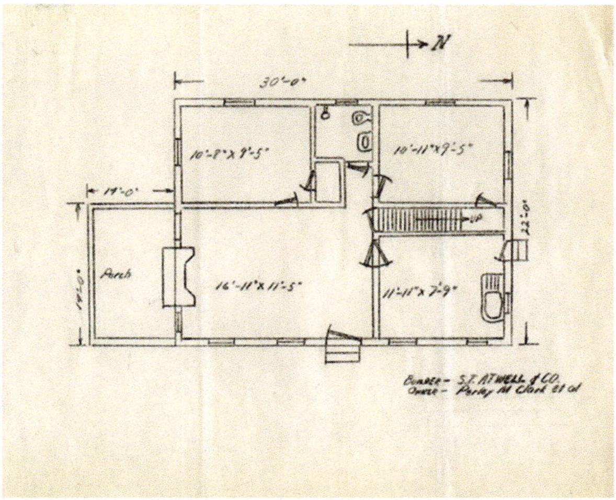

Figure 30: Plans that were attached to the application that Perley M. Clark, Louise H. Clark, Minnie L. Heintz and Caroline M. Heintz submitted. ***Van Sant Collection, Historical Society of Washington, D.C.***

pine; all other exposed finish must be of fir, cypress or cedar; and, they expressly stated that no sap pine could be used on any exposed work. Any such structure was to be for residential use only.

Building regulations that the commissioners adopted on July 19, 1913, still applied to any new building or structural changes costing greater than $20. In advance of an applicant receiving the official building permit from the town's Inspector of Buildings, the inspector had to receive a written application for a building permit, a copy of the plans and specifications, and a building fee ranging from $1 to $100.

One such application was dated July 3, 1936, for a new Cape Cod-type cottage on Block 35, Lot A, at the corner of Magnolia and Cohasset Avenues. Four women, including two from the Heintz family, were the co-owners. The inspector approved a building permit and issued it nine days later.[30] From multiple accounts this property had on it – and may still have – the well that provided water for the former Arundel-on-the-Bay Railroad.

Snapshots of Other Community Activities in the 1930s

Arundel-on-the-Bay Properties, Inc.

8/31/36

630 INVESTMENT BUILDING
CORNER 15TH AND K STREETS. N. W.
WASHINGTON, D. C.

List of Unsold Lots. Arundel

Blk.	Lots	No.
15	D F G H K	5
16	I	1
17	K	1
19	C	1
20	K L	2
21	D I K	3
27	F G H I K	5
28	G H I K	4
29	A B C D H I	6
30	A B C D E F G H I K L M	12
31	A B C D	4
36	A B	2
40	C D E G H I K L M	9
41	A B C D E F G H I K L M	12
42	A B C D E F G H I K L M	12
43	A B C D E F G H I K L M	12
44	A B C D E F G H I K L M	12
46	A B C D E F G H I K	10
56	F G H I K	5
58	A B C D E F G H I K L M	12
59	A B C D E F G H I K L M	12
60	A B C D E F G H I K L M	12
61	A B C D E F G H I K L M	12
65	A B C D E	5
66	A B C D E	5
67	D E F G H I K L	8
67	Front Strip	
70	C D E F	4
73	A B C D E F G J O L	10
89	Entire Block	

Figure 31: Arundel-on-the-Bay Properties, Inc. List of Unsold Lots, in 1936. ***Van Sant Collection in the Kiplinger Library of the Historical Society of Washington, D.C.***

During the early 1930s, the commissioners of Arundel-on-the-Bay submitted an application to the commissioners of Anne Arundel County to construct 1,960 feet of bulkhead. The *Baltimore Sun* reported on July 11, 1935 that Arundel-on-the-Bay had awarded a contract for $20,990 to construct 1,785 feet of timber bulkhead around the waterfront. Two years later, the *Baltimore Sun* reported that the Anne Arundel County engineer had declared nine completed projects efficient including the 1,939 feet along the shore of Arundel-on-the-Bay costing $21,008.48.

In a letter to Mayor Philip Maley dated July 28, 1934, Arundel-on-the-Bay Properties, Inc. applied to the town for removal of restrictions on Lot F in Block 22 (west of Cohasset Avenue and south of Cedar Avenue) to permit the erection of a tearoom or inn. The firm also asked for "permission to sell beer and possibly light wine – no hard liquor to be sold at any time." There's no indication that the request was granted.[31]

The Colonel of the Army Corps of Engineers for the district including Arundel-on-the-Bay, in a letter dated August 22, 1934, informed the commissioners of a complaint that a footbridge obstructed the mouth of Oyster Creek adjacent to Arundel-on-the-Bay. He described it as a light timber footbridge across the Creek, blocking free and easy navigation into it. The Colonel reminded the commissioners that it is unlawful to construct a bridge over a navigable waterway without legal authority and plans approved by the War Department, and asked for "the name and address of the owner of this bridge." [32]

There is no record whether the responsible party was identified. However, the significance of the Colonel's communication was that the Arundel-on-the-Bay commissioners were responsible for matters extending north to Oyster Creek.

In the mid-1930s, Anne Arundel County was struggling to build a by-pass around Annapolis. It was needed to handle the thousands of weekend motorists, especially those from Washington and Baltimore, who were headed to and from shore resorts, including Bay Ridge, Highland Beach, and Arundel-on-the-Bay. The county had the funds but not the 25-50 workmen it needed from the Works Progress Administration, a federal New Deal agency that employed unemployed people to carry out public works projects. The by-pass was to run from a point on the South River Road, south of the former Camp Parole, through the present Chinquapin Round and Annapolis Neck Roads to Bay Ridge Road.[33]

In 1935, the General Assembly of Maryland authorized Arundel-on-the-Bay Properties, Inc. to take over the real estate business within the town. Why the General Assembly took this action is unclear.

"No one would have thought in 1940 that a little over a decade later, a family including "persons of the African, Asiatic or Mongolian blood or descent"–as the odious restriction was worded–would own the former Pyles house."

Meanwhile, on March 26, 1935, Arundel-on-the-Bay Properties, Inc., upon receipt of "good and valuable considerations", deeded to the commissioners of Arundel-on-the-Bay for community and town purposes Lots C-D-E-F-G-H-I of Block 13, subject to the usual conditions and restrictions. That land is today's Arundel-on-the-Bay community beach.[34] It was created in 1935. A year later Arundel-on-the-Bay Properties, Inc. still had almost 200 unsold lots.

Unfortunately, Arundel-on-the-Bay Properties, Inc. was listed in the "1941 Governor's Proclamation Giving Notice of Forfeiture of Delinquent Corporations," for not paying its taxes.[35]

In March 1936, Arundel-on-the-Bay's secretary on the board of commissioners sent to Mrs. J. Chester Pyles of Washington, D.C., a letter outlining the restrictions that applied to lots, including the "FIFTH" restriction, and welcoming her to the community on behalf of the commissioners. Her Lot A in Block 7 on the Bay front, was the former site of the community pavilion, otherwise known as the Arundel Country Club. The Pyles house was erected in 1940 at 1362 Chestnut Avenue across from Idle Wild Cottage.

No one would have thought in 1940 that a little over a decade later, a family including "persons of the African, Asiatic or Mongolian blood or descent"–as the odious restriction was worded–would own the former Pyles house. Suzanne Johnson, a member of the family that bought the house and still enjoys it, recalled living there as a child in the 1950s-60s. She listed some of her delights in a 2012 memoir:

Figure 32: Fast forward to summer 2015, Arundel-on-the-Bay childhood playmates (l-r) Brenda Carpenter Gamble, Karen Neale, Virginia Johnson and Suzanne Johnson in front yard of the former Pyles house on Chestnut Avenue. ***Photo courtesy of Karen Neale.***

> One of my favorite activities was dipping crabs out onto our little pier, or walking along the bulwarks looking for crabs on the pilings, then sneaking a chicken neck on a string down to lure them off the pilings so they could be dipped with a dip net.
>
> Or, fishing with Papa, my grandfather. Of course, he'd put the worm on the hook and he'd also remove the fish. I loved casting out the line, holding it tenderly between my fingers waiting to feel the nibble, then jerking the line and pulling in the fish–or eel.
>
> Loved swimming from the pier to the float in front of the house. The community was so full of kids of all ages! Remember Mrs. Walker's outdoor Sunday School? I also enjoyed the older brothers and sisters, the flashy cars, the music, the glamorous girls and the so-cool older boys. It was a wonderful place to spend the summers growing up![36]

Virginia Johnson, who also grew up summers at the former Pyles house, is a legend. She became a founding member and prima ballerina of the internationally acclaimed Dance Theatre of Harlem. It was founded by Arthur Mitchell and Karell Shook in the Harlem neighborhood of New York City in 1969, following the assassination of Dr. Martin Luther King Jr. Post-retirement, Ms. Johnson returned to the troupe in 2009 as the artistic director and was honored at the White House in 2016.

Late in the evening on Sept. 17, 1939, Arundel-on-the-Bay residents lined the shore to watch the rescue of members of a fishing party out of Laurel, Md., forced to leap into the Bay when their 36-foot cruiser burned and then exploded. The yacht had left Eastport (across the bridge from downtown Annapolis) and had gone as far as the South River. However, when the Chesapeake Bay became rough and the yacht turned back, its electric light plant failed. All five men, including a priest, were saved by the State of Maryland's steamer, *The DuPont*, which was returning from Chestertown, Md. where it had taken then Governor and Mrs. Herbert O'Connor to a dinner with the Board of Governors of Washington College. Both the Governor and his wife participated in the rescue.[37]

Other Memories of the Community: The Madill Memoir

Readers of this community history met Edwin Madill in Chapter 2. In this chapter, his depiction of life at Arundel-on-the-Bay in the 1930s and his revelation of part of the history of Idle Wild Cottage reflect a critical time in our country's history.

Figure 33: The four Madill Family children. ***"Memoirs of Ed Madill" in the Van Sant collection, Historical Society of Washington, D.C.***

In the late 1920s, Edwin Madill married Margaret Agnes Shea, granddaughter of one of the founders of Arundel-on-the-Bay, Nicholas H. Shea. Together the couple enjoyed good times in the community, according to Madill's description of family life at the beach. The family's "reign", as he termed it, actually began in the community on Labor Day in 1936, when the couple's first-born was only two months old, and lasted until 1951, when their four children – Margaret Ann, Edwin J., Mary Paula, and Michael – indicated they preferred to spend their holidays elsewhere.

Madill recalled, "The wonderful thing about Arundel was that our children could swim almost before they could walk." Over the years at Arundel-on-the-Bay, Madill noted that his children played with the Pyles and the Mullen children, whose houses were on either side of Idle Wild Cottage on the Bay front.

Madill described a boat designed for the family as "a Chesapeake Bay bugeye–wide of beam and about 22-25 feet long with centerboard instead of a finkeeler," lamenting that, "It appeared to be my job to paint it every spring for readiness of putting her over." The family assembled its own fleet of watercraft. "All of us were proud of our armada: Nick's boat–a bugeye, *The Oleo*, the Coast Guard cork raft, and the Air Force inflatable life raft that could hold about 16 people. I also bought the children an Elgin outboard-motor to power *The Oleo*."

The proud father recounted his sons helping him build "skids" to get the family "armada" out of the water. "Walter Tyler was very cooperative in getting lumber hard to get during the war," Madill explained; and, "Captain Wells on the inlet would check our fleet."

> *"Do you remember when we used to sail out when the battleships used to anchor [in the Chesapeake Bay]? The Wyoming and the Arizona."*

Prior to World War II, U.S. battleships often were anchored out in the Bay. At the beginning of his family memoirs, Madill asked his children:

> Do you remember when we used to sail out when the battleships used to anchor [in the Chesapeake Bay]? The Wyoming and the Arizona....In those days, the refuse from the ships was dumped into the Chesapeake and [it] floated over to our beach in front of our Idle Wild Cottage. You children could not take a swim for several days. [38]

More Memories of the Community: The Worthington Family

Figure 34: Tom Worthington (1929-2017) during an interview by Bill Semenuk and Pamela Duncan at his home in Sabillasville, Md., November 17, 2012. ***Photo by Bill Semenuk.***

Thomas Worthington, nicknamed "Tommy Carroll", who summered at Arundel-on-the-Bay from 1929 when he was born until the late 1940s, provided a lot of helpful insight into life on the peninsula. The Arundel-on-the-Bay residents who interviewed him call him "Tom".

In the 1920s, empty lots were referred to as "camp." In fact, in 1925, the first year Tom's family owned its property, they camped out. Theirs was the third lot from the end of the Point on Narragansett Avenue. William H. Thomas, his mother's father, built the house and a garage with an apartment above.

Figure 35: Tom Worthington's house and garage on the Point at 3571 Narragansett Avenue about 1930. ***Photo courtesy of Thomas Worthington collection.***

There was sandy beach on the Bay front where Tom lived, but not after 1933. Thomas Point had extended another quarter of a mile; and, after 1933 water cut through the Arundel-on-the-Bay neighborhood called the Point in two places creating what was called "First Island" and "Second Island" as noted earlier in this chapter. Both eventually disappeared.

Tom recalled that the lighthouse keepers used a pier at Arundel-on-the-Bay to deliver food via boat to Thomas Point Lighthouse. He would go out on the boat and into the lighthouse to play, and would be transported home just before the last load was taken to the lighthouse.

Figure 36: In their "fort" on First Island, (l-r) Tom Worthington, Bill Schumacher, Mike Mullen, and Hugo Bezdek in early 1940s. ***Photo courtesy of Thomas Worthington collection.***

Also, Tom reminisced about many of the children with whom he played growing up. He and his cousin Bill Schumacher were born eight days apart in 1929, and shared a crib at the Annapolis Emergency Hospital.[39]

"Bill lived all around," Tom explained, "because his dad was a naval officer, but Bill joined us at the beach each summer." Another cousin, Betty Schumacher (Sain), was prominent in young Tom's life. He recalled that she wanted him to pull her doll baby around in a wagon, but at the same time she looked out for him.

Figure 37: (l-r) Bill Schumacher, Tom Worthington, Florence Clark and Ted Schumacher on the beach in front of Tom Worthington's Grandfather Thomas's house on the Bay front, in mid-1930s. ***Photo courtesy of Thomas Worthington collection.***

Tom also remembered playing with the children at Idle Wild, known then as Madill. Next down from the Madill house he recalled the Mike Mullen house. It was at 1362 Myrtle Ave., the home of John Frederick Warfield, who was introduced earlier in this chapter. His daughter married Mike Mullen.

Next door to the Warfield house at 1363 Myrtle Ave. was the property that Christian Heurich Jr. purchased in 1939 as introduced in Chapter 4. He was the son of the prominent Washington brew-master and German immigrant Christian Heurich, who died in 1945.[40] Heurich Jr., a graduate of the Wharton School of Finance, had assumed the role of treasurer of the Heurich brewery in 1933, then ran it after World War II.

Competition from large brewers, a growing trend toward blander beers, and a bad batch of its popular "Senate Beer" affected the business, and it closed in 1956. The brewery was demolished in 1962 to make room for the Kennedy Center. [41] But the Victorian-era, Christian Heurich mansion (commonly known today as the Brewmaster's Castle) that the father built as the family's residence in the 1890s off DuPont Circle in Washington, D.C., still stands at this writing as a treasured museum and a venue for fine entertainment.

Tom's cousin Betty Schumacher, as a teenager, was a best friend of one of Christian Heurich Jr.'s daughters, Carol Heurich, whom Tom remembered as "drop-dead gorgeous." As a result of the friendship, Carol became Tom's date for his senior prom.

Figure 38: Neighbor Betty Ann Hall and young Tom Worthington visiting on the bulkhead at Narragansett Avenue about 1934. ***Photo courtesy of Thomas Worthington collection.***

Among other childhood memories, Tom cited evidence that the railroad into Arundel-on-the-Bay did indeed end at Narragansett and Magnolia Avenues. He said the children of his era located a well pump that had provided water for the steam train. Tom confirmed that members of the Heintz family bought a neighboring lot where the line had ended.

The Great Hurricane

On August 21, 1933, hurricane warnings were issued for what became known as the 1933 Chesapeake-Potomac Hurricane. It turned out to be the most severe North Atlantic hurricane to hit the East Coast since 1821.

The *Baltimore Sun* reported:

> At Arundel on the Bay . . . the damage was extensive along nearly a mile of shore-line. Along a part of the waterfront, residents had constructed a concrete sidewalk well back from the bank overlooking the beach. A part of this walk remains but it ends abruptly at the edge of the embankment, and broken slabs of concrete on the present beach reveal clearly that the land has been pushed back . . . once was excellent beach . . . occupants have been forced to seek a new and higher level.[42]

Tom Worthington, a witness of the 1933 hurricane, recounted the harrowing experience. He told us that at that time the National Weather Service (known then as the Weather Bureau) was gleaning information about storms from ships traveling through them. Other

Figure 40: Four men survey 1933 Chesapeake-Potomac Hurricane damage at Arundel-on-the-Bay. ***Baltimore Sun, September 24, 1933. Permission from the Baltimore Sun.***

ships, upon hearing a radioed report, would avoid the area, making it easier to lose track of a storm. Since early August there had been rumors of the existence of a large storm off San Juan, Puerto Rico.

Tom's grandfather, William H. Thomas, was a weather-wise descendant of watermen from the Eastern Shore. Observing conditions from the end of the Point at

Arundel-on-the-Bay on a Sunday evening, Grandfather Thomas ordered that the family's boat be taken to Annapolis and tied up at the foot of Conduit Street near the family's city home.

Figure 41: 1933 Hurricane. Looking south from the porch of the Thomas Worthington Cottage toward Thomas Point Island with the Carey Meredith family cottage next door. This photo was taken just before the Worthington family evacuated. ***Photo courtesy of Thomas Worthington collection.***

By Tom's account, on the morning the storm hit the wind already was blowing as Grandfather Thomas and young Tom's father, T. Carroll Worthington, left for Annapolis to open the family's clothing store. After 45 minutes the wind picked up considerably and waves of 20 to 30 feet crashed up against the bulkhead, and caught by the wind, water blew into the house through the French porch doors. Meanwhile Grandfather Thomas received a telephone call from a friend in Norfolk, Va., who reported conditions there of a nine-foot tide and winds of 100 miles per hour.

Tom's father called his wife Lucille Worthington, who still was able to answer the family phone (then located in an oak box with two bells, a crank, and a receiver) and advised her to evacuate. At this point water was in the yard and whitecaps were racing across the lawn.

The hurricane getaway car was a 1927 Buick four-door sedan with a reputation for stalling in damp weather, but Grandmother Thomas, a proper Victorian lady, couldn't be hurried until she was properly dressed. Finally, Tom and his mother and grandmother waded through water already knee-deep for him and up to mid-calf for the ladies. He had opened the garage doors but was unable to close them because of the wind.

The family managed to reach Arundel-on-the-Bay Road where it forks at the road to Thomas Point before the car stopped running. As arranged, Tom's father met them, and, using a tow-rope, pulled the old Buick to Annapolis. It was three or four days before anyone could return to Arundel-on-the-Bay after the storm, because there were many downed

Figure 42: Hank Seely and Louise Linkins Bezdek in Annapolis in the late 1930s. ***Photo courtesy of Bezdek Linkins collection.***

trees blocking the road. A family friend described the community as looking as though it had been bombed.

Tom reported that the homes of neighbors on either side, those of the Merediths and the Edwards, were badly damaged. The two-story Victorian home of Philip Maley had its two porches blown away and windows smashed, and a tower with a water tank to allow running water on the property was destroyed. The Somers' family home on higher land had more wind than water damage. The 1933 hurricane destroyed every pier on the Bay front.

Louise Seely is perhaps the only other survivor today of the 1933 hurricane at Arundel-on-the-Bay. She recounted her experience in a June 2014 letter to Bill Semenuk:

> The hurricane of 1933 was a bad one. I was 20 at the time and spent the day out helping neighbors leave, never realizing my mother wanted to leave. It was too late to do so when I finally went home. Junior Clark and Nick Shea were with me pushing cars through the water. The Bay came up from the front and the Creek from the back and met on the roads. We were back of the Thomas's house in water up to our armpits–Junior holding my hand on one side and Nick on the other, with his other arm around a telephone pole. The water was swirling around us in a pretty strong current. Both of these kids were about 17 or 18 at the time.
>
> The water over the road in front of our garage was about three to four feet-deep, also with quite a current. We watched the community wharf go out. The wind was from the southwest and large sections were lifted up and then fell. These sections must have been about 20 to 25 feet tall before falling.
>
> Mother spent the night going from one porch door to another with a kerosene lantern to see if the water was getting higher. We had branches and sticks under the house that kept bumping the floor. The wind died during the night and the water went down in the morning. A rented house below the Thomases near the end of the Point was the worst hit. Water came in the front and washed right on through and met the Creek coming in.

Upon reading Tom Worthington's account of the hurricane, Louise wrote in October 2014:

> Tom Worthington is not the only person who remembers the 1933 hurricane–I was there and we did not evacuate . . . . We pushed the Worthington car through some of the high water . . . . Langmead's pier was our pier and our houses did not suffer. 'Windows were blown out', Tommy dreamed that one up!

While Tom and Louise clearly had different recollections of some details of storm damage more than 80 years ago, they both recalled the strength and danger of the 1933 hurricane.

Figure 43: Guests of Arundel-on-the-Bay resident Florence Clark on the community's pier with the Point in the background, about 1940. ***Photo courtesy of Thomas Worthington collection.***

In September following the storm, Arundel-on-the-Bay Commissioner Van Sant wrote to the Bay front property owners about the need for additional protection. At the commissioners' September meeting, the point was made that approximately half of the Bay front owners already had breakwaters, and only two had failed. Owners of 15 of the 30 unprotected lots on the waterfront agreed to join in new construction.

Van Sant explained that Smith Brothers Inc., which had built protection at Cedarhurst that stood up during the storm, had quoted a price for protection of Arundel-on-the-Bay's waterfront. The company would charge $295 for each 50-foot lot, including construction of jetties located 16 feet apart. The community would provide protection at the street ends, if the whole thing could be done at once. The street ends would amount to about 10 lots, and there would be stairways providing for access to the Bay, he said. In asking for agreement, Van Sant reminded lot owners: "You will readily appreciate that unless all of the front is protected, the water can seep around and destroy the entire front . . . ." [43]

The 1940s: Developments in Town and Abroad

The 1930 census taker's canvass of Arundel-on-the-Bay still featured Elijah Wells – in the "one-man-town." By then, Capt. Wells was 58. However, on May 30, 1937, Walter Tyler filed a permit request to build a bungalow 22'x30' on Lot E of Block 68 at Saratoga & Oak Avenues. As a result, after the 1940 census, the *Baltimore Sun* reported that Elijah Wells, known as "the one" at Arundel-on-the-Bay, had been joined by other year-round residents, including Walter Tyler and Mr. and Mrs. William Sevier and their two children. Capt. Wells's fame as "the one" officially had ended!

"The Washingtonians kept hold of power!" the *Annapolis Evening Capital* reported two days later.

> *"Owners of unsold Arundel-on-the-Bay property sold their Tract known as "Oyster Creek" therefore paving the way for the eventual community of Oyster Harbor."*

Street lights, sanitation, oiling of roadways, wells and efforts to keep the Chesapeake Bay at bay had dominated the first third of the century, and efficient roads and erosion prevention remained a high priority in the mid-40s. Anne Arundel County authorized revenue expenditures for roads at Arundel-on-the-Bay, but records also showed special local taxes for roads and erosion.

Arundel-on-the-Bay became much less expansive on March 31, 1941, when Carey L. Meredith et al., owners of much of the unsold Arundel-on-the-Bay property, sold the tract known as "Oyster Creek" therefore paving the way for the eventual community of Oyster

Harbor. The buyer was a corporation named Forest Beach. In order to complete the sale, Forest Beach struck a land purchase mortgage with Meredith Lumber for $17,100 payable within five years. This was not necessarily the total amount of the sale.[44]

In the Forest Beach, Inc. deed, there was only one of the "Restrictions" typical of deeds involving Meredith Lumber Company–the "FIFTH" restricting the tract nor any part of it from being sold, leased, transferred to or occupied by persons of African, Asiatic or Mongolian blood or descent… .

In August 1943, the *Baltimore Sun* reported a new public service. Mrs. Isabel K. Shaw became Anne Arundel County's first rural mail carrier. Her route included Arundel-on-the-Bay as well as Bay Ridge, West Annapolis, Weems Creek and Inglehart.

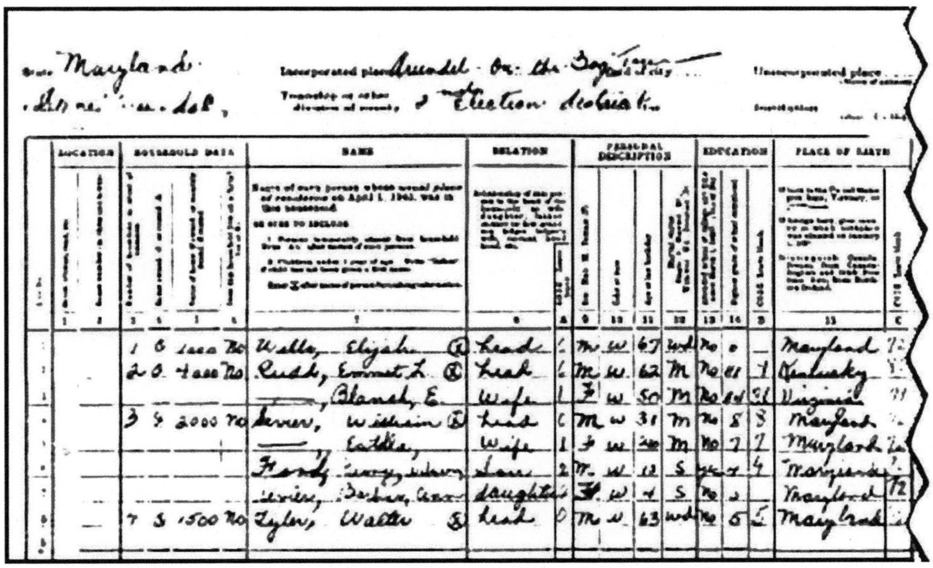

Figure 44: 1940 Federal Census of year round residents of Arundel-on-the-Bay, which shows caretaker Elijah Wells is no longer the sole resident. ***Source: Ancestry.com.***

By Tom Worthington's account, the community pier was located at the mouth of Fishing Creek, otherwise known as "Fishing Cove." A float was anchored in the creek and kids swam to it. Tom described how he and his friends prepared for a crab feast by crabbing for hard-shelled crabs and putting them into a common basket. They would then cross Fishing Creek to Thomas Point Island by boat, he said, crank up a record player, play big band music, dance in the sand, steam their crabs and eat marshmallows with them. Yummy!

Some of the kids from the mini-neighborhoods had grown-up by the early 1940s. For example, Tom Schumacher, one of the children from the mini-neighborhoods pictured in Figure 28 on the Arundel-on-the-Bay beach in the late 1930's, had traveled half-way around the world to serve in World War II, a stark contrast to life at Arundel-on-the-Bay.

During the mid-1940s, a seemingly large number of lots and homes were advertised, with two stories and new amenities beyond those noted in the 1920s:

- "A 3-bedroom, summer furnished bungalow at AOTB on a Lot 100 x 150 for $7,500." [45]
- "A 2-story cottage, Lot 200 x 200, furnished, electric refrigerator and gas, both on 1st floor. Offered at a sacrifice! Only $12,000." [46]

Figure 45: Tom Schumacher, also shown in Figure 28 on the Arundel-on-the-Bay beach in the 1930s, is shown here in North Africa during WWII. ***Photo courtesy of Thomas Worthington collection.***

- Large comfortable cottage directly facing the Bay. Living room, dining room, four bedrooms and bath completely furnished. Gas stove. Garage. $12,000 [47]

Sadly, the caretaker for several of Arundel-on-the-Bay's summer houses, 49 year-old George R. Chinn, who lived alone, was found dead in his home by his next door neighbor Benjamin Rawlings. The county's medical examiner indicated the cause of death was a paralytic stroke.[48]

As World War II ended and more residents lived in the community year-round, newspapers still carried numerous accounts of Arundel-on-the-Bay social activities, such as midshipmen visiting young ladies in the town, residents' celebrations held at Carvel Hall (a hotel attached to and encompassing the area known today as the historic Paca House in Annapolis), and guests visiting over the Christmas holidays.

On July 3, 1945, the *Annapolis Evening Capital* reported a happy event. Cpl. Philip C. Tyler, who'd been reported missing-in-action in World War II, in September 1944, visited his dad, George N. Tyler Sr., at Arundel-on-the-Bay. His wife and son accompanied him.[49] Cpl. Tyler was the second youngest of the eleven Tyler children who grew up in town.

LIBERATED

Figure 46. Cpl. Philip C. Tyler was reported liberated from a German prison camp and returned to the United States after capture during WW II. ***Annapolis Evening Capital, July 3, 1945. Permission from the Baltimore Sun.***

Also in summer 1945, the *Annapolis Evening Capital* reported breakthrough news in Arundel-on-the-Bay. Miss Mary E. Gallagher was elected to serve as a commissioner of the town. Heretofore, through the twenties, thirties and forties, only men were elected. In the July 27, 1946 election, Miss Gallagher ran as an incumbent.

The *Annapolis Evening Capital* reported:

> The election for commissioners, the town fathers for Arundel-on-the-Bay today was described by one of the incumbents as the liveliest contest in the history of the town. Two factions composed of 11 candidates for the seven posts are competing. One is comprised of year-round residents of the bayshore community and the other of

> Washington D.C. citizens who have summer homes there. "We'll determine whether the seat of government will be moved from Washington, D. C. to Arundel," one of the commissioners says.

"Breaking the Ice"

While there was no reported or recorded social interaction with the African American residents of Highland Beach north of Arundel-on-the-Bay, Tom Worthington recalls that Arundel-on-the-Bay residents felt no animosity and recognized that Highland Beach was populated with distinguished, professional people. Tom's mother, however, did not allow him to go there.

One morning, after Tom's father offered him five cents for any soft-shelled crab he could find, Tom was working his way up the Bay front studiously catching crabs, when he looked up and realized that he had ventured too far north into Highland Beach. Tom remembered that a lady in the woods called out to him, "Who are you, little boy, and where do you live?" He answered by pointing to Arundel-on-the-Bay and saying "Up there ma'am." "Are you white or are you passing?" she asked. "White," he replied. "How did you know that terminology then?" she asked. Worthington replied indirectly, "Well, my family taught me to address older colored people as Aunt or Uncle, as a sign of respect."

Actually, Tom knew Mrs. Florence Sparrow, an African American and the owner of the Sparrow's Beach resort. It was located off Edgewood Road and is now in the community of Chesapeake Harbor. Sparrow's Beach was a highly successful venue for entertainment, and one of the major Chesapeake Bay resorts that catered to African Americans between the 1930s and 1960s.[50] Tom's father carried the insurance policy for Sparrow's Beach and was on the board of directors at the bank that Mrs. Sparrow used. She deposited each weekend's proceeds in downtown Annapolis and called Tom, then in his late teens, to help her with the shopping bags in which she carried the money. Tom said he also attended concerts at Sparrow's Beach to see big name acts such as Archie Moore Jr., Dinah Washington, and various big bands of the era.

Disincorporation of the Town of Arundel-on-the-Bay

After World War II, Arundel-on-the-Bay experienced heightened tension between the year-round residents and the summer residents. The *Baltimore Sun* reported on February 1, 1949, that the citizens association of Arundel-on-the-Bay sent a letter, signed by the association president Mrs. Nettie A. Howard, to the county legislative delegation, asking for disincorporation of the town due to the commissioners being summer residents and services ceasing when they leave. Mrs. Howard summarized the petitioners' complaint:

> For a number of years this town has lagged far behind other growing communities because it is and has been totally controlled by the seven commissioners who are only interested in spending a few weeks or months during the summer at Arundel-on-the-Bay . . . . After the summer season, everything has been left absolutely unattended and totally unprotected.

She explained further that residents were paying a town tax on top of state, county, soil erosion, and benefit taxes, and that perhaps de-incorporation could result in reduced taxes.

The *Baltimore Sun* had run an article indicating how taxes for 1950 differed among the eight districts of Anne Arundel County:

> [Rates] will range from $1.69 in parts of the Fifth district (Brooklyn-Glen Burnie), where no special local taxes are levied, to $3.59 per $100 of assessed value in Arundel-on-the-Bay.
>
> Situated in the Second district (suburban Annapolis), Arundel-on-the-Bay property owners must pay the general district tax rate of $1.72 ($.28 general county, $1.17 schools, $.05 roads, $.10 police and $.12 fire) plus an erosion-works levy of $1.60, and a garbage collection tax of $.27.[51]
>
> And this was for a community where most residents used services only during the summer months.

Andrew W. Kahrl, in his book, *"The Land Was Ours: African American Beaches from Jim Crow to the Sunbelt South,"* suggested a different motivation: "Following Oyster Harbor's completion, the white property owners of Arundel-on-the-Bay quickly moved to fortify their own status as a private community by dissolving the town's charter, and on June 3, 1949, reforming as a private homeowners' association." Kahrl noted that the community's action came in the wake of the Supreme Court decision *Shelley vs. Kraemer* in 1948 that ruled covenants on real estate unenforceable [by courts].[52]

"Following Oyster Harbor's completion, the white property owners of Arundel-on-the-Bay quickly moved to fortify their own status as a private community by dissolving the town's charter, and on June 3,1949, reforming as a private homeowners' association."

Figure 47: A visitor, and three young members of the Lofton family who grew up summers between Walnut and Cedar Avenues on Chesapeake Walk, are pictured on the Bay front in early 1960s: l-r. Joyce Jefferson (visiting from Detroit), and Robin Lofton (daughter of Dr. William G. Lofton Jr), Judy McMahon and Carol McMahon (granddaughters of Dr. William G. Lofton Sr.). ***Photo courtesy of Carol McMahon.***

Yet in 1949, there were four African American families—Curtis, Lofton, Ellis and Tyson—with summer homes on the Bay front above Walnut Avenue in Arundel-on-the-Bay.[53] Fred Garrett recalled that the Arundel-on-the-Bay commissioners were angered when a resident built a house on a lot on the Fishing Creek side of Magnolia Avenue, which heretofore had remained unbuilt. Then, the resident advertised it for sale only to a colored family.[54] Helen McMurdock Dodson remembered being told by her mother, who bought their family home at 1358 Hollywood Ave., that the resident had been angered by the treatment of his wife, who happened to be Jewish.[55]

Tom Worthington described great upheaval at Arundel-on-the-Bay after World War II. "It had been all white; became all black in a short period of time," he said. Tom recounted that many families turned to his father, who was in real estate, to sell their homes for them. However, Tom explained, his father refused because he didn't want to profit from actions based on racial animosity, and instead, referred the business to the firm of an African American Annapolitan named Carroll Hynson Sr. Tom said that his family kept its property until his grandfather died and nobody was using it. The family sold it for $85,000 in May 1973 according to land records.[56]

Clearly, there are a number of different explanations for the demise of the Town of Arundel-on-the-Bay. Whatever the cause, in the winter of 1949 the Anne Arundel County Delegation introduced in the General Assembly of Maryland a piece of legislation labeled "House Bill 191," to repeal Sections 129-161 of the County code dealing with the incorporation of Arundel-on-the-Bay. [Appendix C] The General Assembly approved the bill on April 29, 1949.[57]

The dissolution of the Town of Arundel-on-the-Bay, known as "a resort town 10 miles south of Annapolis," quietly took effect on June 1, 1949.

Photograph by Marc Grigsby.

Endnotes

1. "Elijah Wells, Town's Lone Resident, Has No Trouble With Municipal Problems", *Baltimore Sun Newspaper,* October 17, 1930.

2. "Aged Colored Woman Dies at Eastport Home,"*Annapolis Evening Capital,* January 9, 1919.

3. Phone interview of Arlene Wells, great-granddaughter of Philip Booth, by Karen Neale, April 2014.

4. "Hold First Outing at Arundel on the Bay," *Washington Herald,* August 6, 1922, p. 4.

5. U.S. Census, 1920.

6. Interview of Louise Linkins Bezdek Seely by Bill Semenuk, Spring 2013.

7. Interview of George Tyler III by Karen Neale and Bill Semenuk, August 2013.

8. Deed between Meredith Lumber Company (grantor) and Walter Tyler (grantee), in Anne Arundel County Circuit Court Land Records, 1937, Book 161, p. 336, MSA CE 59-505.

9. John F. and Isabel Warfield's children were Freda (1908-1999) and Louise Isabel (1911-1997.) Freda married Harry Rogers Mullen and their children were Patricia Louise (1932-2003), Harry Rogers Mullen (1933-) and John Warfield Mullen (1940-1960). Louise married Arthur Linwood Garrett. Their children were John Frederick Garrett (1937-) and Anita Lynne Garrett (1942-). Arthur Linwood Garrett was the grandson of William Robert Wyatt Garrett, who just had returned from the Civil War when John Wilkes Booth came asking for a place to stay. He and his father told Booth to stay in the barn and the rest is history, according to family historian Stephanie Reese in a May 2, 2014 e-mail.

10. "Arundel Elects Council,"*Baltimore Sun Newspaper,* July 31, 1922.

11. *Baltimore Sun*, Classified Ads, 1921.

12. *Baltimore Sun*, Classified Ads, April 20, 1921.

13. *Baltimore Sun*, Classified Ads, April 16, 1922.

14. Trustees' notice of Chesapeake and Columbia property for sale, Special Collections, from Estate of Frank Van Sant, The Historical Society of Washington, D.C. , MS 401 Arundel on the Bay, Maryland Records, 1898-1938.

15. Deed between trustees and receivers for Chesapeake and Columbia Investment Company (grantor) and Carey L. Meredith and William G. Meredith trading as Meredith Lumber Company (grantee) in Anne Arundel County Circuit Court Land Records, 1926, Book 34, p. 154, MSA CE 59-344.

16. Deed between Meredith Lumber Company (grantor) and J. F. Johnson Lumber Company (grantee) in Anne Arundel County Circuit Court Land Records, 1926, Book 23, p. 247, MSA CE 59-33.

17. Arundel on the Bay Revised Plat, Anne Arundel County, Md., Cabinet No. 1, ROD # A-3, Plat No. 492.

18. Deed between Chesapeake and Columbia Investment Company (grantor) and Laura A. Douglass (grantee) in Anne Arundel Circuit Court Land Records, 1893, Book 45, p. 61, MSA CE 59-60.

19. Deed between Laura A. Douglass (grantor) and Austin M. Curtis (grantee), in Anne Arundel Circuit Court Land Records, 1929 (recorded), Book 61, p. 94, MSA CE 59-405.

20. "Austin Maurice Curtis, 1868-1939," by Dr. Montague Cobb, *Journal of the National Medical Association,* Vol. 46, No. 6, July 1954.

21. Ibid.

22. Ibid.

23. Deed between Edward J. Brosnan (Estate of Jeremiah Brosnan grantor) and Austin M. Curtis, Jr. (grantee) in Anne Arundel County Circuit Court Land Records, 1923, Book 34, p.214 MSA CE 59-344.

24. Accounts provided by Pamela Sue Norris to Karen Neale and William Semenuk, 2012-2013.

25. Phone interview of Mrs. Ruby Kendros Pelicanos by Pamela Duncan and Karen Neale, August 22, 2014.

26. Mini-neighborhoods based on Thomas Worthington's accounts in interviews by Bill Semenuk and Pamela Duncan, 2012.

27. Deed between Carey L. Meredith and William G. Meredith t/a Meredith Lumber Company et al. (grantors) and Robert S. Tiger and Ben S. Hill (grantees) in Anne Arundel County Circuit Court Land Records, 1933, Book 111, p. 258 MSA CE 59-455.

28. Deed between Robert S. Tiger, Ben S. Hill and his wife Blanche E. Tiger (grantors) to Arundel on the Bay Properties, Incorporated (grantee) in Anne Arundel County Circuit Court Land Records, 1933, Book 111, p. 261, MSA CE 59-455.

29. Special Collections, from Estate of Frank Van Sant, Historical Society of Washington, D.C. , MS 401 Arundel on the Bay, Maryland Records, 1898-1938.

30. Ibid.

31. Special Collections, from Estate of Frank Van Sant, Historical Society of Washington, D.C. , MS 401 Arundel on the Bay, Maryland Records, 1898-1938.

32. Ibid.

33. Ibid.

34. Deed between Arundel on the Bay Properties, Inc. (grantor) and Commissioners of Arundel on the Bay, Anne Arundel County, Maryland (grantee), 1935, Book 137, p. 530, MSA CE 59-481.

35. "Governor's Proclamation," *Baltimore Sun*, November 17, 1941.

36. Memoir submitted by Suzanne Johnson, February 29, 2012.

37. "State Yacht Saves 5 From Burning Craft," *Baltimore Sun*, September 18, 1939.

38. Madill, Edwin J., Unpublished memoir "Arundel on the Bay," 1988. Historical

Society of Washington, D.C.

39. The Annapolis Emergency Hospital opened in a large cottage in 1902 and the maternity ward was added in 1919. It was located and expanded at Franklin and Cathedral Streets in Annapolis, and evolved to today's Anne Arundel Medical Center. http://www.aahs.org/aboutus/history.php.

40. Deed between Mary M. Harris and Ada Harris Maley (grantors) and Christian Heurich Jr. (grantee) in 1939 for Lot G, Book 195, p. 352, MSA CE 59-539; and between the same in 1938 for Lots D,E, F, H, I, Book 194, p.174, MSA CE 59-538.

41. "Christian Heurich," *Immigrant Entrepreneurship*, 2016. Http://immigrantentrepreneurship.org/entry.php?rec=38.

42. "Maryland's Receding Shoreline", Stewart Macauley, *Baltimore Sun*, September 24, 1933.

43. Special Collections, from Estate of Frank Van Sant, Historical Society of Washington, D.C. , MS 401, Arundel on the Bay Maryland Records, 1898-1938.

44. Deed between Meredith Lumber Company et al. (grantor) and Forest Beach, Inc. (grantee) in Anne Arundel Circuit Court Land Records, 1941, Book 234, p. 14, MSA CE 74-39.

45. *Baltimore Sun*, Classified Ads, January 28, 1946.

46. *Baltimore Sun*, Classified Ads, June 15, 1947.

47. *Baltimore Sun*, Classified Ads, July 27, 1947.

48. "Caretaker Found Dead at Resort," *Annapolis Evening Capital*, June 30, 1944.

49. "Liberated," *Annapolis Evening Capital*, July 3, 1945.

50. Http://www.blackpast.org/aah/carr-and-sparrow-s-beach-annapolis-maryland-1926-1974.

51. "Anne Arundel Taxes Differ- Local Levies To Vary Rates from $1.69 - $3.59", *Baltimore Sun*, November 14, 1949.

52. Kahrl, Andrew. *The Land Was Ours: African American Beaches from Jim Crow to the Sunbelt South*, Cambridge, MA: Harvard University Press, 2012, p. 111.

53. Phone interviews of Carol McMahon and Robin Lofton, October 2017.

54. Interview of Fred Garrett by Pamela Duncan, October 2012.

55. Interview of Helen Dodson by Pamela Duncan, January 2013.

56. Deed between T. Carroll Worthington and Elizabeth J. Thomas, trustees (grantors) and Henry L. Jackson and Charlotte E. Jackson (grantees) in Anne Arundel Circuit Court Land Records, 1973, Book 2584, p.273, MSA CE 59-2928.

57. Maryland House Bill 191, Chapter 527, p. 1280, Maryland State Archives, Session Laws, 1949.

58. Compilation from *The Chesapeake and Potomac Telephone Company Book of Baltimore City, 1932*, courtesy of Pamela Duncan.

Acknowledgments

Pamela Duncan, who shared research she had begun relative to this chapter before I came on-board, co-interviewed Tom Worthington, and inspired me with historian-like zeal and thoroughness.

Bill Semenuk, who interviewed Louise Linkins Bezdek Seely in Florida and shared her subsequent letters, co-interviewed Tom Worthington, and was the expert on maps and geography in and around Arundel-on-the Bay for this chapter.

Louise Linkins Bezdek Seely, longtime Arundel-on-the-Bay resident who granted a priceless interview, and provided personal memoirs, hand-written letters of explanation, and photographs.

Hugo Bezdek, who provided binders of photos, and assisted his mother, Louise Linkins Bezdek Seely with her contributions.

Thomas Worthington, longtime Arundel-on-the-Bay resident who granted two invaluable interviews, and provided personal memoirs and an extensive photo collection and home movies.

Jane McWilliams, Annapolis, Md. area author and historian who encouraged us, and referred us to Tom Worthington.

William "Buster" Lofton, longtime summer visitor and eventual property owner who provided first-hand accounts of life in the northernmost part of Arundel-on-the-Bay.

Pamela Sue Norris, former resident who provided information on her lineage, "The Curtis Family" as well as helpful tips, and facilitated communication with her uncle, William "Buster" Lofton.

Edwin (Ned) Madill, former summer resident of Arundel-on-the-Bay who provided, and in addition spoke with us about, his father's unpublished history/memoir of Arundel-on-the-Bay.

Ruby Kendros Pelecanos, who camped at Arundel-on-the-Bay a couple summers and shared an early childhood memory that "connected the dots."

George Tyler III, member of the Tyler Family raised in Arundel-on-the-Bay, who gave us practical insight of everyday life in the Town.

Kiplinger Research Library, Franklin Van Sant Collection on Arundel-on-the-Bay, Historical Society of Washington, D.C., which was a treasure trove of the Town's records donated by the Van Sant family and well-preserved by the Library.

Enoch Pratt Free Library of Baltimore, Md. where the Maryland Room and the Periodicals Department held vital information awaiting discovery.

APPENDIX A.

"RESTRICTIONS" applicable to properties sold in the Town of Arundel-on-the-Bay, issued by principals of Arundel-on-the-Bay Properties, Inc. on June 24, 1933, recorded June 24, 1933 and located in Md. Land Records, F.S.R, 111 folio 261.

F.S.R. 111 folio 261

June 24, 1933

EN S. HILL, SINGLE, ROBERT S. TIGER AND BLANCHE E. TIGER, WIFE
AND
THE ARUNDEL ON THE BAY PROPERTIES, INCORPORATED.

RESTRICTIONS

FIRST: That not more than one dwelling shall be erected on any one lot of groun,d which shall cost not less than $2,000.00; shall be thirty feet from the front property linel shall be of artistic apperance and shall have no flat or tar paper roofs; all sills shall be long leaf pine or fir, all porch floor shall be fir or heart pine, and all other exposed finish shall be of fir, cypress or cedar, no sap pine shall be used on any exposed work; and said premises shall be used for resident purposes only.

SECOND: Garages and pump houses shall be exempt from the minimum cost of$2,000.00 but otherwise shall be subject to the same restrictions as dwelling.

THIRD: The rightis reserved by the said grantors, their heirs or assigns, to go upon vacant lots, or cut grass or weeds or plant and cultivate flowers and shrubbery, and to construct or authorize the construction of conduits or poles on any lot for public utilities, wherever possible.

FOURTH: the grantors reserve the right at any time to zone the subdivision with regard to restrictions for business purposes and when so zoned no building shall be built, occupied or used for any business purposes except within said zone, and then under such restrictions and conditions as shall be provided for in said zoning regulations.

FIFTH: The said lot of ground shall not be sold, leased, transferred to, or occupied by any person or persons of the African, Asiatic or Mongolian blood or descent; this privision, however, not to include the occupancy by any servant or employee of any owner or occupant of said property.

SIXTH: No outside toilets shall be constructed upon any of the said lots and no sewerage shall empty into the Chesapeake Bay, or any tributary thereof, but all houses must be provided with such cesspools or septic tanks as may be agreed upon.

SEVENTH: the foregoing restrictions shall apply only to all lots lying to the south of Cedar Avenue, and east of the center line of Blocks Nos. 27, 28, 29, 30, 31, 32, 33, 34, 35 and 36, as shown on the aforesaid plat.

EIGHTH: And further that Lots A and K and an unnumbered Lot 150 feet fronting on Narragansett Avenue in Block 11, Lots A and K in Block 9, Lot A in Block 35, that in Addition to the restrictions set forth above, there shall be a further restriction that no building is to be placed within twenty feet on said lots from any side street

NINTH: The following restrictions and conditions shall apply to all of the rest and residue of the property South ofc Cedar Avenue and not mentioned in the Seventh restriction except as herein noted.

That only one dwelling shall be erected on each lot of ground as designated on said plat, to be used for residential purposes only, and on those lots fronting on Newport Avenue from Magnolia Avenue to Myrtle Avenue, that shall be no building or structure erected at a cost of less than $1,000.00, and shall not have a flat roof, shall not be nearer to the front property line than thirty feet. As to the rest and residue of the property, as shown on said plat, there shall not be erected more than one dwelling on each lot and before any dwelling is erected on any lot, plans and specifications are to be submitted and

(page 2)   F.S.R. 111 folio 261

be inspected and approved by the Grantors or those designated by the grantors.

That garages, pump houses, bath houses, and all other buildings of any character other than dwellings used in connection with a dwelling erected and existing on said property shall be exempt from the minimum cost but shall be otherwise subject to the same restrictions as dwellings. No person orpersons of Asiatic, African or Negro blood, lineage or extranction shall be permitted to occupy a portion of said property, or any building thereon; except domestic servant or servantsmay be actually and in good faith employed by white occupants of such premises.

That no outside private toilets shall be constructed upon any of said lots, and no sewerage shall empty into the Chesapeake Bay, or any tributary thereof, all houses to be provided with cesspools or septic tanks of such construction as may be agreed upon.

That the grantors, their heirs and assigns shall have the righh to go upon vacant lots, vut the grass or weeds, plant and cultivate flowers and shrubbery, and to construct or authorize the construction of conduits or poles or any lot for public utilities hwerever necessary.

That the said parties of the first part shall have the right at any time to zone restricted area with regard to restrictions for business or sport purposes, and when so zoned, no building shall be built, occupied or used for any busines or sport purposes except within said zone and then under such restrictions and conditions as shall be provided for in said zoning regulations.

Recorded June 26, 1933.

APPENDIX B. U.S. Department of Interior map issued by Geological Survey, Annapolis MD, 1957. Note shaded areas of submerged land farthest southeast. Also, dots within Arundel-on-the Bay indicating structures.

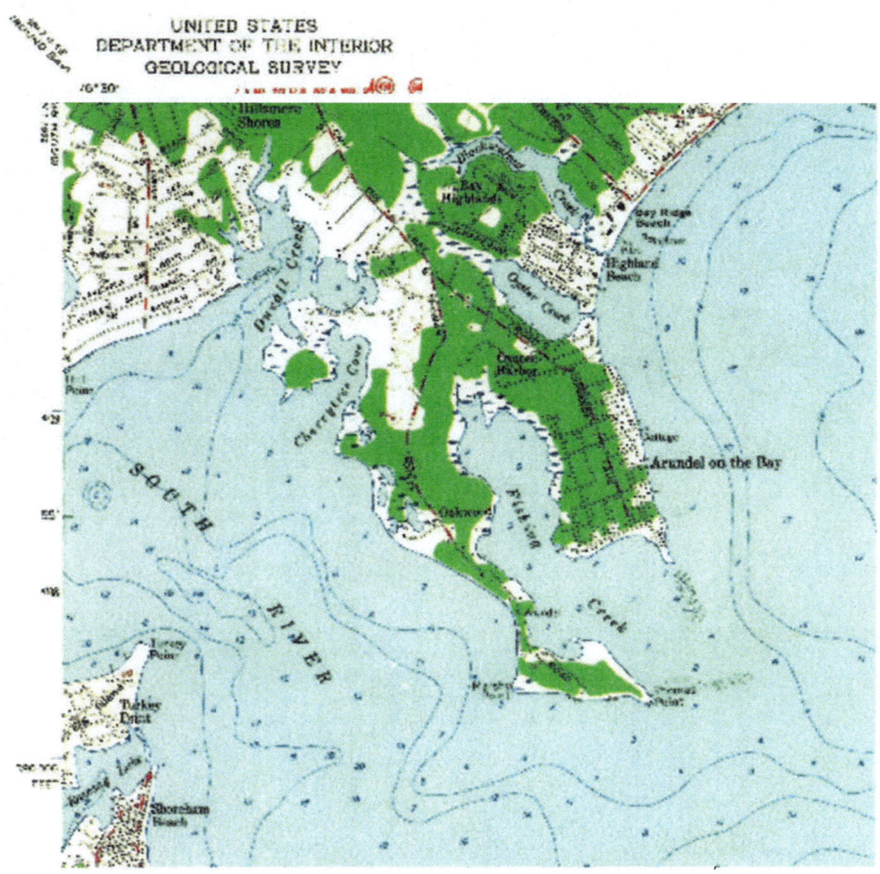

APPENDIX C.

House Bill 191, Chapter 527, p. 1280, Laws of Maryland, April 29, 1949

1280 LAWS OF MARYLAND. [CH. 527

CHAPTER 527

(House Bill 191)

AN ACT to repeal Sections 129-161, inclusive, of the Anne Arundel County Code (1947 Edition), being Article 2 of the Code of Public Local Laws of Maryland (1930 Edition), title "Anne Arundel County", sub-title "Arundel-on-the-Bay", said sections relating to the incorporation of Arundel-on-the-Bay, in Anne Arundel County.

SECTION 1. *Be it enacted by the General Assembly of Maryland,* That Sections 129-161, inclusive, of the Anne Arundel County Code (1947 Edition) being Article 2 of the Code of Public Local Laws of Maryland (1930 Edition), title "Anne Arundel County", sub-title "Arundel-on-the-Bay", be and they are hereby repealed.

SEC. 2. *And be it further enacted,* That this Act shall take effect on June 1, 1949.

Approved April 29, 1949.

Water Blown-Out on Fishing Creek, Thomas Point. ***Photograph by Marc Grigsby.***

Photograph by Marc Grigsby

Chapter Six

Arundel-on-the-Bay: Life in the 1950s and 1960s

Aris T. Allen Jr. and Arend J. Thomas III

The Era of Social Change

One of the most controversial periods in the history of Arundel-on-the-Bay is the era of change in the racial make-up of the community which began after World War II. A clear description in what occurred is contained in an interview with my father that appeared in the *Washington Post* in June 1988:

> When Dr. Aris T. Allen first saw the waterfront vistas of the little community of Arundel-on-the-Bay, it was not the summer haven for black physicians and professionals it was later to become.
>
> Although just south of Highland Beach, an area established in the 1890s as a refuge for Washington black intelligentsia, there were no blacks living in Arundel-on-the-Bay in the early 1950's. And that is what made the sign outside the small cinder-block house, located on a sweep of waterfront land offering a spectacular view of the Chesapeake Bay, even more peculiar.
>
> While Allen doesn't remember the exact wording, the message was clear: For Sale to "Colored" only.
>
> The white man selling the house had built the home over the objections of his neighbors, who didn't want their views of the water obstructed. When he built it anyway, his neighbors ostracized him, Allen said.
>
> So he said, "I'll do the very worst thing I can do to you – I'll sell to colored," Allen recalled. Allen passed up the chance to buy the home, but a Howard University medical professor decided to take the chance.
>
> When the professor moved in, Allen said, white families began moving out. "There was almost a complete changeover from white to black residents," Allen said.[1]

Arundel-on-the-Bay experienced changes that would alter the community forever. It began with the discontent of white property owners who had become angered that Jack V. and Sophia G. Ahrens were planning to construct a one and one half story home on waterfront Lots A & B of Block 37, 1323 Magnolia Avenue next to the Newport Avenue community pier. Concerned that views of the water would be obstructed, neighbors wanted the waterfront lots along Magnolia Avenue to remain undeveloped. The Ahrens, who purchased the lots in 1939 to build a vacation home, were unwilling to change their plans and proceeded with construction of a white cinder-block Cape-Cod style home of approximately 1,000 square feet, with a single car garage and screened porch. They became

Figure 1: The first sale to an African American family since 1916, T. Randolph Waters, Baltimore caterer, purchased 1322 Magnolia Avenue on November 12, 1949. ***Picture taken in the 1950s. Courtesy of Michon Peck Bailey.***

discontented and no longer felt welcome in the community. Upon completion of the house, the Ahrens decided to sell and move. It is reported that during the summer of 1949, they placed a for sale sign on their property that read 'For Sale to Colored Only.' Did this give residents concern that they might have to face racial change in the community? Coincidently during this period, the incorporated Town of Arundel-on-the-Bay was dissolved on June 1, 1949 and re-organized as the Property Owners Association of Arundel-on-the-Bay, Incorporated on June 3, 1949. There were seven directors.

Tensions escalated. Some residents expressed their dissatisfaction by putting their property up for sale, including William C. and Margaret A. Jamar, across the street from the Ahrens, whose water view from their home at 1322 Magnolia Avenue, Lots A & B of Block 38 was blocked. By deed of November 12, 1949, the Jamars sold their property to black Baltimore caterer T. Randolph Waters and his wife Theresa E. for $9,500. The Waters were the first African

Figure 2: The second sale to an African American family since 1916, J. Francis Dyer MD purchased 1323 Magnolia Avenue on November 29, 1949. Dr. Dyer owned the property until 1962. ***Courtesy of Aris T. Allen Jr.***

Americans to purchase at Arundel-on-the-Bay since the sale in 1916 between two African American families, Charles and Laura Douglass to Dr. Austin M. Curtis.

Several weeks later the Ahrens property was sold by deed of November 29, 1949 to Dr. J. Francis Dyer, a black Howard University professor and medical doctor, who had been looking for a waterfront summer home for his family.

These sales concerned many of the residents in this settlement of summer homes occupied primarily by white property owners who became upset at the prospect of living next door to black neighbors. Whites began to sell to anyone able to buy. Advertisements,

Ads for Arundel-on-the-Bay for "Colored People."

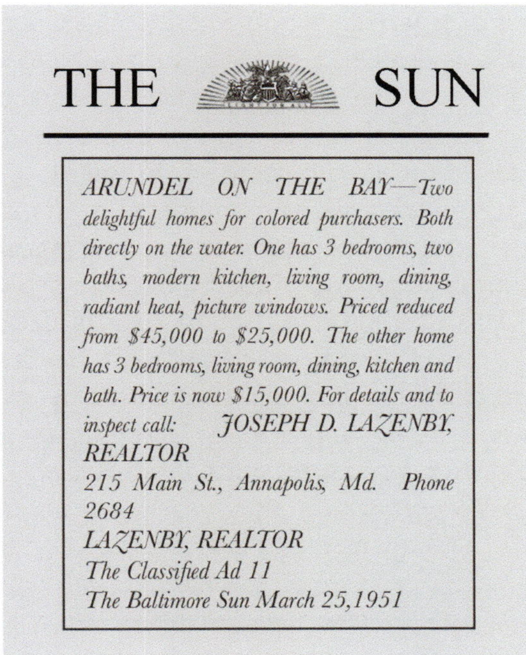

THE SUN

ARUNDEL ON THE BAY—Two delightful homes for colored purchasers. Both directly on the water. One has 3 bedrooms, two baths, modern kitchen, living room, dining, radiant heat, picture windows. Priced reduced from $45,000 to $25,000. The other home has 3 bedrooms, living room, dining, kitchen and bath. Price is now $15,000. For details and to inspect call: JOSEPH D. LAZENBY, REALTOR
215 Main St., Annapolis, Md. Phone 2684
LAZENBY, REALTOR
The Classified Ad 11
The Baltimore Sun March 25,1951

Figure 3: Facsimile newspaper advertisement. ***Text courtesy of Richard Napoli.***

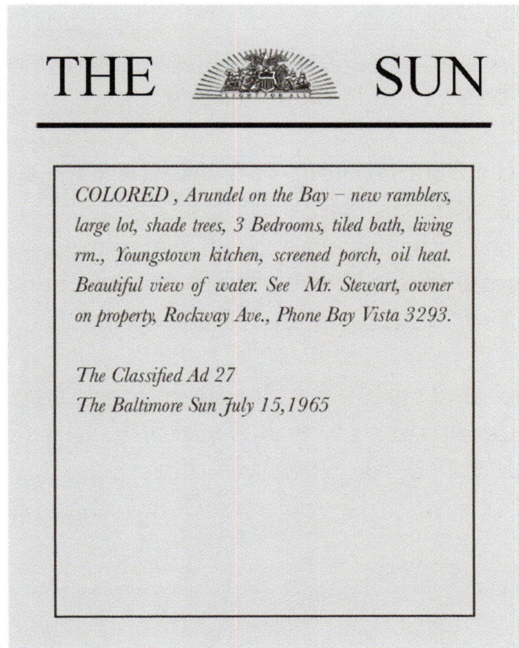

THE SUN

COLORED, Arundel on the Bay – new ramblers, large lot, shade trees, 3 Bedrooms, tiled bath, living rm., Youngstown kitchen, screened porch, oil heat. Beautiful view of water. See Mr. Stewart, owner on property, Rockway Ave., Phone Bay Vista 3293.

The Classified Ad 27
The Baltimore Sun July 15,1965

Figure 4: Facsimile newspaper advertisement by husband and wife builder, Gordon and Elizabeth Stewart who were Arundel-on-the-Bay residents, 1965. ***Text courtesy of Richard Napoli.***

such as the ones above, which appeared in the real estate section of newspapers, targeted black shoppers.

Interestingly, the presence of the Douglass, Curtis and Lofton families who were black and owned property as early as 1893 at the northern end of the community, did not trigger the exodus by white residents that occurred in reaction to the sales of the late 1940s and the 1950s. This white flight afforded opportunities for black professionals to move into Arundel-on-the-Bay who were well-educated and accomplished in a variety of fields including education, real estate, medicine, law, business, politics, government, opera and theater. From 1951 to 1955, Theodore H. Johnson, M.D. served as the first black president of the Arundel-on-the-Bay Property Owners Association, Inc. By 1955, seventy percent of the families were black. By 1966, the number of black families had increased two and a half times.

Carroll H. Hynson, Sr., the first black real estate broker in Anne Arundel County, handled the controversial sale of the Ahrens waterfront house and other sales to black purchasers during the 1950s and 1960s.

Figure 5: Carroll H. Hynson Sr. (1899-1994). ***Courtesy of Carroll H. Hynson Jr.***

His son, Carroll H. Hynson Jr., who continues his father's business, said that his father was inundated with calls from prospective black buyers following the Ahrens sale. Following the U.S. Supreme Court's Brown v. Board of Education ruling of 1954, black professionals, primarily from Washington, Baltimore, New Jersey and Pennsylvania, purchased at Arundel-on-the-Bay. They found this quiet and scenic waterfront community to be a convenient and safe haven. From Memorial Day to Labor Day their homes were filled with families. These residents referred to the travel to Arundel-on-the-Bay as going to "the beach" or going down to "the bay." Black families became acquainted with each other and developed close relationships. Social interaction was commonplace particularly in the summer when the vacationers were in residence.

Figure 6: Carroll H. Hynson Jr. ***Courtesy of Carroll H. Hynson Jr.***

Black purchasers during the 1950s and 1960s bought summer cottages and upgraded or remodeled them. Some who planned to live year-round in Arundel-on-the-Bay often made extensive renovations to be more comfortable. Other black purchasers bought lots and built new homes of various types and sizes that were conducive to their life styles. Gordon and Elizabeth Stewart, a white husband and wife builder team who resided in Arundel-on-the-Bay during this era, were not threatened by the social changes and remained in the community. They constructed speculative one story and split foyer style homes, which they marketed to blacks as shown in the *Baltimore Sun* advertisements on the previous page. Some of the homes they built still exist including their personal homes: a remodeled home at 3545 Rockway Avenue and their final home at 1312 Magnolia Avenue.

Summer residents focused primarily on activities within the community. However, the residents who lived full-time in Arundel-on-the-Bay expanded their interests and awareness and became more involved in the local government, schools and the social climate occurring in the City of Annapolis and Anne Arundel County. Integration of the school system began in 1954 after the Supreme Court ordered the desegregation of the nation's public schools. Black students were no longer limited to attending black-only public schools such as Wiley H. Bates High School, built in 1932, or the Stanton Elementary School. Stanton was initially built in 1903 as the only Anne Arundel County high school for black students. Green Street Elementary, Annapolis Junior High School and Annapolis High School, originally all-white, were desegregated in the 1950s.

Blacks were also no longer restricted to attending the black-only movie theater, the Star Theater. All movie theaters as well as restaurants, hospitals, hotels, churches and other public venues were integrated during this time period.

With integration came challenges. From personal experience, there was racial tension between black and white students, often manifested on the school buses. White students were picked up first. Once the buses arrived at Arundel-on-the-Bay, the white students sometimes denied seating to the black students – an affront that frequently led to physical confrontations.

Arundel-on-the-Bay resident, Philip Brown (1909-2009), was among those who led the successful legal effort to obtain equal pay for black teachers in the local school district and chronicled these efforts for integration and full funding of education for black students in his 1988 book, *A Century of Separate but Equal Education in Anne Arundel County.* Black Arundel-on-the-Bay residents joined civil rights activities in Annapolis and Anne Arundel County in the struggle for equal rights. They organized and participated in local meetings, negotiations, protests and sit-ins.

Play on the Bay and Community Activities

Residents enthusiastically enjoyed each other in Arundel-on-the-Bay. There were numerous planned events for both adults and children. Social gatherings included picnics, beach outings, card parties, holiday parties and house parties. A children's summer recreation program was sponsored by Anne Arundel County, replete with games, arts and crafts, swimming lessons and lifeguard training. Naturally, many activities were water-oriented. Children enjoyed the beach and the water.

They regularly played football and basketball within the community and on organized school teams. Close and long-term relationships developed among adults and children. A children's summer Sunday school was organized by Dr. Orris Walker and his wife Llewellyn which was held in the guest house of their home on Narragansett Avenue. Shorts and swim suits were the accepted attire for the children.

There were winter hayrides and summer parades with decorated bicycles, wagons, and scooters. Children and pets of all ages attended. Prizes were issued for best decorations. During Halloween, the kids would dress-up in costumes and go door to door for trick-or-treating.

Children spent hours in the water turning their fingers into prune-like digits which indicated that it was finally time to come out of the water.

By the end of the day, community kids would head home to bathe, change clothes and eat in anticipation of joining friends for the evening adventures. They would spend the evening hanging out in the community and at each other's homes to listen to music, dance and play cards.

During the summer, residents and guests might be seen enjoying yard parties or picnics that included a variety of foods and sometimes a pig roast. It would not be unusual to see a Hawaiian luau.

They could be found sunbathing, swimming, relaxing and lounging. Other residents could be found climbing trees to build tree houses for their children.

In this water-privileged community, some of the residents owned boats which they used for recreation, fishing and water skiing. The community boat pier, located at Newport Avenue, provided a facility for docking boats as well as for fishing and crabbing.

The annual Arundel-on-the-Bay Christmas Party and New Year's Eve Party were favorites during the holidays.

(See images on following pages)

Figure 7: Beach Fun, 1955, L-R: Aris Allen Jr., Theodore Johnson III and Lonnie Allen. *Courtesy of Aris T. Allen Jr.*

Figure 8: Boyd Children Boating, 1958. *Courtesy of Corrine Boyd.*

Figure 9: Children's Bicycle Parade, 1964, Willie Q. & Joyce McManus leading. *Courtesy of Joyce A. McManus.*

Figure 10: Halloween, 1957, L-R: Jay Walker, Pat Green, Michael Johnson, Gary Dixon, Lance Walker and Ted Johnson. *Courtesy of Lance Walker.*

Figure 11: L-R: Joan Dyer, Aris T. Allen Jr. and Lois Dyer in 1952. *Courtesy of Lois F. Dyer.*

Figure 12: Swimming in the 1950s. The community pier is in the background, L-R: Peggy Amos, Ricky Ellis and Michon Peck. *Courtesy of Michon Peck Bailey.*

Figure 13: Beach Fun in the 1950s, L-R: Peggy Amos and Michon Peck. *Courtesy of Michon Peck Bailey*.

Figure 14: House Party, 1956, teenagers dancing on waterfront porch. Courtesy of *Aris T. Allen Jr.*

Figure 15: House Party, 1956, teenagers dancing on waterfront porch. Courtesy of *Aris T. Allen Jr.*

Figure 16: Waterfront Picnic, 1969, L-R: Faye Allen, guest and Aris Allen Sr. The community pier is in background. ***Courtesy of Aris T. Allen Jr.***

Figure 17: Community Picnic: 1963, L-R: Marc Grigsby and his mother, Lenora Grigsby. ***Courtesy of Marc Grigsby.***

Figure 18: Sunbathing in the 1960s, Gordon & Corrine (Dimples) Boyd. ***Courtesy of Corrine Boyd.***

Figure 19: Picnic on the Lawn at the Walker's residence in the 1960s, L-R: Julia Mae McDaniel and Llewellyn Walker. ***Courtesy of Lance Walker.***

Figure 20: Hanging-Out in the 1960s, L-R: Theodore Johnson, Cecil Burton and Orris Walker. ***Courtesy of Lance Walker.***

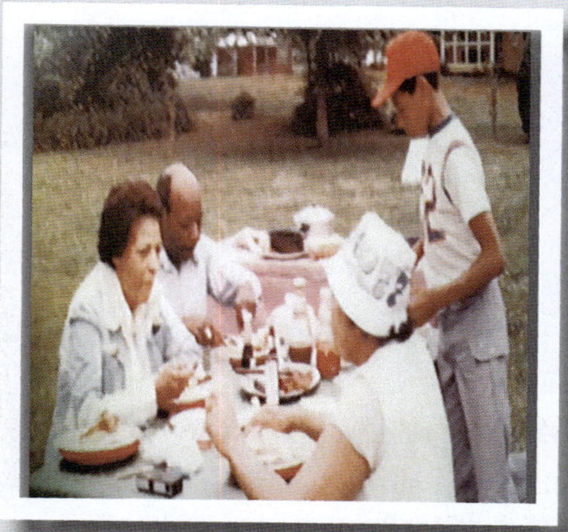

Figure 21: Picnic in the Snowden Yard in the 1960s, L-R: The Snowdens and guests. ***Courtesy of Corrine Boyd.***

Figure 22: Sun Bathing in the 1950s, Robert Peck and Helen Ellis. *Courtesy of Michon Peck Bailey*.

Figure 23: "Profiling" on the Community Pier in the 1950s, Helen Ellis, Inez Wall and Imogene Peck. *Courtesy of Michon Peck Bailey.*

Figure 24: Relaxing on the Community Pier in the 1950s, F-B: Imogene Peck, Pauline Spaulding, Inez Wall, Robert Peck, Dale Ellis, and Wilber Ellis. *Courtesy of Michon Peck Bailey.*

Figure 25: Billy Keyes, the tree house expert, high above the ground in the mid 1960s. *Courtesy of Billy Keyes*.

Figure 26: Boating in the 1950s. *Courtesy of Corrine Boyd.*

Figure 27: The Arundel-on-the-Bay Community Pier in 1966, Faye Allen and her dog. *Courtesy of Aris T. Allen Jr.*

Figure 28: Bragging about the biggest catch in the 1970s, L-R: James Snowden and Gordon Boyd. *Courtesy of Corrine Boyd.*

Figure 29: The Arundel-on-the-Bay Community Pier in 1976, with residents' boats. *Courtesy of Aris T. Allen Jr.*

Figure 30: The Arundel-on-the-Bay Christmas Party in 1967 at the Allen residence, 1315 Magnolia Ave. *Courtesy of Aris T. Allen Jr.*

Figure 31: Arundel-on-the-Bay Christmas Caroling in 1967, A. Cathryn Johnson on the right and friends. *Courtesy of Aris T. Allen Jr.*

Figure 32: Arundel-on-the-Bay Christmas Caroling, in 1967, Helen and John Weatherford. *Courtesy of Aris T. Allen Jr.*

Figure 33: Christmas Caroling in 1967, L-R: Betty Hynson on the left and friends. *Courtesy of Aris T. Allen Jr.*

Figure 34: New Year's Party in 1968, L–R: Thelma Sparks, Helen Edmead, Aris Allen Sr., Helen Chambers, Unknown, Bernice Gibbs, Unknown and Charles Gibbs. *Courtesy of Aris T. Allen Jr.*

Figure 35: A New Year's Party in 1968, L-R: Helen Weatherford, Cathryn Johnson, Unknown, Doris Knight, Unknown, Faye Allen and Thelma Sparks. *Courtesy of Aris T. Allen Jr.*

Fraternities, Sororities and Civic Organizations

Segregation affected black residents of Arundel-on-the-Bay as it did in other communities. They looked to each other for civic and social connection and interaction. As a result, some black residents of Arundel-on-the-Bay became members of, or were instrumental in founding, Greek and civic organizations consisting of neighbors and like-minded friends who had the same ideals and visions. Their purpose and mission was to serve local communities, under-privileged families and youth with a focus on eradicating social injustice and drug abuse, and improving academic achievement, recognizing community leaders and promoting the arts and public affairs. Women affiliated with Greek organizations such as Delta Sigma Theta, Alpha Kappa Alpha, Sigma Gamma Rho, Zeta Phi Beta and Chi Eta Phi and civic organizations like the Annapolis Chapter of the Links Incorporated and the Annapolis Fine Arts Club. Men joined fraternities like Alpha Phi Alpha, Omega Psi Phi, Kappa Alpha Psi and Chi Delta Mu and other organizations such as the Frontiers International.

Figure 36: Annapolis Fine Arts Club, 1968, L-R: *Bernice Gibbs, Gloria Massey, Yevola Peters, Eloise Richardson, *Harriet Abels, Judy Agnew– wife of then Governor Spiro T. Agnew, *Joyce McManus - president, Electa Holland, Jean Jackson, Ana Phillips, and *Vandola King. *Courtesy of Joyce A. McManus*. (*Arundel-on-the-Bay residents).

Annapolis Fine Arts Club

Many residents of Arundel-on-the-Bay supported the Annapolis Fine Arts Club and worked with government and businesses to develop art initiatives. They encouraged youth to widen their horizons and broaden their interests. One of their acclaimed initiatives was the 1968 "Annapolis Today" Wall Art exhibit which showcased student art works and interpretations of Annapolis. This initiative was a joint venture between Farmers National Bank and Annapolis Junior High School students.

Figure 37: Annapolis Chapter of the Links, 1962, L-R Rear Row: *Amanda Nunley, *Betty Hynson, *Emily Johnson, *Faye Allen, *Delores Chambers, Lulu Hardesty and Ana Phillips; middle row: *Bernice Gibbs, *Thelma Sparks, Pauline Maloney, Vivian Beamon, *Xavier McDonald, *Louise Burton and *Alma Hilliard; front row: *Vandola King, the first president. *Courtesy of Errol Brown*. (*Arundel-on-the-Bay residents).

Women of Arundel-on-the-Bay establish the Annapolis Chapter of the Links, Incorporated

The Links, Incorporated, an international not-for profit corporation, was established in 1946. It consists of nearly 14,000 professional women of color in 282 chapters located in 41 states, the District of Columbia and the Bahamas. The Annapolis chapter was chartered in 1962 under the leadership of Vandola H. King with many Arundel-on-the-Bay residents being installed. The organization's mission was to promote educational, civic and inter-cultural activities within the Annapolis area with an emphasis on encouraging youth to continue their education and realize their potential.

Men of Arundel-on-the-Bay Establish a Fraternity

Alpha Phi Alpha Fraternity, Incorporated was founded at Cornell University by seven students in 1906. Subsequent chapters were established at other colleges and universities. In 1959, seven like-minded friends and neighbors, four of whom were Arundel-on-the-Bay residents, aligned themselves to promote brotherhood and established the post-graduate Annapolis Chapter, Eta Lambda.

Figure 38: Alpha Phi Alpha Fraternity, 1959, L-R: Arundel on the Bay residents Aris T. Allen, M.D.; Robert H. Haygood, Lawrence E. Knight and Theodore H. Johnson, M.D.; Samuel P. Callahan, D.D.S.; James R. Randall, M.D. and Jerry H. Luck, Esq.

Memories and Reflections

Current and former residents have vivid memories of the transitional times during this era in Arundel- on-the-Bay. They recall the joy of growing up in a small community surrounded by water for fishing, crabbing, boating and water sports. Perhaps more importantly in that era, they remember Arundel-on-the-Bay as a warm and family-friendly shelter, a community where neighbors were like an extended family. It was a place to live a normal life while major social changes shook the nation. What follows are personal reminiscences–shared with this book's authors over the past several years–that help paint a vivid picture of Arundel-on-the-Bay in the 1950's and 1960's.

Figure 39: Lois F. Dyer. Her family was one of the first African American families to purchase a home in Arundel-on-the-Bay in the 1940s.

Lois F. Dyer

Lois Dyer is the daughter of one of the first black families who purchased a home in Arundel-on-the-Bay after World War II. The Dyers owned their vacation residence at 1323 Magnolia Avenue from 1949 to 1962. Lois is the older of two Dyer daughters. She lives in Washington, D.C., and works for CBS News. Although the years that Lois spent as a young person in Arundel-on-the-Bay coincided with great changes in the community, her most vivid memories that follow are those of good friendships and the joys of living on the water:

Arundel-on-the-Bay was a part of my life at a time when I was too naive to know that not every child had a house on the brink of the Chesapeake Bay and the luxury of carefree days. In the fall of 1949 when I was not quite one-year old, my parents, J. Francis and Lois Dyer, purchased the red-and-white cinder block house and adjacent waterfront property on Magnolia Avenue at Newport, becoming the first blacks, or Negroes as we were known then, to own in Arundel-on-the-Bay. That purchase set up wonderful childhood memories for me that remain more than 60 years later. I recall my parents saying that the seller, Sophia Ahrens, decided to sell to blacks as her way of returning the land to Native Americans who originally inhabited the area, even if her neighbors were not pleased with her decision.

Figure 40: The Dyer Family in 1958, L-R: Lois, daughter; J. Francis Dyer, M.D.; Lois, wife and Joan, daughter. ***Courtesy of Lois F. Dyer.***

By the time I had real memories of beach life, other black families had moved to the community. A white family, the Stewarts, were already there and remained a while. Our next door neighbors on Magnolia were Doctors Aris and Faye Allen and their sons, Tee and Lonnie, who were the first family I knew to have a color television and to host a luau, complete with roasted pig that spent the day cooking underground in their yard and the only people I've ever known to own an Edsel. They were special because they lived at the beach year-around, while most of us then were weekend residents. Directly across the street were Mr. and Mrs. Peck and their daughter, Michon, who like my family lived in Washington, D.C.

My mother and Mr. Peck had grown up on the same block in Washington and he was one of the first black firefighters in the city. Across the street in the yellow house were the Waters and in the blue-trimmed house the McDonalds–both couples were residents of Baltimore, as I recall. Also on our street in the 1950s were the Hynsons, Kings and Goodloes. Other early residents of 'the beach,' as we affectionately called it, were the Duncans, Greenes, McMurdocks, Dixons, Johnsons, Fortes and Carpenters.

I was always anxious to get to 'the beach' to play with my beach friends Tee and Lonnie and Ted and Michael Johnson and to see whether Michon and her family had arrived to spend a few days, too. Bike riding was perhaps the activity I looked forward to the most, while crabbing on the rickety pier next to our house was not on the top of my list. Other vivid memories include walking with my father around Arundel-on-the-Bay and chatting with all we met, my mother teaching me to ride a bicycle, my parents' parties and my parents working in the yard as autumn overtook lazy summer days.

The Fourth of July was always spent at the beach and at a young age I was allowed to hold a sparkler under the watchful eye of my parents. My sister, who was born only months before our third summer at Arundel-on-the-Bay, was no fan of the colorful fireworks and would watch only briefly before our father took her inside. I enjoyed frolicking in the water, whether sitting in an old rubber tire or dodging jellyfish. I loved to swing or just sit in the yard, gazing at the Thomas Point lighthouse or watching the motorboats go by, especially young Carroll Hynson in his boat, *The Kiss*. My sister and I always giggled at that name.

I've not spent a night at Arundel-on-the-Bay since the early 1960s but the days I spent there wove lasting memories and I'm grateful my parents provided us a special haven. A couple of years after my father died, the Allens purchased our property. The red and white house with the awnings and screen porch and stunning view of the Chesapeake Bay is no more but the land, water and grand view remain and all I need to do is close my eyes and I am back there–the smell of the bay, the sound of the waves as I fell asleep, moonlit nights, playing with Tee, Lonnie, Michon, Michael, Ted, Todd and all the rest of us kids who were fortunate enough to also experience Arundel-on-the-Bay.

The breathtaking view I remember from Magnolia Avenue has not changed in all these years and the Thomas Point Lighthouse and the surrounding Bay from that vantage point will always be the most beautiful and calming tableau to me.

Andy Grose

Figure 41: Andy Grose in 2014. ***Courtesy of Andy Grose.***

Andy Grose shares his perspective and memories as a young white person growing up in the community at a time of racial change. His parents owned a home at 3523 Rockway Avenue from 1946 to 1972. When he lived there, Rockway Avenue was named Rockaway Avenue. They moved from Prince Georges County to live full-time in Arundel-on-the-Bay. His family witnessed the gradual racial transition that occurred although social interaction was limited. Andy explains, "I can't say my parents were any more thrilled than other whites who sold and moved out, but my father especially loved that place, and we stayed put. I loved living there growing up. Sadly, I cannot recall ever meeting any of the black neighbors. Neither do I recall any problems or unpleasantness associated with being in the minority there." Following are Andy's recollections and memories:

> Our house was on the NE corner of Rockaway and Oak. Rockaway is now named Rockway. It may have been 10 years ago that I was last there (I live in California). The house was there then. Two structures; the house and a separate two-car garage with a 12:12 roof with a large room over. Our neighbors during our years there (approximately 1946 to 1970) to the south were Ben and Belva Rawlings. My mother worked at NSA and only came to Arundel-on-the-Bay on weekends. Mrs. Rawlings (she was my second mother) who was a very bright and wonderful person often fixed my meals, helped me with my homework and took me with her to visit relatives in the greater Annapolis area.

"The first African American families did come about the same time we moved to Arundel-on-the-Bay full time in 1950. The only family I recall was the Hynsons, who built on a lot at the south end of Rockaway on the water. White families started selling very fast at that point. But a number did not, quite a few actually."

> At the north end of Rockaway on the creekside were Mr. and Mrs. Tracy. Also on Rockaway before getting to the Tracys was Walter Tyler. His father George lived with him early on but died in the 1950s. George was known as Captain Tyler. To the west of us at the foot of Oak at the creek was Captain Boley Tyler. He was George's brother. Both of them were old watermen. Boley Tyler was a veteran of the Spanish American War, with Dewey at Manila Bay. He worked at the Naval Academy in carpentry and retired from that. He was a great storyteller and a great character.
>
> He had restored and sailed a Chesapeake Bay log canoe at the Miles River Regatta for several years. It was named the *Sandy*, after his beagle. It won the Governor's Cup one year in the late 40s. I sailed with him as the bail boy in the 1952 regatta. Those boats would take in water over the gunnels when it was at full sail and a small kid was aboard to bail that water! Captain Boley died about 1954. I still have a large, 30-inch-long model of a pungy, a turn of the 20th century two-masted cargo sail boat that he

had made by hand for his daughter Augusta. I learned a great deal about the water from him. He had a gruff exterior but always treated me great.

My family moved to our beach house to live year round in early 1950. I had gone to school in Bladensburg but transferred to Eastport Elementary in 1950 in 4th grade. Just about two years later we moved back to Bladensburg where I was in 6th grade. The rest of our time owning the property, it was a summer house. My father had a 26 foot dead-rise, the *Mildred*, which we kept at the foot of Oak Avenue. There was a pier there built by Ben Rawlings, who also kept a boat there, first the *Helen* and then the boat that he took several years to build in his back yard, the *Belva Sue*. He died several years ago. His wife died just last year at almost 100.

The first African American families did come about the same time we moved to Arundel-on-the-Bay full time in 1950. The only family I recall was the Hynsons, who built on a lot at the south end of Rockaway on the water. White families started selling very fast at that point. But a number did not, quite a few actually. My father loved that place and, while he was no integrationist, he just continued life as usual, which centered on his boat and fishing. Most of the white families along the bay front sold, as I recall. We only knew one of those families, the Stamatas family. My father was a Greek immigrant (from an island!) and so the connection with that family. The creekside of Arundel-on-the-Bay was the cheaper, blue-collar side. Another family that stayed was the Brinks. He was 'Major' Brink, his wife Mrs. Brink and their son Steck. The Army rank was from WWI. He was retired. They lived in a shake shingle house on Newport about a block back from the water. The foot of Newport was the town pier. I guess it still is.

Steck was about six years ahead of me in school, but he had all sorts of 'toys' including a big train layout that took up most of their enclosed porch. He had his own workshop in the backyard where he built rockets and launched them. His mother loved Canasta and I played a lot of that with her.

The north side of the entrance into Fishing Creek was Lums Point. I never knew the Lums, but they were another white family that did not sell. That was really the only accessible good beach in Arundel-on-the-Bay then. There were two other white families that did not move, at least for a few years. The houses were at the corner of Cohasset and either Linden or Chestnut, the latter I think, both on the west side.

To the north were the Daywalts. Don't know much about them except for their son Jerry, who was my age. We had lots of adventures in what was basically a pretty wooded, open space. Jerry was the kind of guy who had to be the first to swim each spring, regardless of the weather. One day on a walk along the bay-front before the school bus, he found a dead seagull and took it to school under his coat! I think the Daywalts were renters.

"And it was recognized that the non-white families were professionals and educated - more than the white families."

To the south of Chestnut were Tommy and Mary Tyler. Tommy was Walter's brother. Tommy was a carpenter. He built our garage and our side porch. Walter had been a lifelong bachelor. Tommy had lived with Walter and their father until he was perhaps 40 when he married. Walter, by the way, was a practical genius. He built 40-foot boats in his backyard–beautiful boats, great lines. He could also build or repair just about anything, a very smart guy. But if you were just talking to him for the first time, not knowing his genius, you'd think he was learning-disabled. He always referred to his car as 'the machine.'

Another family was the Stewarts. He was also known as 'Major' but his rank was from WWII. And his wife Lizzy was a German war bride. They owned a number of lots in Arundel-on-the-Bay and worked at developing them. They lived in a big New England-style beach house at the corner of Rockaway and Magnolia, on the north side. She was a 'typical' German–a strong woman, and very hard-working. She seemed to be the one who worked. He was the 'brains' I guess, but never saw him do physical work.

I mentioned the Tracys before. She was a homemaker. He drove a truck for some company like Jewel Tea. She loved dogs. She ended up taking our dog after he did not adjust to moving to Bladensburg. She drove. Mrs. Rawlings and Mrs. Brink did not. So once a week on Friday, this group would go to Annapolis to grocery shop. Seems like there was a fourth, but can't recall.

I graduated from college in '62 and after a master of science degree in 1964 went into the Air Force; I lost track of things in Arundel-on-the-Bay. But as of 1970 when we returned from Germany, Walter Tyler was still alive, the Rawlings were still there, Augusta Tyler was living in Captain Boley's house (she had retired from Anne Arundel General Hospital). My family would sell to an African American family sometime not too long after that. The Rawlings would move to Bradenton, Fla., where both their daughters and families had been for a while. Walter Tyler would pass on. So had the Brinks or soon would. I don't recall what happened to the Stewarts or the Tracys.

My observation was that the selling panic of the late '40s and early '50s lasted only a couple of years and then the racial balance stabilized for about 20 years. The white families who did not panic eventually sold but for normal reasons of age, death, family, and so forth. But in the '70s the buyers were still non-white. I was very pleased in returning in the '90s and the 2000s to see greater diversity than at any time in my direct experience.

Those who stayed after the panic, like my father, were hardly enlightened civil libertarians. They were pragmatists who basically wanted little to do with their new neighbors but still enjoyed living there. But things evolved. Neighbors got to know each other to some limited extent. Everyone admitted the place had greatly improved with the new neighbors who built nice houses or remodeled existing ones, all to the better. And it was recognized that the non-white families were professionals and educated–more than the white families.

C. Todd Duncan

Figure 42: Charles Todd Duncan (known as Todd) in 2013. Grandson of opera singer, Todd Duncan, the first to sing the role of Porgy in George Gershwin's opera.

C. Todd Duncan is a photographer, journalist, and world traveler who is living in St. Louis. He is the third generation of his distinguished African American family to have enjoyed Arundel-on-the-Bay.

C. Todd elected to commemorate his grandfather, Todd Duncan (1903-1998), a renowned baritone, who gave more than 5,000 opera and solo classical concerts and performances in 50 countries. Todd Duncan regularly practiced his singing which was often heard emanating from the house. He was affectionately called "Far-Far" by Todd, which means father's father in Norse. The name "Far-Far" was given to him while performing in Norway when he received the announcement of grandson C. Todd's birth. In July 1954, his grandfather, and grandmother, Gladys Jackson Duncan (1896-2005), purchased the Warfield home at 1362 Myrtle Avenue in Arundel-on-the-Bay. Reportedly, his grandfather decided to purchase the house without entering, saying 'This is it!" C. Todd shares his recollections and wonderful anecdotes of his famous grandfather, Todd Duncan:

> Among the things that my grandfather loved – teaching, fishing, entertaining–high on his list was gardening. Each June he would excuse his voice students until September, and he and his wife went to their retreat at Arundel-on-the-Bay. Every summer I was lucky enough to go with them; and what a sweet deal it was for my parents!

Todd Duncan, opera star. First to play Porgy on Broadway

Figure 43: Todd and Gladys Duncan at Arundel-on-the-Bay in 1960. *Courtesy of the Duncan family.*

Figure 44: Todd Duncan on the pier of his Bayfront home in the 1950s. *Courtesy of the Duncan family.*

Figure 45: Todd Duncan lecturing to a group in Annapolis. *Courtesy of the Duncan family.*

Figure 46: Todd Duncan tends his beloved roses in 1955. Behind him to the right is the cottage at 3520 Narragansett Avenue. *Courtesy of the Duncan family.*

When he wasn't in the yard, Porgy-like on his knees digging in the dirt "It's soil, son, not dirt," he would gently remind me, then he was on the porch reading about it. Books on gardening and voice were his favorites, and his libraries were crammed with titles on both.

He collected rainwater in always-rusting steel barrels because he preferred it to well-water for his flowers and tomatoes. He kept a compost pit in the farthest corner of the yard, and would pick through our trash for valuable additions my grandmother might have overlooked.

Once—and only once—he came home with the back seat of his Cadillac filled to overflowing with rich topsoil from some construction site he had driven by. As long as his plants got what they needed, he felt it was worth the blistering response he surely knew awaited him from Gladys. The car smelled 'earthy' for months and was never again quite clean in back. But that summer, his plants prospered. For him, that was enough.

C. Todd Duncan's grandfather, Todd Duncan, was renowned for his role as the original "Porgy" in George Gershwin's great American opera *Porgy and Bess*. In addition to Gershwin, his repertoire included works by Brahms and Schumann, and audiences across the nation heard his rendition of "Unchained Melody" in the 1955 movie *Unchained*. He was music professor at Howard University and taught voice privately.

C. Todd Duncan's father, Charles T. Duncan, was a Harvard educated lawyer and the first Corporation Counsel of the District of Columbia under the Washington, D.C., Home Rule Act of 1968. He later served as Dean of the Law School at Howard University and as an arbitrator at the Iran-U.S. Claims Tribunal in The Hague, the Netherlands, from 1995 until 2000. Charles Duncan (1924-2004) and his wife, Todd's mother Dorothy (who died in 1972), summered in the home. Charles and his second wife, Pamela, resided in the home from 1995 until his death. Pamela has continued to live in the home.

Figure 47: Arundel-on-the-Bay resident, Keiffer J. Mitchell, MD, 2012.

Keiffer J. Mitchell, MD

Keiffer J. Mitchell, MD, internist with specialty in gastroenterology, is a third generation son of the politically famed Mitchell family of Baltimore nationally recognized for their role in civil rights and social justice. His family owned 3544 Narragansett Avenue from 1951 until the early 1990s. In 2012, Dr. Mitchell (1941-2015), who lived and practiced in Baltimore, shared his memories of his family and of Arundel-on-the-Bay:

> My grandmother, Dr. Lillie May Jackson, was the president of the Baltimore branch of the NAACP and raised funds for the legal battle against restrictive covenants. (This battle) went to the Supreme Court, which struck down the restrictive covenant in place preventing African Americans from owning property in Arundel-on-the-Bay.
>
> My parents bought their home in 1951, and I spent summers there. Arundel-on-the-Bay was unique in that it was an island in the middle of Anne Arundel County, which would not allow overall integration of eating facilities and public beaches. My mother, Juanita Jackson Mitchell, filed the legal suits that desegregated those public accommodations, and my brother, Clarence Mitchell III, was in the state legislature and ensured that law upheld full integration of public accommodations in Maryland.
>
> I chose medicine as a vocation, and this is my forty-fourth year in the practice of gastroenterology and internal medicine. My son, Keiffer Mitchell, Jr., represented the 44th Legislative District in the House of Delegates of Maryland from 2011 to 2015. He spent summers at Arundel-on-the-Bay as a five year old.
>
> He continues to work in the legislature for laws that affect in a positive way communities like Arundel-on-the-Bay. In January 2015, Keiffer, Jr. left his legislative seat and took a position as Special Advisor, Governor's Legislative Office. He also serves as a member of the President's Advisory Council of the Baltimore City Community College.
>
> I feel that the history of how Arundel-on-the-Bay was open to African Americans to buy property and live free of segregation must be known to future generations.

The Mitchell family's involvement in civil rights and elected politics on both the state and national levels was unique and unprecedented. Here is a snap-shot of Dr. Mitchell's family. His grandmother, Dr. Lillie Carroll Jackson, was president of the NAACP's

Baltimore office. His father, Clarence M. Mitchell, Jr. was head of and lobbyist for the NAACP's Washington office and his name appears on the Baltimore City Courthouse, the Admission Building at the University of Maryland and the Engineering School at Morgan State University. His mother, Juanita J. Mitchell, was the first black female to attend the University of Maryland Law School and the first black female to be admitted to practice law in Maryland. His uncle, Parren J. Mitchell, was the first black to graduate from the University of Maryland graduate school, the first black to be elected to U.S. Congress and his name appears on the Art & Sociology Building at the University of Maryland. His son, Keiffer J. Mitchell, Jr., served in the Baltimore City Council. Two brothers, Clarence M. Mitchell III and Michael B. Mitchell, Sr., served in the Maryland State Senate and the Baltimore City Council respectively. His nephew, Clarence M. Mitchell IV, served as a Maryland State Senator.

Figure 48: Juanita Jackson Mitchell, Esq., Arundel-on-the-Bay resident and first black women to attend the University of Maryland School of Law and the first black women to practice law in Maryland. ***Courtesy of Keiffer J. Mitchell, MD.***

Gloria Forte Henderson

Gloria Forte Henderson is an administrator in Washington, D.C., public schools. Her family owned 1362-1364 Linden Avenue from 1950 until the mid 1960s. In the following text, she shares her conviction and enthusiastic belief that this community provided her with her greatest memories:

Figure 49: L-R: Allan U. Forte Jr., Bertha B. Forte and Gloria Forte Henderson, 1977. ***Photograph by Dr. Allan U. Forte. Courtesy of Gloria Forte Henderson.***

My family and I began spending summers at Arundel-on-the-Bay in 1950. Prior to this, our summers were spent in the hot inner city of Baltimore. During this time, my family's housing choices were limited because of the unwritten racial segregation rules that prevented us from buying a new home in a less congested suburban park-type neighborhood. Also, the use of public pools and other such amenities were off limits as well. So, the only relief from those sizzling July and August days were trips to the park, visits to relatives in less cosmopolitan areas and visits to the two local black beaches, Carrs and Sparrows. Without question, the excursions to the beach were the best. Thank goodness these places were available, because I really loved the sand and waves. In fact, my parents told me that first time I went at age 4, I did not even wait for my dad to unload the car. I ran immediately for the water. It was truly love at first sight.

Figure 50: L-R: Bertha B. Forte, Allan U. Forte Jr. and Gloria Forte Henderson in 1953. ***Photograph by Dr. Allan U. Forte. Courtesy of Gloria Forte Henderson.***

This love for the beach probably inspired my dad to investigate and explore surrounding areas for a permanent residence close to the water where his family–my mother, baby brother and I–could spend relaxing fun times in the summer. Probably this was why he always felt so fortunate to find such a great piece of property in Arundel-on-the-Bay, which stretched from the corner of Narragansett Avenue and Linden Avenue to the shoreline of the Chesapeake Bay. This property included a large four-bedroom home, a one-bedroom guest cottage and a big two-car garage. A very narrow roadway separated the larger house from a steep embankment that ended at the edge of the bay; this area had been shored up by a wall of rocks and jetties. Luckily there was a wooden staircase there that led down to a small pier that extended out over the water, providing a means to swim, fish, catch crabs, board small boats and enjoy a wonderful up close and personal view of the Chesapeake Bay.

After the property was purchased, renovations were made to the main house, including wood floors and plumbing upgrades that included a new pumping system for our well water and a new furnace so that we could stay there at any time of the year. From that point in time, every summer, as soon as school closed, we would leave our home in Baltimore and move to the bay until Labor Day. However, on many occasions we spent Christmas at Arundel-on-the-Bay, and the following day my parents celebrated their anniversary with a party there.

Arundel-on-the-Bay was definitely a great place to be. Each day the atmosphere was very comfortable and casual. Bathing suits could be worn most of the day because dips in the bay were taken so often. During the beginning years of our stays, there were other white and black families who also spent time there. However, as black families moved into the area, the whites followed the typical trend of those times and slowly moved out.

> *"Every summer a community get-together was held which featured a picnic and a bicycle rodeo. Prizes were given for races, best bike tricks and decorations."*

Back in the 1950s, Arundel-on-the-Bay had a country atmosphere, with lots of wooded areas between each home. I spent most of my time swimming, bicycling to enjoy the views, picking blackberries and blueberries for pies, and visiting the new friends I made there. From Monday to Friday, these included Paula Peacou, Eula Lum, Pat Greene and Arend Thomas, Margret and Robert Nelson, Wally Gibbs, Jay and Lance Walker, Victor McPherson and his sister, Lorenzo Snowden, Tee and Lonnie Allen. On the weekends and other times we were joined by others, including Jimmy, Barry and Brenda Carpenter, Michon Peck, Gary Dixon, Bonda Lee, Lesley Gross, Jill Collins, Keiffer and Michael Mitchell. Most of these families came from Washington and Baltimore.

There were always a lot of fun things to do. Fortunately, Anne Arundel County provided a recreation program for children. A young adult came Monday-Friday and gave us opportunities to play games, dabble in crafts and increase our swimming skills.

Over the years, some of us were able to earn junior and senior life-saving status. Also, the county public library system provided a bookmobile that came every two weeks. Each time it came, we were allowed to borrow and return books.

It wasn't long before, the adult property owners decided to incorporate and form a formal association. They met often to discuss plans for maintaining and improving the overall environment of Arundel-on-the-Bay. As an offshoot of these meetings, every summer a community get-together was held which featured a picnic and a bicycle rodeo. Prizes were given for races, best bike tricks and decorations. On some occasions, trips were sponsored to the nearby Naval Academy on Wednesdays to watch the midshipmen display their parade skills. Every weekend Sunday school was provided by Mrs. Walker, Jay and Lance's mother. It was always nice to see everyone sort of dressed up and in a more serious mode. At the end of the summer, her husband, Dr. Walker, would prepare a fantastic closing breakfast, which he prepared on a large brick barbecue grill. Occasionally, the children also enjoyed 'bike hikes' with Mrs. Snowden, Lorenzo's mom. We would meet her early in the morning with a small lunch in tow and ride about two or three miles to La Chappell, a small nearby mom-and-pop grocery store. This was exciting because before our bike hikes, we were only allowed to ride around the quiet roadways in Arundel-on-the-Bay. However, when we were with Mrs. Snowden we got a chance to ride on the main roads. As time went by, my friends and I reached pre-teen and teen years, we spent much of our time riding in small speed boats, water-skiing, playing bid whist and pinochle, listening to current rock-and-roll music and of course dancing, which was especially enjoyable after my parents converted our two- car garage into a big recreation room with plenty of space to do all the latest steps. Also, we occasionally got to drive our parents' cars around Arundel-on-the-Bay and to neighboring Highland Beach, a neighboring historic black beach community. We always had a multitude of fun! On many occasions, each of us would invite our young relatives and friends to visit us, and this always added extra enjoyment to whatever we were doing.

Nevertheless, the real enjoyment of Arundel-on-the-Bay came from observing all that was happening on the Chesapeake Bay. It was always interesting to see the many different types of boats and ships. On many days, there would be a beautiful array of sailboats. Their white sails looked so pretty gleaming against the blue water.

On other occasions, naval maneuvers could be observed, including ships and planes, occasionally breaking the sound barrier. Tankers and commercial ships also could be viewed traveling to and from Baltimore's port. However, one ship, *The Bay Belle*, which made daily trips carrying passengers between Baltimore and Norfolk, Va., had special importance to all of my friends and me because when it came into view at dusk, it signaled our curfew to stop whatever we were doing and head home . . . (or else).

However, without question, the most spectacular bay views included gorgeous sunrises, sunsets and moonlight glistening on the water. Also, this was especially beautiful after the Bay Bridge was built because at night, the cars looked like diamonds moving across it.

Living in Arundel-on-the-Bay includes some of the BEST MEMORIES of my life! It was truly a fantastic place to be!

Alma Carlisle

Alma Carlisle, an architect living in California, has witnessed three generations spending summers at the family's waterfront home at 1362 Chestnut Avenue, from the early1950s to the present. She provides her recollections and experiences:

I don't remember exactly when my parents, Clarence and Alma Murray, purchased the summer cottage at Arundel-on-the-Bay, but it was between the time when I graduated from college in 1950 and I got married in 1953. When they purchased the cottage they also purchased lots at Oyster Harbor.

My parents loved the outdoors – camping, picnics, gardening and the beach. Every year they would rent cottages at various beaches and spend most of the summer 'at the beach'. My mother was a schoolteacher in Alexandria, Va., where the winter home was

Figure 51: Alma Carlisle's children and nephew, L-R: Judith Carlisle, David Carlisle, Kurt Johnson and Carolyn Carlisle in the 1960s. ***Courtesy of Alma Carlisle.***

located. My father worked for the United States government as a railroad mail clerk. They would arrange summer vacations at various beaches. Annapolis and the Chesapeake Bay were close to home, and the family spent many summers at the Bay before they moved to Arundel-on-the-Bay.

The cottage on Chestnut Avenue was great for family vacations from spring until fall. Usually extended family and friends stayed there with them. The cottage has a great porch for getting together for dining, games, yoga, napping, and just enjoying the view of the Bay. We swam every day. When we didn't swim in front of the cottage we walked to Oyster Harbor for swimming from the beach there. They built a stairway to what we called 'the lower level,' a 'boardwalk' on the lower level, a mini-pier for fishing, crabbing with a ladder down to the bay for swimming and to go out to our float in the Bay. (It washed away in a hurricane).

We learned about the history of Arundel-on-the-Bay from a Mr. Tyler, a long-time resident. My aunt, Madeline Pinn Rogers, loved the cottage and spent many summers there. My sister Madeline Murray Johnson and her three children, Suzanne, Virginia and Kurt, spent summers there, and I would travel from California with my three children, David, Carolyn and Judith. (I've sent a photo of the children, when they were young, at the stairs leading to the 'lower level,' and a view of the Bay from the yard.)

Arundel-on-the-Bay was a wonderful place for my family and our friends to get together for a relaxing and fun-filled summer. I've always loved it there—it's one of my favorite places in the world.

Arend J. Thomas III

Four generations of Arend's family have lived in Arundel-on-the-Bay. A retired pharmacist, he has lived in the home he built at 1361 Chestnut Avenue since 1972. Arend, one of the major contributors to this book, shares his fond memories of growing up as a child and living here as an adult:

My memories of Arundel-on-the-Bay begin in the summer of 1951. My father, Arend J. Thomas Sr.—nickname 'Bo'—and mother Mary Ellen Anthony Thomas, known as 'May', purchased two wooded lots on the northwest corner of Chestnut and Narragansett Avenues. The lots were cleared in anticipation of constructing the family home. The roads leading to the property were of an oyster shell base with black gravel chips soaked with oil placed over some of the oyster shells. Later that year, my parents purchased two more lots across the street on the northeast corner of Chestnut and Narragansett Avenues. This is where the family home was built. The lot cost was $400, the house cost $7,000 and taxes were $90. Most of the homes for sale in the community were summer cottages without insulation. Most of these wood framed houses had fireplaces and screened porches with wood siding.

Figure 52: Arend J. Thomas III, Co-author of Chapter 6.

Figure 53: L-R: John Moses, Michon Peck and Arend Thomas in 1967. ***Courtesy of Michon Peck Bailey.***

The Arundel-on-the-Bay area allowed many of us as kids to have several experiences. To survive here it was necessary to have a bicycle. We started with balloon-tire bicycles and later moved up to English racers. Mrs. Tealye Snowden, (mother of Lorenzo) would take all the children on bike tours through the various surrounding communities on Saturday mornings. We would ride to the C and C store on Bay Ridge Avenue, which sold groceries, alcohol, had a walk-in meat freezer, and slot machines.

Our parents kept us occupied with various activities. They partnered with the Anne Arundel County Department of Recreation to have a summer recreation counselor assigned to the Arundel-on-the-Bay community. One of our first counselors was Mrs. Doris Knight. Recreation started on Chestnut Avenue between Cohasset and Narragansett Avenues. There was a large wooden box with a lock on it to secure the board games, balls, various nets for badminton, volleyball and basketball. There was a pole placed in the ground for tetherball. After the association purchased the lots on Newport Avenue, the recreation area and equipment was moved to that location.

"We had summer parades with decorated bicycles, wagons, and scooters. The parade had children and pets of all ages."

We had summer parades with decorated bicycles, wagons, and scooters. The parade had children and pets of all ages. There was a yearly scavenger hunt. The whole community was used to seek out the prizes from questions placed at various homes. We had to run all over the area. The Anne Arundel County Library had a bookmobile that came to the community frequently and we selected books to read. Dr. Michael Ivy taught most of us how to swim at the Hollywood Avenue street end beach. He taught us the basic strokes, and how to float and paddle on a large surfboard. Lorenzo Snowden, the Walker brothers, Orris (Jay) and Lance, and I had rowboats that were kept at the end of Redwood Avenue on the Fishing Creek side of the community before the boat ramp was added.

We had summer water activities. There were swimming events and row boat races, single and double. These events would take place at the Hollywood or Walnut Avenue street ends on the Chesapeake Bay side. Dr. Burrell, (father of Bunky and Michael), Dr. Nelson, (father of Margaret, Robert, Ralph, Ramone, and Natalie), and Dr. Goodlowe, (father of Lynn), often took us for cruises on their yachts up the Severn River. Todd Duncan (stepfather to Charles) and Aris T. Allen, MD. (father of Lonnie and Aris Jr.) taught us how to water-ski.

We swam everyday and partied every night, day after day, never stopping. When we were young children we would party at the guest-house of Maude Pecou (mother of Paula). When we got older, the Walkers' rumpus room and the Fortes' club room were used quite often, although we rotated social activities through other homes. Mr. Robert E. Peck and other

Figure 54: L-R: April Moses and Michon Peck in 1967. ***Courtesy of Michon Peck Bailey***

parents would take us to Highland Beach to see the Saturday on-the-Beach movie in the pavilion. Some would watch the movie and others would sit on the pier.

The channel between Venice Beach and Oyster Harbor wasn't deep or wide at that time. We would carry our bikes through the water avoiding crabs and snakes to the other side of the channel to visit our friends at Venice and Highland Beaches. Most of us weren't good at climbing trees, so tree houses were built on the ground in the woods out of scrap wood and trees. We called them forts.

Mrs. Llewellyn Walker held Sunday school in her front yard on Sunday mornings with the children. We selected officers for Sunday school, which taught us leadership skills. We sang and learned Negro spirituals. Out of this experience Orris Walker Jr. became the Episcopal Bishop of Long Island. Dr. Orris Walker Sr., DDS, would cook an end-of-summer-school breakfast just before Labor Day. Sometimes "Big Daddy" Lipscomb, football star of the Baltimore Colts would be here as his guest. We would toss the football with "Big Daddy".

Some of us tried to start a community newspaper called *The Arundel Highlights*. We selected our own positions such as publisher, editor, reporter, photographer, and circulation manager. We were going to sell the one-page paper for two cents. I remember one issue was produced and then we had no more news to print.

"The water was so clear you could see your feet on the bottom."

Wooden steps were placed at the end of the street ends on the Chesapeake Bay side to allow residents and guests to enter the water to swim. The water was so clear you could see your feet on the bottom. Crabs and fish were plentiful. Bluefish were not kept or eaten, and were thrown back into the water. The Chesapeake Bay blue crabs caught were mostly extra large or jumbos in size. Female crabs were not kept and were thrown back in the water. We had been taught to throw females back so they could produce more crabs.

The home of Mr. Nathaniel and Harriet Dixon (parents of Gary) was known as the "jazz house" because the only music heard there was jazz. Jazz great Billy Taylor and his family lived at 1362 Sycamore Avenue which is now owned by the family of Mr. Osce and Juanita Madden (parents of Navarro and Barbara). Basketball was played by all at the Mitchell home owned by Mr. Clarence Mitchell and Dr. Juanita Jackson Mitchell (parents of Keiffer, Clarence Jr., Michael and George). Opera singer Todd Duncan used to give his students voice and piano lessons with the windows wide open. He and his students could be heard singing for blocks.

On many days we would watch the Naval Academy training pilots in their vintage bi-wing seaplanes off of the Arundel-on-the-Bay shoreline. They would land and take off over and over again between buoys placed in the water. Times have changed.

Trisha Quarles-Goodman

Trisha Quarles-Goodman lived at Arundel-on-the-Bay with her grandparents. They owned 3441 Rockway Avenue from 1964 to the 1990's. She is a marketing executive for Creating Total Wellness which specializes in nutritional therapy, weight loss and lifestyle balancing to bring the body and mind into harmony. Trisha shares her memories:

One of the fondest memories for me living in Arundel-on-the-Bay was the imaginary fun two of my adventurous friends and I used to have. Paul Greene, Shannon Marshall and I would pretend we were lost on an island and walk along the mushy banks of the community, moving all of the water grass and other vegetation out of the way. We would spend hours in peril and distress, but we had each other and we would collect neat shells and stones and pieces of wood along the way. The old boat house at the end of Rockaway, which is now Rockway, would be our landmark to let us know we had found

Figure 55: Trisha Quarles-Goodman. ***Courtesy of Trisha Quarles-Goodman.***

our way home . . . until, of course, I saw a snake and went screaming all the way home. I don't believe we played that imaginary game again.

"And it didn't matter whose house we showed up to get a drink or even a snack.
Our community, now that I look back on it, was exactly how communities should be: loving and nurturing..."

The community itself was a great place to play; the small beaches were perfect for us kids to hang out and swim without our parents being worried. We rode bikes all day long, playing bike tag, or the girls would take the boys' bikes. And it didn't matter whose house we showed up to get a drink or even a snack. Our community, now that I look back on it, was exactly how communities should be: loving and nurturing enough to take care of its young, and influential enough to give them good role models and direction. I would like to take this time to thank everyone in our community who had a part in helping make me the person I am today. I had a beautiful childhood.

Sandra Mullen Barrett

Sandra Mullen Barrett is a guidance counselor retired from the D.C. public school system and the second generation of her family to own the home at 3454 Narragansett Avenue. Her parents, Robert and Almareta Mullen, purchased the lot in 1950 and built the home in 1960. She shares her experiences, particularly the memory of the surrounding waters that captured her imagination as a young person and maintains their hold today:

My earliest memories of Arundel-on-the-Bay go back to age four (that was in 1950) when my parents, Robert S. and Almareta D. Mullen, came to look at the community. Even at that young age I was truly drawn to the fact that there was water all around the community. The water became very important to me. My parents were a young couple, so they purchased a lot with a plan to build a summer home by the time they were 40. Their dream was realized, much to my delight. Prior to building the house, though, we spent weekend days and time during the summer at Mr. Stewart's home. He and his wife had that beautiful, large house at the end of Rockway, just before Magnolia.

I remember Mr. Stewart as the go-to person for buying lots and building the one-level, 2-3 bedroom homes that dot Arundel-on-the-Bay. It seems to me that, for that time in the early 1950s, he single-handedly was responsible for a lot of the re-development of Arundel-on-the-Bay.

Figure 56: Sandra Mullen Barrett, 2010. ***Courtesy of Sandra Mullen Barrett.***

My aunt, Mildred D. Holloway, was the first family member to learn of Arundel-on-the-Bay, and she actively began sharing the dream with family and friends. Mrs. Marian Burrell, Mrs. Pearl Jackson, Mr. and Mrs. Velmo and Dorothy Little, the Gross family, the Summers family, all purchased lots and built homes. There were several of our extended family members who purchased lots but never built homes.

When I reached my teen years, I found that several educators from Washington, D.C., had built in Arundel-on-the-Bay. Because segregation in D.C. during my parents' era limited the number of high schools—and because almost all of these educators had attended Miner Teachers College with my parents—they all knew each other. Some were dear friends to my parents or to my aunt, Mildred Holloway. Arundel-on-the-Bay began to feel like 'old home week.' Aunt' Marian was on Rockway, 'Aunt' Dorothy was on Newport and then on Narragansett. My Aunt Mildred was further down Narragansett. Mr. and Mrs. Jackson were next door. Bill Keyes, the Quarles family, and others, whose names now escape me, were all around. It's hard to describe the sense of warmth, comfort, and welcome this provided me. Arundel-on-the-Bay has always been a safe environment, and I felt so free to walk or cycle the roads, dropping by to visit whoever could receive company.

In my teen years did we have fun in the summers of the early 1960s–boating, swimming, crabbing, fishing, and walking up and down the roads! In the evenings we would gather at someone's home or yard for music and dancing. There was a place called Della's carryout that became a Mexican restaurant located next to the Ebb Tide. Up and down the road we'd go–with whomever had access to a car–for fries, sodas, and other fast foods. Where the garden shop is now, there was a gas station for the 25 cents-per-gallon gas.

Arundel-on-the-Bay provided security and acceptance during an era when stepping out into an upscale "white" or previously "all-white" setting would have met with discouragement. I don't want to change the tone of this remembrance, but I have to admit that from the 1980s on I have experienced some 'head turns,' like: 'What are you doing here?' from our new white neighbors. It has given me pause.

"It concerns me that starting in the '80s newer residents began trying to barricade the streets near their homes that were close to the water with large planters, plantings, and sometime chains and locks."

My parents taught me that residents had access to every Arundel-on-the-Bay road and access to the water by these roads. I still have the old rules book. Chesapeake Avenue was a street and now it's a "walk" and still quite beautiful. It concerns me that starting in the '80s newer residents began trying to barricade the streets near their homes that were close to the water with large planters, plantings, and sometime chains and locks. You used to have a view of water from two blocks into the community and you didn't have to have a three-story house to see the water. The Arundel-on-the-Bay right-of way areas were open and clear. You could appreciate that you were surrounded by water. It really made the community the attractive, beautiful community it was. I digress.

In those days it was easier to access the water. Down Narragansett and all the way through Oyster Harbor you could go down the bank of the channel and half-wade, half-swim over to Venice/Highland Beach. Using this route, the youngsters from three communities could get together more easily. Fun, fun, and more fun.

There was a beach area at Hollywood Avenue where residents gathered and swam. Magnolia had a much deeper sand area that went directly into the water. There was an open road into the cove that had a little beach area. Before further development, my aunt Mildred's home, which was almost at the end on Narragansett before going into Oyster Harbor, had a fabulous view and the sandy/grassy land across the road led right into the water. We swam there, laid out on the sand and grass, picnicked and played games.

After 62 years, and now the owner of the house my parents built, I still get a tingle when I know I'm going to Arundel-on-the-Bay. I still look over to the right at the water you see from Arundel-on-the-Bay Road. I look to the left to see the water at the end of an Oyster Harbor road. Before going to my home I ride down Cohasset and turn on Magnolia to see the cove/creek/bay and slowly drive along Narragansett, watching the Bay-side water all the way.

Ed Lee Johnson

Ed Lee Johnson shares memories of his family and living at Arundel-on-the-Bay since the mid 1960s. He grew up in the community and is living here as an adult second generation resident. Ed's son and grandson are third and fourth generations who also live in Arundel-on-the-Bay.

> My parents were educators. My father, Dr. Ras Oliver Johnson, was Chief of Education Programming for Africa, USAID, where he oversaw the establishment of teacher training colleges. He was featured in the 1956 documentary, *The Splendid Americans*. This was a response to the movie, *The Ugly Americans*. When my father passed while traveling abroad, it was time for us to start a new chapter and Arundel-on-the-Bay was to be our new beginning and home. With the assistance of real estate agents, Cecil Burton and Carroll Hynson, my mother purchased waterfront lots with a small cottage that overlooked the Chesapeake Bay. I was sixteen in the late 1960s, when a new house was built with views of the Bay Bridge and Thomas Point Lighthouse.
>
> My mother, Allyce Cathryn Johnson, was an educator and principal in the Anne Arundel County School System. She was selected to serve on the Board of Directors of Anne Arundel Community College of which she later became Chairperson. The A. Cathryn Johnson Building is named in her honor at the Anne Arundel Community College. I attended Annapolis High School which was integrated. I was shunned by some of my black fellow classmates because I lived at Arundel-on-the-Bay. White students were more accepting of me. I am still remembered for my track team achievements and stair monitor duties at every class reunion I attend. There were happy times with my gang of neighborhood friends who liked to ride bikes, go boating, play cards and party at each others homes while eating any food in sight.

Figure 57: Father and Son: Ras Oliver and Ed Lee Johnson in 1958. ***Courtesy of Ed Lee Johnson.***

> After earning a Bachelor of Science Degree from Tennessee State University, I returned to work in the Anne Arundel School system. I spent forty years as an educator, administrator and Principal. I retired in 2010. I served on the Property Owners Association of Arundel-on-the-Bay as Secretary, Vice President, President (1983 to 1985), Board Director and Chair of the Board of Directors.

Annis Gazaway

Annis Gazaway is a retired administrator of the county social services department. Her husband, Preston Gazaway, was the former superintendent of Boys Village, a state institution for delinquent boys. They have two children, Cheryl and Preston Jr. (Chipper). She still resides in the family home at age 90 and is excited to share her memories of living in Arundel-on-the-Bay:

> Many of the black residents learned about Arundel-on-the-Bay while visiting with church and social groups from Baltimore and Washington, who had sponsored Saturday and Sunday trips to Carrs and Sparrows Beaches in Annapolis. We became interested and retained local real estate agent, Carroll H. Hynson. He located the lots that my husband and I purchased in 1959 and we built our home.
>
> The community was very appealing and a safe place to raise our daughter and son. Husbands and wives were professionals, all graduated from colleges and universities. We became friends and socialized with each other. My husband held a Bachelors and Masters Degree from Western Reserve and Howard University respectively in social work. I received a Masters Degree from the University of Pennsylvania. We embarked on professional careers, experiences and adventures while at the same time raising our children. I am proud to say that our daughter, who was the oldest child, earned a Bachelors Degree and a Masters Degree. She retired as Director of Childrens's' Welfare

Figure 58: Annis Gazaway. ***Courtesy of Annis Gazaway.***

Services in New Jersey. Our son distinguished himself as the first black student in his private school to join the crew team. He earned a Bachelors Degree, graduated from Medical School and resides and practices in Baltimore.

"Lovingly referred to as 'The Village Mothers". We became good friends and often accompanied each other to social and civic affairs, luncheons and other activities."

Families in Arundel-on-the-Bay looked out for each other's children and we were lovingly referred to as 'The Village Mothers.' We became good friends and often accompanied each other to social and civic affairs, luncheons and other activities. A leisure activity that I remember enjoying with the ladies of the neighborhood was the tea and pinochle party hosted by a resident. My husband was an avid golfer. When he wasn't on the golf course, he and our son were on the boat. In 1963, I accepted the position of secretary of the Property Owners Association.

In the midst of whites selling and moving out, there was a white man, Mr. Tyler, who was at home in Arundel-on-the-Bay and had no plans of leaving. I became friends with him and recall that he taught me how to clean fish. In turn, I took him to the market on Saturdays because he had no car after his old Ford broke down. He had never married and was not close to his brother and sister, so I would invite him to Sunday dinner and then drive him home. Mr. Tyler was an excellent carpenter and agreed to build a china cabinet in the corner of our dining room that still remains today. What comradeship during a time of racial transformation !

Figure 59: L-R: Governor's Mansion, Annis Gazaway, Emily Haygood, Rachael Brown, Helen Weatherford, Thelma Sparks, Front: Faye Allen, MD., 2002. ***Courtesy of Aris T. Allen Jr.***

"Memory is like the night that never dies. Forever and everlasting, our souls and our spirit will remember, reflect upon and treasure our neighborhood, just as an infant loves, cuddles and tightly hugs their first teddy-bear."

African American Property Owners of Arundel-on-the-Bay during the 1950s and 1960s:

Arundel-on-the-Bay experienced a significant racial transformation from white to black families in the 1950's and 1960's. By 1955, there were 68 black families and 30 white. By 1966, there were 176 black families. The following list of approximately one hundred property owners is a snap-shot of the level of their accomplishment in the fields of education, real estate, medicine, law, business, politics, opera, theater and government. Let us know of any omissions for further editions of this book.

Cedar Avenue

Curtis, Austin M. Jr. & Fannie: medical doctor.

Chesapeake Walk

Lofton, William: medical doctor.

Coleman, Edward & Josephine: university professor.

Nash, Barbara Jackson: educator.

Gregory, Monroe: medical doctor and university professor.

Sockwell, James & Katherine: nursery school and day care owners.

McGuire, Robert G. & Virginia H. / Robert G. Jr. & Elinor H.: morticians.

Savoy, James & Mary: dentist.

Golden, Ann B., beautician.

Forte, Allan & Bertha: medical doctor & educator.

Walnut Avenue

Chambers, Phillip & Helen: businessman & educator.

Snowden, Jackie Dacus: federal government.

Sycamore Avenue

Taylor, Billie, jazz musician/Madden, Oceola & Juanita: business owners.

McDaniels, Robert & Julia Mae: medical doctor & educator.

Rector, John & Theresa: lawyer & historian.

Redwood Avenue

Cumby, Frank & Esther: federal government & educator.

Linden Avenue

Johnson, Ras O. & Cathryn: USAID/State Dept. official & educator.

Anderson, Stanley: D.C. city councilman.

Terry, Ethel: D.C. government.

Gazaway, Preston & Annis: psychologist & supervisory social worker.

Chestnut Avenue

Johnson, Stewart & Adele: medical doctor & dental hygienist.

Murray, Clarence & Alma: federal government & educator.

Davis, Avery & Sarah: railroad & government.

Burton, Cecil & Louise: real estate broker & educator.

Myrtle Avenue

Duncan, Charles T. & Dorothy: attorney, Howard U. law school lecturer and dean & educator.

Duncan: Todd & Gladys: teacher/classical singer & social activist/educator.

Christmas, Bernard N.: dentist.

Oak Avenue

Johnson, Theodore & Emily: POA-AOTB president/medical doctor & educator.

Hunt, Richard & Delores: medical doctor & POA-AOTB president/educator.

Morgan, Ray: POA-AOTB president/accountant.

Hollywood Avenue

McMurdock, Robert & Helen: dentist.

Ewell, James & Aliene: business.

William LeRoy & Lilian Berry: medical doctor.

Henson, Calvin & Doris: business & educator.

Narragansett Avenue

Henson, George & Helen: farmer.

Mullen, Robert & Almareta: educators.

Thomas, Arend & May: businessman & educator.

Brown, Phillip & Rachel: educators/authors.

Walker, Orris & Llewellyn: dentist & educator.

Snowden, James & Tealye: educators.

Boyd, Gordon & Corrine: Secret Service/Tuskegee Airman.

Carpenter, James & E.H.: medical doctor.

Watts, William & Pauline: medical doctor & educator.

Nunley, Amanda: home economics educator.

Mitchell Family:

> Parren J.: first Maryland African American elected to US Congress, founding member of the Congressional Black Caucus.
>
> Clarence M. Jr.: civil rights activist and head of the NAACP Washington Office; buildings named after him at U of MD, Morgan U. and Baltimore City Courthouse.
>
> Juanita J. (Clarence Jr.'s wife): NAACP activist and first African American female admitted to practice law in MD.
>
> Clarence M. III: Maryland State Senator.
>
> Clarence M. IV: Maryland State Senator.
>
> Michael: Baltimore City Councilman.
>
> Keiffer: Medical Doctor.
>
> Keiffer, Jr., Baltimore City Councilman.

Hilliard, Herbert & Alma: POA-AOTB president/educator & educator.

Mussenden, Glenford P. & Lydia: medical doctor & nutritionist/educator.

McEddy, James & Evelyn: real estate.

Jackson, Nelson & Ruth: business owners.

Wilkerson, Victor & Diane: medical doctor & educator.

Cohasset Avenue

Bonds, Maceo & Geraldine: fireman & educator.

Covert, John & Bettie: educators.

Pinkett, John & Sally: real estate/construction.

Knight, Lawrence & Doris: educators.

Gibbs, Charles & Bernice: educators.

Smith, Cleveland: medical doctor.

Nelson, Robert & Adele: medical doctor & nurse.
Sparks, Vernon & Thelma: psychologist & educator.
Ivy, Bertha & Lawrence: educators.
Dixon, Nathaniel & Harrvette: government & educator.
Adams, Robert & Jeannie: painter & patient care technician.
Sneed, Ralph & Marion: POA-AOTB president/government & government.
Plummer, Hazel: mortician.
Green, Vernon and Catherine: lawyer & educator.
Weatherford, John & Helen: educators.

Magnolia Avenue

Randall, Julian & Dorothy: Secret Service.
Boxley, George: businessman/real estate.
McDonald, George & Xavier: medical doctor.
Waters, Randolph & Theresa: caterer sold to Butler, medical doctor who sold to Fred and Mary Ferguson, pharmacist & federal government/entrepreneur.
Dyer, Francis & Lois: medical doctor/university professor & educator.
Peck, Robert & Imogene & Tulip: fire chief & federal government.
Allen, Aris T. & Faye: medical doctor/politician & medical doctor.
Hynson, Carroll & Betty: real estate broker/bail bondsman & educator.
King, Douglas & Vandola; educators.
Madden, Nathaniel: businessman.
White, Bernard E. & Fannie M.: government & government.
Godlowe, Joseph: medical doctor.
Phillips, John & Myrtle: dentist.
Wilson, Elroy: mortician.

Newport Avenue

Edmead, Edmund & Helen: federal government.
Lansey, Teackle: business owner.

Rockway Avenue

Haygood, Robert & Emily: educators.
McManus, Willie Q. & Joyce P.: POA-AOTB president, educators & musician.
Brown, Maudella: veterinarian.
Quarles, James & Catherine: educators.
Moss, Joseph & Hilda: liquor store owner & nutritionist.
Keyes, William & Annie: educator/artist/author.
Ables, Kermit & Harriet: mortician & D.C. government.
Motley, James & Cora: POA-AOTB president, military/business & educator.
Grigsby, Richard & Lenora: law enforcement & federal government.
DaCosta, William & Frances Mae: POA-AOTB president, educators.
Snowden, George & Jessie: educators.

Saratoga Avenue

Cook, Archie & Helen: educators.
Amos, Thelma: P.E. educator.

Endnotes

1. Barnes, Robert, "Little Town on the Bay Grows Up," *Washington Post*, June 11, 1988, p.21.

A Bonfire on the Community Beach at Christmas. ***Photograph by Marc Grigsby.***

Houses on Fishing Creek. ***Photograph by Marc Grigsby.***

Chapter Seven

Arundel-on-the-Bay - 1970 to Present

Edie Dolberg, John Moses and Wilma Coble

Introduction:

The last four decades have been a time of change and challenge for the community of Arundel-on-the-Bay.

In 1970, the community was still heavily treed in places, with secondary growth thickets dispersed within its boundaries. Quail nested in the grass and kudzu spread along the former frontage road, Chesapeake Avenue, which was later renamed by the U.S. Postal Service as Chesapeake Walk to differentiate from an already existing street name within the county.

Figure 1: The southernmost point of Narragansett Avenue. ***Photo by R. M. Grigsby.***

On occasion, birds provided residents with a tasty meal. The last remaining duck blind located off Chesapeake Walk, which had provided its owner with fresh fowl and rental income for decades, disappeared in 1970 during a particularly heavy icing of the Bay, thought to be at least 12 inches thick.

In season, blue fish abounded, and there appeared to be an eagle's nest in the wooded 10-acre parcel that would eventually become the Fishing Cove development. This was well before the fox eating the quail and silencing their "bob-white" call forever. There is now even a resident coyote sharing one of the few remaining empty lots with feral cats, which neighbors have been having neutered.

By 1975, the once-white summer colony, which had become a black summer enclave by 1955, was evolving into a year-round, integrated, suburban community. While a few white families remained, it was estimated by residents in 1975 that Arundel-on-the-Bay was now at least 95 percent black. By 2005, after the installation of a county sewer system, which caused a rising interest in the community, it was perhaps 50 percent white and by 2015 it was estimated to be 60 percent white, 35 percent African American and 5 percent

Figure 2: Log Canoe *Eagle* on Fishing Creek in 1972. ***Photo taken by Tom Worthington, courtesy of Linda Worthington.***

Hispanic, Asian or other. The 2015 statistic is the result of reviewing the last Arundel-on-the-Bay list of property owners.

By 1975, social changes were presenting the community with unanticipated real estate challenges. A new generation of African Americans growing up in Arundel-on-the-Bay was facing far less housing discrimination – and other forms of discrimination – and they were looking elsewhere for places to live and vacation. This left aging parents and grandparents faced with the prospect of selling their property below fair market value. As we will see, this left them exposed and potentially vulnerable to the plans for waterfront developers, who saw Arundel-on-the-Bay real estate opportunities as a profitable path toward the development of vacation and boating facilities.

It was believed, perhaps because the community in 1975 was substantially African American, that financial institutions and elements of the county government treated it as unable to defend its own interests. With a substantial Bay and creek frontage, some in the local business community viewed Arundel-on-the-Bay as a waterfront investment opportunity. This potential opportunity, however, was not to include most of the current residents, many of whom were aging and had begun to sell their property at below fair market value. Because the children of the then-current property owners faced far less housing discrimination – and other forms of discrimination – than their parents had faced, there was a loss of interest in the community by many of those children, who could now choose to live and vacation elsewhere.

Public Service and Relations with County Government

During the early 1970s, the neighboring community of Oyster Harbor – once part of the municipality of Arundel-on-the-Bay – had a sheriff, Andy Richardson, who took it upon himself unofficially to look out for Arundel-on-the-Bay as well by occasionally patrolling our streets in his dilapidated Volkswagen. In addition to his badge, Andy carried a shotgun in his Volkswagen. Whenever he spotted a suspicious car, Andy would follow it, and if it stopped within the community, he would approach the car with his shotgun and badge. If he did not approve of the car's occupants or their stated reason for being in the community, Andy would tap his head a couple of times and tell the occupants that he had a steel plate in his head from the Korean War. He then warned them that he never wanted to see them in his community again. Per his widow, Barbara Madden, Andy recalled that this strategy did not work too well with many fishermen who would just keep on fishing. But it apparently did work with any possible criminal element. In those days, many residents felt secure enough to leave doors unlocked during daylight hours. There was no crime.

Generally, Arundel-on-the-Bay has had a good and steadily-improving relationship over the last four decades with the Anne Arundel County government, once it became clear that residents would take whatever steps were necessary to continue as a residential community and to protect and maintain the look and feel of the community that they had all moved here to enjoy. Career county employees were almost always very helpful once they understood the residents, and the residents in turn understood the county culture.

"The inspector said that the ham sure smelled delicious, and that he loved bourbon. Subsequently the authorization was given, and the drains got cleaned. That was life in the 1970s Arundel-on-the-Bay."

For example, the community needed county help in unclogging the drains along the roads back in the 1970s. One savvy Arundel-on-the-Bay resident happened to have a Virginia ham and a bottle of bourbon in his car trunk. When the county inspector came by and was reluctant to authorize cleaning of the drains along community streets, the resident opened his car trunk and let the aroma of the ham escape, and then closed the trunk. A little while later the trunk was reopened. The inspector said that the ham sure smelled delicious, and that he loved bourbon. Subsequently the authorization was given, and the drains got cleaned. That was life in the 1970s Arundel-on-the-Bay.

During the late 1960s and early1970s, a small group of residents was very interested in building a community center on four community-owned lots. A committee was established and a constitution and by-laws were written. Dr. Delores Hunt was elected chairman and Mrs. Bertha Ivy was vice chairman. The committee spent several years in organizing and conducting activities for the purpose of raising funds to build the center.

The majority of the residents, however, were not in favor of the community center project. After more than $60,000 was raised, the project was cancelled. In accordance with the constitution, the money was donated to two organizations that had been designated in advance. The Eastport Fire Department in Annapolis, which served the community at that time, received $20,000 and the United Negro College Fund received $40,000.

As Arundel-on-the-Bay began to evolve from a summer residency into a year-round suburban community, interest in neighborhood financial improvement began to increase. Of the three types of special taxing districts in Anne Arundel County, Arundel-on-the-Bay has two, namely: the Special Community Benefit Tax District and a Shore Erosion Control Tax District. The funds for the community budget are collected by the county in the form of property taxes, and budgets are managed by the Arundel-on-the-Bay Property Owners Association. The Shore Erosion Control Tax District was secured in the mid-1970s, and the Special Community Benefit Tax District was attained in 1979. To qualify, the community was required to present petitions containing more than 50 percent of the residents' signatures for the community benefit district and a petition with over 75 percent of the community residents' signatures for the shore erosion control district.

Special Community Benefit Districts have been formed for a variety of purposes, including maintenance of community property and private roads, special security or special police protection, improvements to community facilities, and insect and pest control. Shore Erosion Control Districts are formed for more specialized purposes, including construction, repair and maintenance of facilities for erosion control and building or repairing of bulkheads and dredging of channels. The improvements constructed through erosion control districts are funded by no-interest state loans to the county on behalf of the districts.

Zoning and Growth

The 1970s started with considerable concern by the community as to its zoning designation. The purpose of the zoning designation is to identify the housing density approved for building in a specific area. An R-2 designation allows only single-family homes to be built, while an R-5 designation allows for the building of denser multiple housing like town houses, for example. To that end, an R-2 designation stipulates that building is restricted to two houses per acre or ½ acre lots per house. With regard to the platted lots of Arundel-on-the-Bay, in practical terms this would mean that if one owned a single 50-foot lot, or two or three adjoining 50-foot lots, you could build a single house on your property. However, if you owned four adjoining 50-foot lots, then you would be able to build up to two single family houses if you desired.

Figure 3: Ronald Kelly enjoying the Arundel-on-the-Bay beach off Hollywood Avenue along the Chesapeake in 1970, with the Lewis Payson House (1895) in the background. *Photo courtesy of Rosalind Larry.*

At that time, Arundel-on-the-Bay had an R-5 zoning designation. The zoning designation R-5–or five houses per acre–allowed a far greater density of development than had actually occurred in Arundel-on-the-Bay until then. Oyster Harbor, Bay Highlands, Highland Beach and Venice Beach, although unlike Arundel-on-the-Bay in that they had originated as totally African American summer communities, also had R-5 designations; neighboring Bay Ridge, however, had an R-2–or two house per acre–designation. All five of these communities were originally platted in 40 to 50-foot wide building lots. Like Bay Ridge, Arundel-on-the-Bay had many single-family homes on double or even triple lots and a substantial amount of undeveloped land. The Director of Planning and Zoning informed our community that R-5 zoning was better than R-2. In order to preserve the character of the neighborhood as it had been initially intended, however, residents desired the R-2 designation protection being enjoyed by the Bay Ridge community. At the time, it was the opinion of many in Arundel-on-the-Bay that the only difference between the two communities was that Bay Ridge was all white.

In 1972 the county government abruptly changed the Arundel-on-the-Bay zoning designation from R-5 to R-2. The change in designation was believed to have been prompted by the fact that the office of the U.S. Attorney in Baltimore had received information, supplied by John Moses and compiled by Andy Richardson, the sheriff of Oyster Harbor, that the county government might be working with several developers who were planning to convert Oyster Harbor and Arundel-on-the-Bay into a commercial resort. Arend Thomas was one of a few residents who was approached about selling their land, so that a large hotel chain could erect a hotel/motel with a floating dock for yachts on their property. Apparently, it was assumed by a group of local businessmen that Arundel-on-the-Bay was a dying community. There was in fact a lapse of interest in the community by the children of property owners at Arundel-on-the-Bay and other African American potential purchasers, largely due to the decline in housing discrimination. As a result, the retail value of homes and properties in the community did not rise as rapidly as did those in similarly-situated white communities. As Arundel-on-the-Bay has now evolved into an integrated suburban community and then a majority white community, this is no longer the case.

Some residents believed that changing the zoning designation to R-2 would allow Arundel-on-the-Bay to maintain its then-current look and feel, even while it continued to grow. This was due substantially to a county regulation passed in 1970, which required adjacent lots to be combined if building permits were not obtained by 1971. With respect to black communities, however, this requirement was honored more in breach than practice due to a novel legal concept known as "Developer's Interest." This idea was a concept created in 1984 by the Anne Arundel County executive, in order to evade the requirements in the 1970 county law that required lot owners to combine lots to meet subdivision standards.[1]

During the mid-1970s it appeared that the county's health department imposed a general building moratorium in the area. This was not a lot-by-lot moratorium, but rather was thought to be applied only to properties owned by African Americans in an area that encompassed Fishing Creek, Oyster Creek and Black Walnut Creek. One house was built by an African American family in Arundel-on-the-Bay during this moratorium, and one by a single white man in Highland Beach. The health department justified the moratorium on a general assumption that none of the land would pass a "perc test." Such tests for the rate of water percolation are conducted on vacant lots that are otherwise eligible for housing development but do not have access to a public sewer system. The test determines the ability of the land to absorb and process the material from an on-site septic system. Despite the moratorium, however, the county allowed the development of an unnamed subdivision adjacent to Black Walnut Creek on land that was in the affected area. It was generally rumored that this new development was built on land purchased from an elderly black

Figure 4: Bulkhead repair along the Arundel-on-the-Bay shoreline in 1982. ***Photo by Arend Thomas.***

woman, whose property taxes were alleged to have been raised so steeply that she could not pay them, forcing her to sell the land.

Erosion and Water Control

With continual pounding of surf and storms on the bayside, coastline behind the existing Chesapeake Bay bulkhead–constructed in the 1930s by the Works Progress Administration with federal funds–wore steadily away through the 1970s. In order to protect the peninsula, the community pursued a shore erosion control project. The Arundel-on-the-Bay Property Owners Association worked with the Maryland Department of Natural Resources and the county to develop plans for the project. The cost of the repair work was estimated at $400,000 for which the association received an interest-free loan from the State of Maryland payable over the period of twenty-five years.

Repairs were made on the Chesapeake Bay side of the peninsula from Cedar Avenue to the south end of Narragansett Avenue. The project was accomplished over time with the assistance of many people. The planning phase for the project was begun during the Association presidency of Dr. George Snowden, and the blueprint phase was completed during the presidency of Willie Q. McManus. Wilma Coble was president during the bidding of the contract and the construction stages.

The contract was awarded to Crandell Marine Construction Co., and the work was completed in 1982. As part of the construction, existing bulkheads were repaired, new wooden bulkheads were built, and large stones–termed "rip-rap" when used in shoreline protection–were placed on the water side of the bulkhead. The county informed the association at the time that this was the largest community project ever completed in Anne Arundel County.

Arundel-on-the-Bay faced another kind of water issue with a law enacted in 1977, which required all communities without public water to have 5,000-gallon water tanks buried every 2,000 feet for use by firemen in the event of a fire. This requirement for water storage tanks in suburban communities seemed to be unique to the State of Maryland. In 1982, Anne Arundel County announced that it planned to bury a 10,000-gallon water storage tank in our community by the end of the year, to supplement water carried on fire trucks.[2] It was not until 1984, however, that the county sent a letter to then-Association President Wilma Coble, stating that the Department of Public Works would move forward with the installation of an underground water storage tank in Arundel-on-the-Bay at Myrtle and Newport Avenues.

After the installation was finally completed around September 1994, it has only been used by the fire department on a few occasions. Since then, the community takes comfort in the closer Annapolis Neck Fire Station, which was built at the corner of Bay Ridge Avenue and Arundel-on-the-Bay Road, and water drafting sites that were installed at the water end of several streets in the community in 2015.

New Development at Arundel-on-the-Bay

In 1985, the county government decided that Arundel-on-the-Bay did not qualify for protection under R-2 zoning because it could not show that there was a Developer's Interest in lots conveyed by the original developers of Arundel-on-the-Bay, thereby removing protection against overdevelopment. This decision resulted in Arundel-on-the-Bay seeking advice from a local law firm, when a developer, Wendell Lilly Jr. Co., acquired the undeveloped 10-acre parcel of land in the northwest corner of the community from Gordon and Elizabeth Stewart and proposed to build 50 homes on the site. The local law firm gave the community the following opinion:

> Notwithstanding the minimum lot area and width requirements of this title, a residential dwelling may be constructed on a properly recorded lot recorded on or before the implementation date set forth in Section 1-108 (June 1, 1972) of this Article, if the other requirements of this Article are met.
>
> Since Arundel-on-the-Bay was developed before June 30, 1952, all the lots in the subdivision are buildable even though they do not meet today's minimum requirements of R-2 zoning.

Believing this advice not helpful, Wilma Coble, April Moses and John Moses sought another opinion from the law firm of Harry Blumenthal. After much discussion, Mr. Blumenthal advised the county that Arundel-on-the-Bay was protected by Developer's Interest. Accordingly, only 25 houses could legally be built on the 10 acres owned by Lilly. Unfortunately, Mr. Blumenthal could no longer represent us, because of a conflict of interest, leaving the community back at square one on the issue.

At this point, resident Joyce McManus contacted Councilwoman Maureen Lamb, who took the issue to the county council. After intense negotiation with the Lilly Company, the number of home sites proposed was reduced from 50 to 39 houses. This was the best

Figure 5: Sign advertising the project being developed by Lilly company. ***Photo courtesy of Wilma Coble.***

that the community could do without very extensive and expensive litigation.

At the same time, the community was also able to convince the county council to pass emergency legislation setting more stringent requirements for development in areas not served by county-supplied water. This provided at least some protection from denser development. During negotiations with the council, Arundel-on-the-Bay sought the names of those communities not having the "Developer's Interest" designation. Of the nine communities named, eight were predominantly black, the sole exception being one white community on the Mayo Peninsula. When this was pointed out to the council members present, one member dismissed the concern as irrelevant, stating that it sounded like "stuff from the 70s."

Construction at Arundel-on-the-Bay

When construction started on the homes built by the Lilly Company, the development site was referred to as "Lillyville" by many Arundel-on-the-Bay residents. In advertising issued by the builder to draw perspective buyers to the homes, the development was called "Fishing Cove" rather than "Arundel-on-the-Bay." Since Arundel-on-the-Bay was considered to be a predominantly black community, community residents believed that the builder wanted his housing to draw a wider interest base and be viewed as a completely separate development.

"After the completion of sewer lines, the floodgates seemed to open for development in Arundel-on-the-Bay."

In addition to the new construction by Wendall Lilly, two talented local professionals played a significant role in the building or renovation of homes at Arundel-on-the-Bay in recent years; Raymond Strang and Associates, Architects, now of Stevensville,

Figure 6: Two examples of Strang homes in the community. ***Photos by Marc Apter.***

Figure 7: Examples of Allen homes in the community. ***Photos courtesy of Aris T. Allen Jr.***

Homes Built by Ray Strang and Aris Allen Jr.

Strang's work appears throughout the community and can be recognized by its contemporary form and use of natural, often unpainted wood. Either he built fresh on previously unbuilt lots or renovated or demolished older properties. Among the homes he built are:

Narragansett Avenue
3126, 3406, 3426, 3448, 3450, 3528 and 3530

Hollywood Avenue
1343

Saratoga Avenue
3516 3530, 3532, 3436, 3548

Myrtle Avenue
1294

Rockway Avenue
3452, 3501, 3502, 3528

Cedar Avenue
1391, 1393, 1395

Magnolia Avenue
1290, 1292, 1299

This is not an exhaustive list of the work of architect Ray Strang in the community but rather a product of a recent "windshield tour" of Arundel-on-the-Bay taken one afternoon by history researchers Marc Apter and Pamela Duncan in the company of Mr. Strang.

Likewise, the work of Aris Allen Jr. appears throughout the community. Beginning in the early 1970s, he designed, developed and oversaw the construction of new and renovated homes. His projects include:

Allen's design/build projects include:

Chesapeake Walk
3402

Narragansett Avenue
3557, 3559, 3508, 3510

Cohasset Avenue
3539

Saratoga Avenue
3505

Walnut Avenue
1373

Magnolia Avenue
1323, 1328

Sycamore Avenue
1358, 1363

Rockway Avenue
3461, 3463, 3465, 3508, 3510

And his renovation projects include:

Chesapeake Walk
3422, 3440

Narragansett Avenue
3463

Cohasset Avenue
3463

Sycamore Avenue
1360

Linden Avenue
1365

Rockway Avenue
3412, 3444, 3501, 3522

Maryland, as well as Arundel-on-the-Bay's own Aris T. Allen Jr. of Allen and Associates Inc., now retired from his design/build/development practice.

In 1983, Ray Strang bought three waterfront lots at Oyster Harbor and built there. Soon thereafter he purchased three lots at the Fishing Creek end of Magnolia Avenue and built a house for himself. In total, Strang estimates that he has constructed or renovated more than 50 properties at Arundel-on-the-Bay. Some of these projects were undertaken in association with Architect Stephen Halpern of Annapolis and/or developers Daniel Ruegg and Dennis Williams of Arundel-on-the-Bay.

Allen's design approach for waterfront sites was to orient as a minimum the living spaces and master bedroom so that a water view could be achieved, and he often incorporated a featured tall window in his designs in addition to enlarged windows facing the water. Aris T. Allen Jr. received his Master of Arts in architecture from Columbia University in 1973. When asked to describe his design philosophy, the ever-modest Allen said, "You know the usual, form follows function…and budget…and site constraints…and client requirements." His intent, was to give clients what they desired within the budget that was established.

Another milestone for the community came in 1977, when county contracts were awarded for the installation of sewage lines into Arundel-on-the-Bay, Oyster Harbor, Venice Beach, Highland Beach, Anchorage and Thomas Point. The Arundel-on-the-Bay sewer work was started in February 1979.[3] After the completion of sewer lines, the floodgates seemed to open for development in Arundel-on-the-Bay. The transition from a relatively sparsely-populated summer community to a more populated suburban neighborhood was not without controversy.

Since all Arundel-on-the-Bay homes have their own wells, there was fear among a few residents that the increased construction would result in saltwater intrusion into the Aquia aquifer. This could make it very difficult to obtain financing for construction or home mortgages and thus could drastically reduce the value of homes, again leaving Arundel-on-the-Bay open to exploitation. The fresh water Aquia aquifer under Arundel-on-the-Bay dropped from 10 feet above sea level in 1952 to a foot above sea level in 1986.[4] At the time, 95 percent of the wells in Arundel-on-the-Bay tapped into that aquifer. Strangely, the county health department did not seem to be concerned about possible saltwater intrusion into the water supply.

Figure 8: Test wells installed off Magnolia Avenue. ***Photo by Bill Semenuk.***

In 1986, attorney Claude Roxborough filed a pro-bono law suit on behalf of Arundel-on-the-Bay, requiring that the proposed 39 homes in the Wendell Lilly development access the deeper Magothy aquifer, which lies below the Aquia aquifer. The judge ruled from the bench that he would not interfere in the property rights of the developer. Fortunately, resident April Moses was able to persuade the state government to require that all new construction in Arundel-on-the-Bay use the Magothy aquifer for its water supply. After the state government put pressure on the county, all new development in Arundel-on-the-Bay was and continues to be required to access the Magothy aquifer. As part of the continuing effort to monitor saltwater intrusion in the Aquia aquifer, three test wells were drilled on the community beach on Magnolia Avenue. These test wells are monitored by the Maryland Geological Survey on a regular basis.[5]

Tales of Fish and Fire

Because Anne Arundel County does not have many direct water access sites for the general public, Arundel-on-the-Bay became a popular destination for local fishermen. In 1972 the community was invaded by trespassers in the form of determined fishermen anxious to take advantage of the large schools of bluefish along our shores. It was not long before the area of Magnolia Avenue at the Chesapeake Bay end of the street was overrun by fishermen, both residents and non-residents, for fishing and other social activities. Each year from 1974 through 1980 the problem became a greater nuisance for nearby neighbors. Some of these visitors came from as far away as Baltimore and Washington, D.C. to fish without any restrictions. According to Wilma Coble, as time went by, the fishermen became increasingly more comfortable in the community and began to make the waterfront their own. They went so far as to actually cut gaping holes in the community-built bulkhead on the Chesapeake Bay, through which they would drag their fish. The fishermen also began to enter adjacent homes when the owners were not there, to "borrow" cooking utensils so they could cook and eat their catch on-site.

The Property Owners Association was aware of these problems but was unable to eliminate them. During the period, the association only had those funds collected from membership dues of $20 per year and, unfortunately, only a small number of residents ever paid their dues. Therefore, funds were not available to hire the security services that were needed to enforce order. The association's security volunteer worked hard to stop the problems, and property owners living in close proximity to the favored fishing areas also attempted to help, but neither were successful. Property owners experienced several confrontations while trying to stop the fishermen from using the community for a social gathering place.

Each summer brought in more fishermen and more problems. Often as many as twenty cars would be parked on the street ends by the water. As the number of fishermen increased, so did incidents of unlawful activities. A long-time resident stated that at the northern end of Chesapeake Walk there was heavy drug use, and there was even a rumor of soliciting for prostitution.

In June 1980, the *Annapolis Capital* newspaper reported that two Arundel-on-the-Bay summer cottages were destroyed and another damaged in a "suspicious" two-alarm fire. The fire appeared to have started in the Magnolia Avenue cottage owned by Clyde and Wilma Coble, and spread to the others. Although the cottage had undergone substantial renovations, it was an original summer home built in Arundel-on-the-Bay in 1895 by former congressman Lewis Payson. The fire department had difficulty drawing water from the bay to fight the fire, and the house was destroyed. Residents suspected that these fires might have been a response to attempts to limit the activities of the fishermen, a suspicion reinforced by the discovery of a gas can at the very active fishing area. There was a possible second explanation: a storm had struck the community a few days earlier, dropping two large trees onto the house and

Figure 9: The original Payson house (1895) as renovated by the Coble family before the fire in 1980. ***Photo by Arend Thomas.***

Figure 10: The Coble house after the fire in 1980. ***Photo courtesy of Wilma Coble.***

possibly damaging the cottage's wiring.

The Cobles built a new house on the site of their destroyed cottage. Wilma Coble went on to be elected president of the Property Owners Association in 1981 and served three terms. The board of directors and the association closed the Magnolia Avenue street end to vehicular traffic, and a sign was posted stating that trespassers would be arrested. The trespassing and fishing problems on Magnolia Avenue appear to have been resolved.

Another incident of note occurred on the bay front at Magnolia Avenue during the spring of 1982. A small private plane crashed into the water near where the bulkhead was being repaired. Fortunately, the airplane ditched into the water before reaching the newly rebuilt Coble house where a committee meeting was being held. The plane came to rest right where the bulkhead was being rebuilt. The pilot was not injured in the crash, but it took several days to remove the plane from the water.

Another fire broke out in the community in the 1980s, along Chesapeake Walk. A

Figure 11: Small plane ditched by the beach in the Bay in 1982. ***Photo courtesy of Wilma Coble.***

resident burning trash in a barrel on a winter afternoon decided to dispose of a dried-out Christmas tree. After the tree was put into what had been a small fire, it exploded into a large one. A gust of wind from the south sent the flame to a new source of fuel provided by a part-time resident's uncut grass, and from there on the fire spread to the rear of the resident's house.

The fire department was called, but because at the moment all of their usual trucks were on other calls, they responded with a vintage fire truck with only one fireman. He broke out a window in the back of the burning house and climbed onto the roof where he cut a hole to let the heat out; unfortunately, this provided a draft for the fire. Neighborhood spectators were recruited to help deploy a fire hose to fight the fire, which by then had grown. The hose was soon manned by several residents who made substantial progress in subduing the flames, while the fireman went off to locate the community's underground water tank.

As those people manning the hose began to tire of their duty, resident John Moses offered to relieve them. The offer was accepted and the hose turned over to John, whose only previous experience with hoses had been with the garden variety. Once John grabbed hold, the hose turned into a writhing python. John could not let go of the hose because he was afraid that the heavy nozzle left unrestrained would have beat him to death. Water shot out everywhere, including into the crowd of spectators. When the hose finally pulled John to the ground, he crawled away as fast as he could. To everyone's relief, the fireman reappeared and shut off the water. Around the same time, a full-sized truck with a normal complement of firemen arrived and got the fire under control. Fortunately, only the rear section of the house burned.

Although the problem of trespassing fishermen had been resolved at the end of Magnolia Avenue, they continued to make many residents in other parts of the neighborhood weary of "the general public," contributing to a determination to reserve all private roads accessing the waterfronts for the use of property owners only. The need for keeping access private was further occasioned by gatherings of fishermen on Chesapeake Walk just north of Walnut Avenue. Most of these fishermen were not residents. Ultimately, there was a dispute over the strip of land long used by residents to fish from what was then called Chesapeake Avenue. In September 1994 this escalated to an incident in which one resident pointed a gun at another, as reflected by court records.

Community Evolution

Although the Property Owners Association of Arundel-On-The-Bay was incorporated on June 3, 1949, it was not until February 9, 1976 that a constitution and bylaws were ratified. These documents clarified the purpose of the association to promote and protect the general interest, welfare and properties of the community of Arundel-on-the-Bay, as well as establishing terms for the officers. The officers' terms are one year and the board of directors are two year terms. In 1983, the term for the President and Treasurer were changed from one year to a two-year term. A number of community-spirited residents have served as president of the association, giving their time and energy for the betterment of the community.[6]

During the 1970s and 1980s, community residents enjoyed activities held on the beach for Halloween and Christmas. Instead of door-to-door trick-or-treating, children received their treats as they gathered on the beach to play games. Another enjoyable event that took place each year was Christmas caroling on the beach around a decorated Christmas tree. Community Christmas parties were held at the residence of Drs. Aris T. and Faye Allen. These parties were always well-attended with plenty of good food, dancing and socializing with neighbors. Events hosted by Willie and Joyce McManus included such notable guests as Alex Haley, the author of *Roots*, and famed bebop and modern jazz musician Dizzy Gillespie.

Before the Special Community Benefit Tax district status was enacted in 1979, fund-raising events such as crab feasts and dinners were held on the beach during the summer

Figure 12: Alex Haley and Lois Haley visited Arundel-on-the-Bay during the dedication of the Kunta Kinte monument in Annapolis. Shown here are (left to right) Arundel-on-on-the-Bay residents, Willie Q. and Joyce McManus, Alex Haley and his sister, Lois Haley Butts of Annapolis, in Sept 1981. ***Photo courtesy of Joyce McManus.***

months. These activities continue year-round to this day and are supported by community dinners, admission charges and other fundraising.

In the late 1980s and early 1990s, Arundel-on-the-Bay was embroiled in several internal disputes. Some residents wanted a basketball court, a tennis court and a tot lot built on four community-owned lots; others objected to these plans. One resident accused the board of taking money earmarked for the benefit of Fishing Creek-side residents and using it for the benefit of Chesapeake Bay-side residents—a dispute termed "Arundel-on-the-Bay versus Arundel-on-the-Creek." When the board of directors reduced the erosion fund tax to cover the cost of the proposed playground by reallocating tax funds, it angered some residents even more.[7]

In the mid-1990s and early 2000s, four lawsuits arose over the issue of fences erected across platted rights-of-way and community streets with fee simple titles. The initial litigation was filed by the Arundel-on-the-Bay Property Owners Association itself. In 1994 the association requested a report on the title to street beds in Arundel-on-the-Bay, through its counsel Wayne Kosmerl, a principal in the Annapolis law firm of Council, Baradel, Kosmerl, and Nolan, PA. Edward Albert, a highly regarded title expert, prepared a comprehensive summary of the devolution of title in Arundel-on-the-Bay. He concluded after reviewing 272 title instruments that there were "no set of restrictions...reserving title to street beds, nor reservations on recorded plats." The Albert report also stated:

> It is also noted that Maryland Law generally extends an owner's title to the center of street beds which bind along property lines, unless title to the beds is reserved in the

Figure 13: Philip Brown, Educator, Author, Treasurer of the Property Owners Association for 27 years, and resident, Lolly Thomas, ca. 2008. ***Photo by Arend Thomas.***

> grantor. However, street beds are often subject to the rights of others to use them even though ownership is invested in others.[8]

Despite the Albert opinion, a suit was filed by the association against property owners Portner and Durant, requiring them to remove a fence and asking the court to declare the association the owner of the portion of the street that had been enclosed by the fence. While settlement of the issue of ownership of the road was the purpose of the association suit, the court required removal of the fence but declined to rule on the issue of fee simple ownership of the street.

In another attempt to settle the title issue, the association then brought legal action against a long-time resident, requiring the removal of a fence across Saratoga Avenue separating two plated portions of her deeded property. Again the court did not rule on the issue of title but rather decided that the defendant as the long-time property owner had acquired adverse possession of the adjacent "paper" street and need not remove the fence.

In the meantime, another property owner brought suit against the officers and board members of the association over title to the portion of Chesapeake Walk adjacent to her property. She sought damages from the association for having encouraged residents to trespass on her property, which abutted the former Chesapeake Avenue, a plated street that had eroded. Two other property owners joined the suit, and all three plaintiffs were successful in having the court declare them the fee simple owners of the streets adjacent to their property. The end result was the removal of a fence across Chesapeake Walk and a clear right of easement to other Arundel-on-the-Bay property owners to continue walking along Chesapeake Walk.[9]

The community faced other challenges during this same period. John Moses reported—and other Arundel-on-the-Bay residents suspected—that there was a certain amount of drug smuggling arriving by boat at either the community pier or beach, passing through the community into Oyster Harbor and then proceeding into other parts of Annapolis. There were sightings of unknown cars and people loitering near the Magnolia Avenue beach and pier and wading into the water at odd hours of the night. Because Arundel-on-the-Bay Road was the only road out of the community, the so-called "smugglers" would drive up Narragansett Avenue from the Magnolia Avenue beach and into Oyster Harbor, affording them a choice of exits from both communities onto Arundel-on-the-Bay Road. There was also talk of hearing three to four gunshots one night; some residents even commented that they heard bullets whistling through the trees.

In order to stop this traffic from coming through its small residential community streets, in 1989 the president of the Oyster Harbor Civic Association put heavy planters across the northern end of Narragansett Avenue between the two communities to block the road. This action required all traffic leaving Arundel-on-the-Bay to follow Cohasset Avenue out of the community. The heavy planters were in place for several years but were eventually replaced around 2008 by removable bollards, after firefighting efforts were hampered during a major fire in Oyster Harbor, when emergency and fire vehicles were unable to pass through from the Arundel-on-the-Bay side. This fire resulted in the destruction of three houses along Shore Drive and caused concern for the Arundel-on-the-Bay residents nearest to the area. One resident reported that he could feel the heat from the flames while standing on his pier at Walnut Avenue.

Up to this time, the community would communicate with residents through a series of unscheduled notes and notices. In 1989, the association started publishing a bi-monthly newsletter, called *The Pier.* The first editor was Frank Enty.

In 1990, the community again looked into the possibility of establishing a playground, but this time on the empty lots right on the Bay at Narragansett and Magnolia avenues. A

Figure 14: Under the leadership of resident Lori Strum, colorful and safe new playground equipment was installed on the playground and its surface treated with wood carpet to make it softer for young persons. The finished site was dedicated in May 2014. ***Photo by Edie Dolberg, December 2017.***

resident who was concerned that this would affect the view he currently enjoyed from his home hired an attorney to look into the matter. The attorney's findings stated that building a playground on those lots along the water was prevented by a deed dated May 25, 1949, from the commissioners of Arundel-on-the-Bay to Edward P. Neill, et al., as well as an agreement executed between the Property Owner's Association and John Carter, containing restrictive covenants prohibiting the placement of permanent structures such as picnic tables, swings or playground equipment, so as to retain unobstructed views and access to the water. The playground was ultimately built on the four community-owned lots on Newport Avenue in 1991. Seventeen projects to improve the community were cited in the July-August 1991 edition of *The Pier*.[10]

Figure 15: Arundel-on-the-Bay resident, William Keyes, author of *Keyes to a Long Life*. Photo by Fern Underdue.

At the Fishing Creek end of Linden Avenue lies a little piece of community-owned property, used by residents to fish and crab. For many years this little gem of the neighborhood had been maintained and improved personally by longtime resident, William Keyes. In February 1991, thanks to a grant obtained by Mr. Keyes from the county, the community added to that site a 50-foot crabbing pier, used to this day by residents who want to fish or just walk out to enjoy the view. In May 1981, Mr. Keyes took a photograph of Arundel-on-the-Bay while sky-diving from 5,000 feet. A subsequent report of the event published in *The Pier* for 1989 alleges that Keyes landed in the community dumpster, "unharmed;" Keyes has acknowledged the feat but denied that he ended up in a dumpster. He is the author or a memoir, entitled *Keyes to a Long Life*, edited by resident Fern Underdue and published privately in 2014 when Keyes turned 93.

In 1991, during the June general membership meeting, the Board of Directors of the Property Owners Association recommended renaming Magnolia Avenue as "Aris T. Allen Avenue." While general sentiment favored honoring the late Dr. Allen in some way, it was thought that naming a street in the community would preclude having a street in the larger Annapolis community named in his memory. Because of his stature as a community resident, longtime doctor, a member of both the Maryland House of Delegates and the state Senate, and the first black chairman of the state Republican Party, the board worked to have a street named for Dr. Allen in the City of Annapolis.

Figure 16: Arundel-on-the-Bay resident Aris T. Allen Jr. stands next to the statue of his father, Aris T. Allen, installed on Chinquaphin Round Road at the intersection with Forest Drive and dedicated on October 8, 1994.

The State Highway Administration (SHA) was planning to build a spur from U.S. Route 50 to Forest Drive in Annapolis. The original plan called for the road to cut through an established neighborhood. Dr. Allen influenced the SHA to realign the freeway's path further north along Forest Drive and away from the threatened neighborhood. Construction on what was called the Patuxent Spur began in 1989 and was finished in early 1992. On Oct. 31, 1992, the Maryland Department of Transportation dedicated MD 665, formerly Patuxent Boulevard, named to honor Senator Aris T. Allen who had died the previous year.

Figure 17: Ribbon cutting ceremony for the opening of Aris T Allen Blvd. Participating (l to r) Anne Arundel County Councilman Carl O. Snowden, Lonnie W. Allen, son of Aris T. Allen Sr; Annapolis Alderman Samuel L. Gilmer, Aris T Allen Jr., Alderwoman Sheila M. Finlayson, behind her entrepreneur Dallas R. Evans, Transportation Secretary O. James Lighthizer, former Anne Arundel County Executive Joseph W. Alton, Faye W. Allen MD, widow of Aris T. Allen Sr; County Executive Robert R. Neall, behind him State Senator Clarence W. Blount and Rev. Leroy Bowman of the Forest Baptist Church in Annapolis. ***Photo courtesy of Aris T. Allen Jr.***

Transportation Secretary James Lighthizer said of Dr. Allen, "This tribute to Senator Allen is well deserved. He was a caring man who was deeply involved in serving the community."[11]

Happy 100th Birthday Arundel-on-the-Bay

The U.S. Congressional Record for June 28, 1990, contains the following statement by U.S. Rep. Charles Thomas McMillen (D-MD):

> Mr. Speaker, I rise today to pay tribute to the community of Arundel-on-the-Bay. Arundel-on-the-Bay is celebrating its 100th birthday this week, celebrating the longevity of a town that displays the type of civic pride and individual involvement that provides the base for the county.
>
> Located on a peninsula jutting into the Chesapeake Bay, the citizens of the town formed the Property Owners Association of Arundel-on-the-Bay, Inc. to expand their influence over the issues that most strongly affect such small communities. This expression of concern has resulted in the maintenance of the coastline to prevent erosion, and the establishment of special services that have acted to knit this community together.
>
> Arundel-on-the-Bay is a model community; proving that civic virtue is thriving in the towns of Maryland. These 300 property owners and their families, and 100 years of history, deserve the well wishes of all of us. I congratulate Arundel-on-the-Bay on its 100th birthday celebration.

Congratulatory citations from Anne Arundel County, the Maryland State Senate, and the county executive were received, and on July 7, 1990, as Congressman McMillen had announced, the Arundel-on-the-Bay community actually celebrated its 100th birthday. The festivities included a parade from the entrance of the community down Cohasset Avenue to the community beach on Magnolia Avenue, a dedication

Figure 18: Association President Wilma Coble holding citation plaque at the Arundel-on-the-Bay 100th Birthday event. ***Photo courtesy of Wilma Coble.***

ceremony at the beach, concession tables, games, and refreshments. In the evening, there was dinner and dancing under the stars. Wilma Coble, serving at that time as president of the Arundel-on-the-Bay Property Owners Association, had sent letters of invitation to members of the Anne Arundel County Council, as well as to Maryland's U.S. senators and state delegates, several of whom attended the festivities.

Sea Stories

Being situated on a peninsula jutting out into the Chesapeake Bay, Arundel-on-the-Bay has the benefit of some magnificent sights, sounds and experiences. The visual treats for residents include the sight of ships lined up in the Bay waiting to pass under the Chesapeake Bay Bridge, sailboat regattas, cruise ships coming and going to Baltimore, the U.S. Navy Blue Angels practicing their aerial acrobatics prior to the Naval Academy's Commissioning Week, sunrises over the Bay and magnificent sunsets over Fishing Creek (otherwise known as the Creek), families skiing and tubing on the Creek, the Thomas Point Lighthouse, the ospreys returning to nest in the spring, an occasional bald eagle, a beautiful moon reflecting on the water, and the swans returning every winter.

The sounds include the waves lapping to shore, the Blue Angels practicing, the haunting drone sound of fog-horns over the Bay, and cigarette boats and personal watercraft passing by in the summer. During WWII current resident John Moses remembers hearing the Naval Academy midshipmen practicing take-offs and landings on the Bay while in his crib at Venice Beach, located across Oyster Creek from Arundel-on-the-Bay. For many years the Navy used N3N-3 floatplanes, known as the Yellow Peril, for midshipman takeoff and landing practice off our shores. In 1961 the Yellow Perils, the last biplanes in U.S. military service, were retired.

And, of course, the experiences of living right by the water include living through the damage of 2003's Hurricane Isabel, which destroyed four houses on the Narragansett Avenue point and every pier on the bay side, and the massive rebuilding and renovations that had to be done to many homes afterwards; power outages; damage from trees falling

Figure 19: An osprey nest, crabber and the Chesapeake Bay Bridge. ***Photo by R. M. Grigsby***

on both homes and power lines during many storms; and jellyfish entering Fishing Creek during the summer.

Although beautiful to look at, the Chesapeake Bay constantly reminds us of the power of nature, as can be attested to by the many sea stories from the boaters in the community. One such story is the following recounted by resident Lolly Thomas in a paper for her memoir writing class:

> That weekend in August, 1992 had been wonderful. On Friday we [Lolly and husband Arend Thomas] cruised to Baltimore, excited with the promise of a fun-filled weekend. The sun was hot and the bay was calm. From Back Creek in Annapolis to the Inner Harbor in Baltimore, at cruising speed, the trip was about two and a half hours.
>
> The annual event we were attending was the Sweetheart Dinner-Dance sponsored by the Seafarers Yacht Club [African American Yacht Club], located in the Eastport section of Annapolis. Perhaps fifteen or so boats participated in the cruise. Guests and non-boat owners reserved rooms at the local hotels.
>
> The Saturday party was held on the twenty-first floor of the Trade Center at the Inner Harbor, with spectacular views of the harbor and the yachts below. We danced the night away to the talented XPD's Band a well-known group of Annapolis African American musicians.
>
> The following morning, we awakened to a cloudy, drizzling, gray day. Some boat engines were revving up but many remained silent. We turned on the ship-to-shore radio to get the Coast Guard's report about the weather and bay report. They reported two- to three-foot seas. Not a problem we agreed.
>
> Two boats pulled out about a half hour before we did; another about twenty minutes after us. Everyone else decided to wait until Monday.
>
> We gassed up at the marina and started down the Patapsco River. Never before had we seen waves in this body of water but on this day there were easily one-footers. Strange we thought, since the river was always calm, but we continued on.
>
> When we turned south into the bay, the two- to three-footers as reported by the Coast Guard were more like three to four. Our boat tossed and turned in the roiling sea. I had been in heavy seas before, but not in a twenty-five-foot single-screw boat. I

Figure 20: Mr. and Mrs. Arend J. Thomas III (Lolly) in sailing whites, 1994. These Arundel-on-the-Bay residents are active members of the Seafarers Yacht Club.

began getting nervous but tried not to show it. In all of that turbulence we actually passed two men in a smaller boat, fishing!

We continued on, becoming more and more uncomfortable. When we heard the two boats ahead of us on the radio, Arend attempted to contact them. That's when we discovered that we could receive but couldn't send. Visibility had dropped to about a quarter of a mile. The boat behind us turned around and headed back to Baltimore.

We had our dog, Ginger, a Pekingese, on board. She became so frightened that she attempted to jump overboard. I went below to get her leash so she could be secured to the table. Once below, I was thrown from one side of the boat to the other as there was nothing I could hold onto. It was impossible to stand up in the boat. Things that had not been secured crashed to the floor.

I finally got the leash for Ginger and tied her to the table. Suddenly Arend said, 'Roll up the canvases because right now they are creating resistance which is making us roll even more.'

As we continued south, he heard the captains of the two boats ahead of us talking. The one in the lead said that he was approaching Sandy Point and the water was swirling in an undefined direction and was much rougher. Emphatically he said, 'I am catching hell!' I was ready to turn back; however, had we attempted at this point we would have risked being swamped.

Approaching Sandy Point, the waves seemed to come from different directions and instead of rolling; our boat was being picked up on one wave and slammed down in the trough. There were times when the waves at the stern lifted us and pitched us forward. Arend recalled later that he was positive he saw the sandy bottom of the bay. Each time we came down I knew the boat would split apart. How much punishment could this boat handle?

Between Sandy Point and the Bay Bridge waves approached five feet. We began praying. I could look at Arend and see how exhausting it was to keep the boat under control. It took skill and knowledge to keep us safe. He dared not take his hands off the wheel for that could spell disaster.

Once we cleared the bridge, Arend said, 'I'm going to tack down the bay just like a sailboat and let the wind and waves work for us, not against us.' This exercise worked to our advantage and in close to an hour later we were tying up, safe but shaken.

A year later, we traded that *Mai Gem Too* in for a thirty-three-foot Carver Mariner; a boat we felt was larger and safer. Twenty years later we remember; the first *Mai Gem Too* was twenty-five feet long, had one engine and held fifty-five gallons of gas. We could travel to and from Baltimore on one tank of gas. However, that Sunday in August, due to the elements, we burned approximately forty-seven gallons on the return trip. And a trip that normally took two and a half hours was increased to almost four hours.

Another, very different story, was relayed by resident Michael Postlewaite as he tells of his experience one pleasant evening in 2004 when he set out to do a little fishing:

I thought that I had covered everything. I had brought along an extra can of gas, and an extra battery. I had the small trolling motor. I only expected to be out for about an hour puttering around Thomas Point, so I didn't bring either my cell phone or

Figure 21: Thomas Point Lighthouse. ***Photo by R. M. Grigsby.***

> the portable emergency two-way radio. My troubles began when I tried to move to a different spot and engaged the throttle – the motor stopped. I put the throttle in neutral and turned the key. She started right up. I engaged the throttle to go forward and she cut out. I tried to go in reverse, and again the engine cut out. I kept trying, but no luck. I'm killing my battery and drifting farther and farther out into the bay.
>
> There hadn't been another boat in sight since my troubles began. I thought that if I could just hook up to a channel marker, I could tie the boat to it and sleep until morning when the fishing fleet would show up. I tried to tie a rope around one of the pilings holding a net. It was raining now, and the boat began dashing against the piling violently, almost throwing me into the water.

By the time Michael realized that his boat would be torn to pieces if he didn't get away from the pilings, his propeller was caught in the net. At the same time, breakers were washing over the side of the boat, and filling it with water. He put a fishing knife between his teeth, and jumped over the side into the water. The cold water stunned him, and the waves tossed him about. He was finally able to fight his way back to the boat, and had to dive under to find where the net was caught. In the process of cutting the net free, the knife slipped from his hands and sank. Holding what little breath he had left, he struggled to get the net free with his hands. When he at last felt the net give way and swing free, he felt he was close to unconsciousness. Holding onto the shaft, he managed to pull himself to the surface. The boat was totally awash and submerged just below the surface. Just about everything he had in the boat had floated away. He spent a harrowing night in a partially sunk boat in the middle of the Chesapeake, in a storm. Sometime during the night, he somehow drifted off to sleep due to sheer exhaustion. When he awoke, the storm was over and the sun was up, and he was drifting all alone in the Bay. Eventually he spotted something on the horizon, and kept his eyes glued to it. He could finally make out that it was a large sailboat, and getting closer, but it was not heading in his direction. Michael started waving his arms and yelling to get the boat's attention. He did eventually get the attention of the sole occupant on the sailboat and it turned in his direction.

After pulling Michael out of the water and hearing his story, his rescuer told him "I've been sailing these waters for thirty years and nothing like this ever happened to me before. Do you mind if I take your picture?"

Afterward, Michael said that two days later when he and his father-in-law went to get the boat, they saw what had happened as soon as they got it on the trailer. The bow rope that was attached to the cleat just under the bow had fallen off of the boat unnoticed. Once it was all in the water, it was invisible to anyone on the boat. Though one end was still clamped on the cleat, the other end of the bow rope had snaked its way under the boat and wrapped itself around the prop. Once on the trailer, he tried to turn the prop by hand. It was locked in place like a vice grip. That rope held down the entire engine. In the middle of the prop was a huge slipknot.

Fortunately, most ventures out onto the water by Arundel-on-the-Bay residents are of a more enjoyable and relaxing nature.

The Beginning of the 21st Century

The damage from Hurricane Isabel in the fall of 2003 resulted in the rebuilding of the Newport Avenue pier with new slips, and it encouraged greater ecological awareness in Arundel-on-the-Bay.

The community shelved plans to install impervious surfaces on streets leading to the shoreline and is resurfacing most of these streets with gravel. Dog waste stations have been set up at strategic points throughout the community for the use of the many residents who enjoy walking their dogs along the streets. Projects to limit pollution of the bay and to control shoreline erosion are underway. Water retention swales along Chestnut and Newport avenues, supported by a $500,000 grant from the Environmental Protection Agency and directed by the South River Federation, were completed in 2014. This project was initiated by former Arundel-on-the-Bay resident Julie Winters. In an effort spearheaded by Association President David Delia and Roads Chairman Alan Hinman, drafting sites for fire engines to access Bay water in the event of a fire were also installed at six waterfront street ends in 2014.

Figure 22: Hurricane Isabel flooding at Hollywood and Narragansett Avenues. ***Photo by R. M. Grigsby.***

The community population has shifted again. The wonderful diversity of this eclectic community can be found in the real estate statistics. Records show that 133 properties were sold in Arundel-on-the-Bay from 2001 to 2012, with a settlement price ranging from $127,000 to $1,585,000. During the same period, 14 building lots were sold at prices ranging from $73,000 to $785,000. During 2012, 10 houses changed ownership with the prices running from $150,000 to $1,150,000. Based on the April 2015 resident directory, Association President David Delia and resident Philip Allen estimated that the total population is about 1,000 owners and family (750 residents, the rest absentee) and some 100 tenants in a total of some 350 properties.

The community continues to be a combination of small older cottages and larger newer homes. Some of the cottages have been or are being renovated. Others are being torn down and replaced with larger, raised multi-storied homes.

Arundel-on-the-Bay is a wonderful blend of residents of all ages and ethnic backgrounds. The community is home to newcomers who are drawn to the waterfront, as well as families that have been here for decades. In some cases, there are several generations of families that own a home in the community. Among the notable people who have made Arundel-on-the-Bay their home or home away from home during this time period are operatic baritone Todd Duncan, who was George Gershwin's personal choice for Porgy in "Porgy and Bess"; entrepreneur Toni Ray, who started the successful Hobo International handbag brand out of her home here; and Kurt Schmoke, former mayor of Baltimore and current president of the University of Baltimore.

Arundel-on-the-Bay continues to be a delightful community with events and fundraisers now being held on the beach year round. The current community activities include an adult Wine Tasting and Jazz Fest in the spring and a family cookout with a moon-bounce and water slide held on the community beach in the summer. Arundel-on-the-Bay resident Marc Apter initiated these two events in 2009, and with the help of community volunteers continues to manage them yearly. In the winter, there is a collection for the Annual Annapolis Santa Run of toys for the needy at the beach with a visit from Santa Claus on a fire truck, followed by a bonfire, refreshments and socializing. Organizer former resident Allison Buckler reported that Arundel-on-the-Bay has become known as the community with the most gifts collected for several years in a row. In addition to the toy drive, Allison has also started an annual 5K run through the community. Throughout the year there are also fund-raising lunches or dinners organized by Margaret Delia at various restaurants to encourage fellowship and supplement the community social activities fund. Life is good and tranquil at Arundel-on-the-Bay.

Life continues in the community, and as long as it does, history will continue to be made.

Figure 23: Quinn Budimir, Andrea Bush and Ashleigh Bush surveying damage from Hurricane Isabel. ***Photo by R. M. Grigsby.***

Figure 24: Four generations of the Grigsby family at Arundel-on-the-Bay. (First row left to right) Michael James Grigsby, Richard Magee Grigsby, (second row left to right) Michael Marc Grigsby, Richard Marc Grigsby, a photographer who made major contributions to the book. *Photo courtesy of R. M. Grigsby.*

Figure 25: Community gathering for Christmas toy donation and socializing. *Photo by R. M. Grigsby.*

Figure 26: Chapter author Edie Dolberg is second from the left at a community picnic on the beach. ***Photo by Marc Apter.***

Figure 27: Community residents enjoying the 2016 Summer Family Picnic at the Magnolia Avenue beach. ***Photo by Marc Apter.***

Endnotes

1. Based on experience of John Moses.
2. *Annapolis Capital Gazette,* April 2, 1982.
3. *Capital Newspaper* Sept, 17, 1980.
4. *Kent Island* newspaper, Oct 5, 1988.
5. Department of Natural Resources, Maryland Geological Survey Administrative Report 2006.
6. Partial List of Presidents for the Arundel-on-the-Bay.

Property Owners Association

1951-1955	Theodore H. Johnson
1956-1957	Ralph Sneed
1967-1968	William DaCosta
1970-1971	Herbert S. Hilliard
1971-1973	Raymond Morgan
1973-1976	Delores Hunt, PhD
1976-1978	Willie McManus
1978-1980	George Snowden
1980-1983	Wilma Coble
1983-1985	Ed Lee Johnson
1985-1987	John Moses
1989-1991	Wilma Coble
1991-1993	April Moses
1993-1997	Augie Stasio
1997-1998	Bedford Bentley
1998-1999	Barry Dempsey
1999-2001	Maureen Donohue
2003-2007	Frank Florentine
2007-2009	Harvey Young
2009-2013	Andrew Grannell
2013-2017	David Delia
2017-present	Dawn Davis

7. *Capital Gazette,* August 13 & 20, 1993.
8. Albert memo to Kosmerl dated January 18, 1994.
9. Circuit Court for Anne Arundel County Case # C-06-115184 dated 8 November 2008.
10. These projects were identified in the July-Aug 1991 copy of *The Pier* seen below.
11. Department of Transportation Press Release No. 5862, October 31, 1992.

The PIER

Property Owners Association of Arundel on the Bay Inc.

A Bi-Monthly Publication **July - Aug. 1991**

THANKS TO EVERYONE:

My term as President of the Association will end on August 3, 1991. It has been a pleasure for me to serve in this capacity during the past two years. I am most grateful for everyone's support in working to improve the community. With the help of the committee members, officers, and Board of Directors of the Association we have collectively made a difference. Some of our accomplishments and the persons most responsible for getting the job done are as follows:

1. The completion of the Magnolia Avenue Beach Project - Steven Ford

2. Resurfacing of Narragansett Avenue North of Walnut Avenue - Steven Ford

3. Construction of the Crabbing Pier at Linden Avenue Park - Billy Keyes

4. Landscape Design and Drafting of the berm at Magnolia Beach and the front entrance gate - Grace Schneider

5. Work on the Erosion Control Project on Narragansett Avenue south. The Maryland Department of Natural Resources will bid the project this fall.- Jackson Taylor

6. Bayfront Erosion Control Project between Myrtle and Hollywood Avenues, work to start in August - Ray Morgan.

7. Celebration of Arundel-on-the-Bay 100th Anniversary - Carmita Thomas.

8. Installing Purple Martin Bird Houses in the community - April Moses and Carmita Thomas.

9. Clearing of two community-owned lots and continuing to work to install playground equipment on the lots on Newport Avenue - Lynn Grigsby.

10. Gardening work at the entrance last spring and planting trees on community property - Mark Krawczewicz & Grace Schneider

11. Editing and publishing The Pier Newsletter - Frank Enty & Mark Krawczewicz

12. Arranging and monitoring the dumpster for community clean-up - John Weatherford

13. Organizing and supervising the community Halloween and Christmas activities - Valerie Allen

14. Having Anne Arundel County to replace two large culverts on Magnolia Ave. and re-excavation of the drainage ditches - Carmita Thomas and George Henson.

15. Acting as Recording Secretary - Toni Ray, Nancy Resnick, and Eric Campfield.

16. Planting of Trees on community owned property - Nancy Resnick

17. Preparation of the Special Benifit Budget (91-92) Edmund Mead & Horst Kleinsorg

To those who worked on committees, project and activities and whose names I did not mention, I thank you ever so much for your help.

Sincerely,

Wilma Coble

L-R, Philip Allen, Karen Neale, Aris T. Allen Jr., John Moses, Marc Apter, Pamela Duncan, Arend Thomas, Bill Semenuk and Wilma Coble on the porch of the Duncan home. Edie Dolberg, missing from this photograph is pictured on page 204.

Authors

Aris T. Allen Jr.

Aris T. Allen Jr. is a second generation resident of Arundel-on-the-Bay (AOTB). His parents resided in this community and he currently resides here with his wife. He has fond memories of growing up in this water privileged community. His professional work has included museum planning and design, residential design and construction and development, of which 27 new and renovation residential projects have been completed in Arundel-on-the-Bay. Mr. Allen has served three terms as Vice President of the Property Owners Association of Arundel-on-the-Bay as well as serving on the Board of Directors. He has served as Chair of the Pier and Boat Ramp Committee and Chair of the Newport Pier Rebuilding Committee. He has provided oversight for the community's shore erosion and phragmites control efforts and has served as a member of the Arundel-on-the-Bay History project, which produced this book about the community from the beginning to the present.

Philip Allen

Philip Allen has dwelt on Rockway Avenue in Arundel-on-the-Bay since 2005 with his wife, Dr. Susan Allen, and their beloved French bulldogs, Hugo, then Jolie. Allen edited the community's newsletter from 2007 to 2015, played Arundel-on-the-Bay parliamentarian since 2008, and initiated the sequence of historical interviews on video that preceded this volume. He is Emeritus Dean at Frostburg State University, a former US Foreign Service Officer, and the author of five books on Africa, the Indian Ocean, and Madagascar. Now in semi-retirement, Allen still consults sporadically on African matters, participates in Fulbright Scholar alumni activities, and dabbles in political, literary, and musical life.

Marc Apter

Marc Apter is the director of this book project. He has lived in Arundel-on-the-Bay in Annapolis since 1988. He loves the water and has a collection of small sailboats and a runabout. He races on larger sailboats on weekends. Apter is on the board of the Chesapeake Chapter of the Public Relations Society of America.

Apter is an experienced communicator with award-winning public relations and marketing experience. He currently heads a PR firm, Image Power Inc. (MarcApterPR.com), whose clients have included the Maryland Historical Society, Maryland House and Garden Pilgrimage, Chesapeake & Washington Heart Care, concert pianist Brian Ganz, DC Sail, the National Philharmonic at Strathmore in Bethesda and the Chesapeake Orchestra based in St. Mary's County. He is the publisher of the Mid-Atlantic Media Directory.

Apter has provided PR counsel to St. Mary's College of Maryland as well as trade associations, government agencies and corporate clients. Apter was awarded the Public Relations Society of America's Thoth Award (the Oscar of the PR profession) in September of 2014 for his successful PR campaign to promote the unveiling of the Annapolis monument commemorating the 250,000 Civil Rights Foot Soldiers who marched on Washington in 1963.

Wilma Coble

Wilma Coble has lived in the community of Arundel-on-the-Bay since 1970. She has been very active in the Property Owners Association and has been elected to serve as President for three consecutive years (1981-1984) and again for a two-year term (1991-1992). She was also elected to serve the Board of Directors, as Chairman, for four years (1985-1989). Some of her major accomplishments during her terms in office are as follows:

1) An interest free loan was granted by the State of Maryland for $400,000 for the renovation project of the Chesapeake Bay shoreline. Wooden bulkheads were installed and/or repaired with stones placed on the Bay side of the bulkheads. The project was completed from north to south in 1982.

2) The Special Community Benefit Tax was activated to pay for improving Myrtle Avenue between Cohasset and Newport Avenues to install an underground water storage tank for fire fighting.

3) The first newsletter, *The Pier*, was published to provide community news to all property owners.

4) The Constitution and Bylaws were amended to change the term of the President to serve a term of two years instead of one year.

5) The community beach was improved by placing a low profile wooden bulkhead at the shoreline and stone revetments were placed in the water to prevent any further erosion.

Edie Dolberg

After working for many years as Contracts Director for a government contractor in Northern Virginia, upon retirement Edie was more than happy to step into the less hectic lifestyle of Annapolis. She was familiar with Arundel-on-the-Bay because her daughter, Kim Miller, and her family have been residents for over twenty years. In 2010 Edie and her husband, Charlie, along with their dogs Ramsey and Otis, moved from their weekend house in Eastport to a larger home on Narragansett Avenue so they could more easily accommodate and entertain a growing family. They couldn't be happier about the move. Since they were new residents, Edie was excited to become a part of the small group of people proposing to pull together the history of this wonderful community. "What a fun and interesting project!" said Edie.

Pamela Thurber Duncan

Pam moved to Arundel-on-the-Bay with her husband Charlie in the summer of 1995. She knew Arundel and Highland Beach as a teenager, and grew to know the Chesapeake Bay area better while sailing with him on his boat "Deliberate Speed."

A lover of history and old buildings, she left her career in District and federal government to obtain a master's degree in Historic Preservation Planning at Cornell. Afterward, she worked at the National Trust for Historic Preservation and volunteered with Europa Nostra- a cross European preservation organization. Locally she volunteered at the Kuethe Library of Historical and Genealogical Research of the Ann Arrundell County Historical Society, Inc., becoming a member of the Society's Board and later Vice-President and President. She also served as Secretary of the Property Owner's Association of Arundel-on-the-Bay.

When not tracking down an obscure historical reference in this labor of love, she enjoys the company of her nephew, John Anthony Thurber, and her Cocker Spaniel, Spice, who share the Duncan home.

John Moses

As a child, John spent summers in a nearby community (Venice Beach) and first remembers coming to Arundel on the Bay in about 1943 to visit the small enclave of homes just north and south of Cedar Avenue along the Bay. During his later childhood and teens, he continued to visit Arundel-on-the-Bay as its summer population continued to grow and change.

In 1971 he stumbled upon a house for sale on the Bay. He and his wife April have lived there ever since, John commuting daily to northern Virginia to work as a patent attorney for 43 years. Because they lived in Arundel-on-the-Bay, their three children grew up with a sense of place and a curiosity about other places, and with a delight in the Bay but with respect for its intermittent ferocity.

John has served as President of the Arundel-on-the-Bay Property Owners Association and as a member of its Board of Directors. During that time John worked with the community association and with members of the Annapolis Neck Federation to force Anne Arundel County to adhere to the current zoning regulations, including passage of new legislation regarding antiquated lots. He also worked with the State to protect the Aquia aquifer from overuse as summer communities became suburban developments. He continues to walk the community, to observe growth and change, and to meet new neighbors. Working on this book has reminded him how different it was to be one of fewer than two dozen year around families 47 years ago, and how many hours he spent on Route 50 in order to live here. As he awaits the return of the Ospreys, and watches traffic in the shipping channel for stock market clues, he thinks it's been worth it.

Karen Neale

Karen Johnson Neale grew-up summers at the Arundel-on-the-Bay waterfront cottage formerly known as "Bay View" off Narragansett and Chestnut Avenues. Her parents,

Stewart and Adele Johnson, were part of the wave of black professionals in Washington D.C. who purchased property at Arundel-on-the-Bay in the early 1950s. Karen now lives a few doors away in the house that her uncle and aunt, Cecil and Louise Burton, built in 1956. They came to Annapolis in the early 1940s to teach at Wiley H. Bates High School.

After raising a son together with her late husband, Theodore Neale, completing her career as an environmental lobbyist on Capitol Hill, and retiring to Arundel-on-the-Bay, Karen feels her life has come full circle. Once again she treasures life in the community and the Chesapeake Bay views, but wishes her grandchildren could enjoy the Bay as pristine as it was many summers ago.

Bill Semenuk

Bill is an electrical engineer born in Detroit, Michigan who attended Gonzaga High School and obtained his MEA from George Washington University. He served overseas in Vietnam and Ethiopia, retiring from Lockheed Martin. He is currently researching the history of the Chrysler Missile and Space division which built the Redstone, Jupiter, and Saturn missiles on which the first U.S. satellite Explorer 1, the first U.S. astronaut John Glenn, and SKYLAB were launched into space. An avid sailor and past Commodore of the Arundel Yacht Club with a voracious appetite for all things aeronautic, Bill resides at 3452 Rockaway adjacent to the Arundel-on-the-Bay Crab dock.

Arend Thomas

While studying at Howard University College of Pharmacy, Arend Thomas was required to learn about many scientists and physicians. He worked at Freedmen's Hospital which was built for and by freed slaves after the Civil War. Freedmen's was given to Howard University by the United States Government to serve as a teaching institution. Arend established his own businesses and retired as Director of Pharmacy at Howard University Hospital.

Arend's parents purchased land and built a home in Arundel-on-the-Bay in 1953. This project renewed his interest and led to his recollection of many events and noteworthy people.

Bob Meissner, Editor

Bob and his wife of more than 50 years, Dina, are both natives of Menominee in Michigan's Upper Peninsula. (For readers, think of Hemingway's *Two Hearted River,* the classic *Witness for the Prosecution*, and the novels of Jim Harrison.) He graduated in 1966 from Michigan State University with a bachelor of science degree in geology.

Bob served as an officer of the U.S. Navy during two deployments to the Gulf of Tonkin in the Vietnam War. Out of the Navy and returning to the Upper Peninsula, he managed a motorcycle and power products shop for a dozen years, then took time to write and try to market a science fiction novel, and later worked as an Associated Press award-winning reporter, then editor, of his hometown daily newspaper. While in Menominee, Bob had leadership roles in supporting local musical and literary arts.

In 1995 Bob took a job in D.C. as press secretary for U.S. Rep. Bart Stupak (D-Mich.), and seven years later as press secretary for U.S. Sen. Debbie Stabenow (D-Mich.). In 2004 he became press secretary and later deputy director of communications for the health care advocacy organization Families USA. Former resident of Arundel-on-the-Bay, now officially retired, Bob lives in Chesapeake, Va. He has recently become active in the local Rotary Club and the Friends of Chesapeake Public Library. Most sadly, Dina, who set up Drop Box for the History Project and educated us in its use, died on June 4, 2018.

Index

Entries for images are shown boldface and italic.
Entries for some heavily used topics are only cited for their first appearance and when subject of the text.

C

D

E

F

G

H

P

Q

R

S

Y

Z

Printed in Great Britain
by Amazon

42984795R00137